CRIME AND SOCIAL CONTROL IN 'CENTRAL'-EASTERN EUROPE

Crime and Social Control in 'Central'-Eastern Europe

A guide to theory and practice

ALEKSANDAR FATIĆ

Routledge
Taylor & Francis Group
LONDON AND NEW YORK

First published 1997 by Ashgate Publishing

Reissued 2018 by Routledge
2 Park Square, Milton Park, Abingdon, Oxon OX14 4RN
711 Third Avenue, New York, NY 10017, USA

Routledge is an imprint of the Taylor & Francis Group, an informa business

A Library of Congress record exists under LC control number: 97074441

ISBN 13: 978-1-138-61156-6 (hbk)
ISBN 13: 978-0-429-46359-4 (ebk)

Contents

Introduction

In the mid-1980s, the Hungarian-born legal theorist R.N. Berki addressed the dominant, liberal tradition in political theory and the theoretical interpretation of law, in the proposition that the famous phrase 'law and order' is a conjunction of two terms that explain the law on two different conceptual levels. According to Berki, law and order are not two things, one of which is the end and the other the means for the accomplishment of that end. Order is not merely something that is achievable by law. More precisely, there is also a braver interpretation, according to which a certain socio-political order is also, in an essential sense, a presupposition and a source of law. Only by accepting a certain moral and cultural order, constituted by a certain order of values, the law becomes possible as a normative framework within which the relationships of legitimate mutual expectations between members of society are constituted, and which gives meaning to what is these days increasingly called 'the social capital of trust' in the institutions.[1]

In this context, the question of social order or régime is an essential presupposition for a meaningful discussion of any set of specific problems of social policy, including the problem of internal security, which is the traditional subject of criminal policy. Berki's position is based on the notion that the social order is constituted only through and on the basis of an appropriate structural order of the state and of political organisation.

The relevance of the idea of an essential relationship between the political and ideological structure of a social system and the state of criminality is clear in central-eastern European societies in the period of post-communism. This period is marked by the so-called 'transition' from socialist-communist towards liberal-capitalist forms of socio-political organisation. The analysis of criminal policy and its connections with socio-political and ideological foundations of the system in three representative countries of the region is the subject of much of this book. This analysis should illuminate some aspects of the role of ideology and the state in the constitution of the internal security crisis, as well as the social responses to that crisis through criminal policy.

The most important intention of this book is to determine the role of the community and its consensus about dominant social values within the context of questions about the constitution of legitimacy of social control. This is attempted primarily in the framework of political and social changes in the post-1989 central-eastern European countries. In most of the literature, 1989 is usually taken as the official beginning of the political transition of the region, because of the famous November 1989 events in Prague which were later called 'The Velvet Revolution', and similar events and developments in other countries of the region — Hungary and Poland. This transition has dramatically different appearances in various parts of central-eastern Europe. In central Europe, generally speaking, it was and is being conducted in an orderly and clean manner, along with a systematic deprivation which remains the price of systemic and ideological change. In other countries, such as the former Yugoslavia and the former Soviet Union, it had the form of chaos and disintegration.

The general motivation for the exploration of changes in criminal policy is usually an impression, or a conviction, that there are reasons to doubt the effectiveness of the existing arrangements and institutions of social control. This conviction is certainly present in central-eastern Europe at the end of this century, and it is reflected in the concentrated public debate on issues of crime control. The consequences of the widespread perception of a security crisis include both social disruptions and considerable changes to the value and role of the community in the constitution of feelings of trust in the law and the legal institutions of social control. The debate itself has led to major changes in criminal legislation — all countries are striving to streamline their legislation with that of the European Union member countries, and thus in much of the region criminal laws have undergone, or are undergoing, very significant technical and essential changes.

It is often argued that the rise in criminality is a sign of backsliding of social relationships, and that particularly severe and intrusive forms of crime control are a sign of the impotence of social institutions to resist that backsliding adequately and productively. The decay in social relationships and trust is assumed to constitute the specifically social dimensions of criminality. If this assumption is correct, then it is probably also correct to conclude that the social tissue in post-communist central-eastern European countries is extremely threatened today.

Along with the advent of the ideal of the international liberal state in central-eastern Europe and the universalist aspirations of the political world of the 1990s, international crime, terrorism, drug-trafficking, money-laundering, industrial espionage, and mass fraud are also on the rise.[2] At the same time, and probably more importantly, from a strictly social point of view, the rates of those types of criminality that are usually taken as indicators of internal societal crises and the disintegration of civil, economic, and legal institutions are also increasing.[3] This applies primarily to violent crimes which, because of the immediacy of the threat they pose, often play the deciding role in the formation of attitudes of the population towards both the legitimacy and the effectiveness of the institutions of social control. They have a particularly destructive potential for the social tissue, because they lead to high publicity and have the ability to generate negative and often romanticised deviant stereotypes that call for imitation and following.[4]

On the one hand, these violent types of criminality in the overall amount probably do not cause such global damages, and do not lead to such global security crises, as do international terrorism or organised narcotics-trafficking. On the other hand, they directly reflect the damages to social fabric that characterise many contemporary societies. By generating an intensive fear in the population, they contribute to the erosion of trust in the ability of the criminal justice system to offer adequate protection. This is precisely why violent crime, traditionally seen as an internal or domestic type of criminality (terrorism or drug-trafficking can be seen in some way as international), worries the populations of democratic societies most of all, and induces them increasingly to opt for strategies of repressive dealing with criminally deviant individuals and groups. This sort of discourse of political legitimation is reflected today in the popular initiatives in many countries for the introduction or reintroduction of the death penalty, for increased use of life imprisonment, and for other Draconian penal responses to criminality.[5] The democratic public is increasingly worried about crime, probably more so than about other equally grave social policy problems, such as the chronic lack of living space, unemployment, underage parenthood, dramatic negative social stratification, etc. Even the political programmes of leftist political formations all around the world are turning, increasingly, towards the paradigms of collective deterrence, retribution, and even revenge.[6] The rightist social policy, on the other hand, is stable in its traditional position, demanding 'tough' or 'iron fist' strategies, elevated in its social profile by the current tide of fear of crime. Its traditional programme, based on the concepts of criminal 'desert', 'just retribution', etc., continues to be increasingly attractive for the average voter in most 'western' countries.[7]

The populations of central and eastern European countries, after the disintegration of the Soviet Union which provided the ideological umbrella for the former systems in the region, are no less caught by this tide of worry about the questions of security and social control policy, particularly regarding criminal policy. Their recently liberalised societies are experiencing changes which are fully representative of the well-known phenomena of security crises in advanced liberal systems, but are also, in important aspects, a novelty for societies once governed by an ideology and a Party that maintained a firm direction of control. These societies are not used to high rates of irrational individual crimes, such as the so-called serial murders, or highly organised drug-trading or money-laundering chains. The rebellion against the security crisis is loud, and the confusion is even greater. What Emil Durkheim called 'anomie', a lack of clear social norms or a mutual clash of norms, is an overwhelming reality in the post-communist world.[8] Criminology and criminal law, like elsewhere in the world, seem unable to offer a quick and conclusive answer to this confusion and to the questions that arise from it. Part of the reason for this is in the very structure of the transition of post-communist societies, and particularly of those in central Europe. The silence of criminology and criminal law is greater and deeper where the emphasis of explanatory efforts is not on the questions of social justice and possibilities for a benevolent and minimally intrusive social control, but almost entirely, and almost only, on economic questions. The latter relate to conditions for a stable influx of capital and foreign investments, penetration into the foreign markets in western Europe and Asia, liberalisation of trade and other economic aspects of the legislation, harmonisation of the taxation system with the systems of the closest western markets (for central Europe, this refers mainly to the European Union market), etc.

All these aspects of social policy and legislation are, of course, essential in the existing political, social, and institutional circumstances in the region. The problem is that, particularly in central Europe, along with an almost absolute emphasis on the economic aspects of transition, the voice of social justice is silenced, as well as the voices of concern for the moral and legal security of society and social relationships from the arbitrary consequences of an uncritical application of market principles. There are aspects of social life that require contexts of consideration and values that are not necessarily, or completely, compatible with the market principle of maximisation of cumulative welfare. Some truths about criminality, its causes and the results of various forms of institutional policies of crime control, are thus easily lost from sight in this part of the Continent, obsessed with economic aspects of the 'liberation'. In this way, central-eastern Europe, and particularly its central part, together with the economic and political changes, experience the destructive consequences and omissions that characterise the *negative* side of capitalism and representative democracy. These include the introduction of stricter and more intrusive forms of control in many legal systems, a diminution of concern about the preservation of standards of benevolence and fair treatment in the process of social control, leading to the emergence of populism as a vulgarisation of the legitimate democratic tendency to achieve a maximum level of public support for particular forms of social policy.

The aim of this book is to offer a special synthesis of theoretical and practical considerations and material, which would be a source of relevant information in the area of criminal policy and theory, as well as a guide through the specific problems of security and criminal policy that are characteristic of contemporary central-eastern Europe. It is not an exhaustive critical study of all criminal legislation in the region, nor does it set out to present all aspects of social control in it. Rather, it attempts to be a comparative interpretation of the picture of the emerging criminal policy in the region in the immediate aftermath of communism.

Work on *Crime and Social Control in 'Central'-Eastern Europe* took place between 1993 and 1996. Most of the empirical material was collected and analysed during a study stay in the countries of central Europe, a large portion of which was spent in the Czech Republic in 1994 and 1995. The collection of this material, as well as travel necessary for the completion of this project, were made possible by the financial support provided by the Research Support Scheme of the Central European University in Prague. A considerable part of this research was also made possible by a research fellowship from the Serbian Ministry of Science and Technology, which facilitated work on the comparative political aspects of this book at the Institute of International Politics and Economics in Beograd. The book was given its final form in the course of 1996 at the Institute of International Politics and Economics in Beograd.

Notes

1. Berki, R.N. (1986), *Security and society: Reflections on law, order and politics*, J.M. Dent & Sons, London, especially the second chapter, 'The state as law and order', pp. 44–114.

2. A wealth of statistical information confirming this is systematised in the UNICEF study of central-eastern Europe in transition, entitled *Central and eastern Europe in transition: Monitoring public policy and social conditions*, Economies in Transition Studies, nos. 1–2, UNICEF, Innocenti, 1993–95. Also see Barr, N. (ed.) (1995), *Labour markets and social policy in central-eastern Europe: The transition and beyond*, Oxford University Press, Oxford.

3. This institutional disintegration stretches from disintegration of the family as the basic social institution through to crises of the entire legal, and especially judicial, systems.

4. More detailed discussions and information in this context are present in the comparative part of this book. Some observations and anecdotal evidence in the social context of the contemporary Serbia can be found in Knežević, A. & Tufegžić, V. (1995), *Kriminal koji je izmenio Srbiju* (*Crime that changed Serbia*), Radio B-92, Beograd.

5. In the central European region, this is probably to the greatest extent the case in the Czech Republic. The Czechoslovak government abolished the death penalty in 1990, immediately before the splitting up of the country.

6. One of the most obvious examples today is the introduction of the 'three strikes and out' legislation by the 'left' Clinton Administration in the USA (any third criminal offence, however trivial it might be, is automatically punishable by mandatory life imprisonment). Another example is the 1994–95 discussion in Great Britain, between the Conservative government of John Major and his Home Secretary, Michael Howard, on the one hand, and the 'left', Labour opposition, led by Tony Blair, about criminal policy, in which the left positions were considerably shifted towards the right and the more repressive forms of crime control. Thus, the left side of the debate hardened its position on the use of imprisonment and the acceptable amount of police discretion. It is also well known that, during this period, a provision was introduced in British criminal legislation which abolished the right of silence of an arrested person, that is, the right not to answer police questions without the presence of an attorney. In a majority of democratic countries this right is considered fundmental to the protection of individual liberty and for avoiding coerced self-incrimination.

7. For a relevant angle of discussion of this phenomenon see, for example, Fox, J. (1984), 'The new right and social justice: Implications for the prisoners' movement', *Crime and social justice*, vol. 20, pp. 63–75. For an extended discussion also see Hall, S. (1979), *Drifting into a law and order society*, Cobden Trust, London. For economic aspects of the use of penal measures see Janković, I. (1977), 'Labour market and imprisonment', *Crime and social justice*, vol. 9, pp. 17–31.

8. For a discussion of the relevance of Durkheim's ideas about social control in the context of crime control, see Garland, D., 'Durkheim's theory of punishment: A critique', in Garland, D. & Young, P. (1983), *The power to punish: Contemporary penality and social analysis*, Heinemann Educational Books & Humanities Press, London & New Jersey, pp. 37–61.

1 The ideological meaning of social control and its procedural democratic legitimation

Definitions and hypotheses

When the ideological dimension of social control in its legitimational context is the issue, it seems appropriate to start the discussion with the definitions of three relevant concepts. This should help to delimit the area within which the arguments of this study will operate. These concepts are (i) ideology, (ii) social control, and (iii) legitimacy. All three terms have a wide range of meanings, not all of which are directly relevant to the context of this discussion, because they reach through an array of disciplines, methodological approaches, and political assumptions. In this book, the three concepts will be used with the following meanings:

(i) 'Ideology' will mean the body of socio-political values adopted by social institutions which guide the social policy of a particular society in a particular time in all its important aspects.

(ii) 'Social control' will mean those aspects of social policy, primarily including crime control, whose purpose is to prevent significant transgressions of norms and values stemming from the adopted ideology, as well as to form and maintain those models of behaviour and reacting that are most in accordance with the ideology. The main context of the forthcoming discussions is crime control and its relationship with the ideological values and norms of a political community.

(iii) Finally, 'legitimacy' will mean the set of dominant characteristics of *decisions* of social institutions which result in specific forms of social policy, and which justify the respective social policy in the context of the dominant ideology and the socio-political system based on that ideology. The greatest part of the discussions addresses the *democratic* context of legitimation, because democratic forms of socio-political order present themselves as dominant social realities and socio-ideological tendencies in the post-communist Europe, at least since the late 1980s.

The main hypothesis from which this book starts is that there are systematic relationships between ideology and crime control which do not always or necessarily correspond with the social realities. Ideological visions of crime control and their legal, policing, and other control implications do not necessarily take into account wider aspects of the relevant social realities. Social policy is liable to developmental regularities arising from ideology. Similarly, deviance and criminality are flexible entities whose quality and quantity probably depend on the ideological structure of society. It is possible, however, that one and the same ideology influences deviance and criminality on the one hand, and social policy on the other, in very different ways. This means that a disparity between the directions and circumstances of the development of deviance and criminality on the one hand, and social control on the other, is a real possibility.

The main context of these discussions is the socio-political circumstances of transitional societies of post-1989 central-eastern Europe, or more precisely, the socio-political changes that have occurred in those societies in the course of their transition from socialist-communist towards liberal-capitalist forms of social organisation. This transition is proceeding at differing paces and in somewhat different forms in particular countries of the region, but all of them are passing through an ideological and social re-structuring which makes the regularities governing the relationships between political ideology and social policy particularly obvious.

In the sphere of social control, with the main emphasis on crime control, the relationships between the conceptions and public perceptions of deviance, the significance of the community's consensus for the legitimation of repressive forms of social control, and the domain and role of the rights of dissensual parts of the community in the definition of dominant forms of social control in that community are particularly important. To better understand the socio-political implications of the legal instruments for crime control discussed in chapters two, three, and four, it is necessary to consider briefly the meaning and significance of the categories of deviance, social reactions to it, the community's consensus in the context of democratic legitimation of social policy, and the rights of dissensual groups who are the primary target of social control.

Deviance and deviation

In the general social theoretical perspective, when considering social control one usually starts from the assumption that its primary subject is deviance or deviant behaviour. Generally speaking, deviance is a social characterisation that is based on the notion of social inadaptability. Those forms of behaviour that digress from social norms, especially those that are perceived by the majority as ill-adapted, or even anti-social, are considered deviant. They are controlled by an array of mechanisms, penal, supervisory, and combined investigative and preventative measures, which is the case with criminal forms of deviance, or by more informal social, group, and family mechanisms and sanctions, such as happens with non-criminal forms of deviance, sexual promiscuity, transgressions of the norms of family behaviour, or of an informal community such as the neighbourhood, etc. Concepts of deviance used in social theory are so diverse that this term is sometimes used to designate any sort of behaviour that threatens or disturbs the majority (this is the case with theories that insist on the importance of social consensus as the legitimational basis for sanctions), and sometimes it is used exclusively to designate criminal behaviour. Some theories even mention positive deviance, which digresses from the usual standards of behaviour in the sense that it transgresses the upper limit of socially constructive behaviour itself, thus causing suspicions that hidden and potentially socially destructive motives might be involved. One of the more persuasive discussions of this problem is from the pen of Jerzy Kvaśniewski, who points out some examples. People who insist on voluntarily donating blood above the limits considered usual, or people who fight corruption in the workplace, alone and against powerful cliques, are sometimes seen as deviant individuals who follow a hidden strategy of exclusive service to their own (unknown) interests. This is the sense in which ironic expressions such as 'smart ass', 'genius', 'great hero', etc., are sometimes used.[1] The theme of these discussions, however, is negative deviance, and primarily criminal deviance and its socio-political milieu, as well as the influence of ideological and socio-organisational circumstances on the perspectives of formation, growth, and control of criminal deviance and social responses to it through criminal policy.

'Deviance' is not only an objective characteristic of an individual or group. It also includes the appropriate social perception, meaning that it is an objective characteristic which, in the relevant socio-cultural and political context, meets a stigmatising characterisation. It is a phenomenon that varies in space and time. Deviance is directly dependent on the appropriate normative assumptions in a particular social context.[2]

It is precisely for this reason that some theories of deviance define it as the *product* of institutional stigmatisation of individuals who, only afterwards, identify themselves with the ascribed deviant roles.[3] Other theories derive from this assumption the conclusion that the massive institutional practice of stigmatisation of deviance leads to the formation of entire deviant subcultures, which intensify the reproduction of deviance through imitation, idolisation, and idealisation of deviant stereotypes, as well as the more technical transmission of knowledge about how to engage in deviant activities.[4]

The point here is really that the repetition of criminal stereotypes becomes entrenched, among other reasons, because the very identity of the criminal group, or the criminal subculture more generally, is largely defined in a particular, semantically negative way: not as a set of affirmative values, but rather as a body of *negations* of the respective affirmative values coded in the law of the mainstream society. Criminal subcultures, in other words, see their identity not in seeking out the realisation of specific, even if socially unrecognised, or even illegal values; on the contrary, they determine and define themselves through their very *opposition* to the values present in the law. This means that, according to the subcultural explanation, the criminal destructivity of these subcultures is founded in their very essence, because even if the law changed, if it favoured some other values, that would not necessarily represent a reason for criminal subcultures to start to obey it, because they do not follow any affirmative values. In other words, this means that the law cannot even theoretically offer a social context in which a full integration and inclusion of this type of generalised culture of criminality is possible.

From a theoretical point of view, one could argue that the reason for this a priori 'deficit of perspective of inclusion' is that criminal subcultures do not determine their objectives and identity in a *substantive* way, that is on the basis of certain directions filled with a positive normative content; instead, they do that in a purely *relational* way. If the substantive values coded in the law are labelled 'x*, x**, x***, (...)', then one could argue that criminality *as a social attitude* — and this is its meaning which is fundamental for subcultural criminological explanations — does not have any other, different substantive values, e.g. y, y*, y**, y***, (...), but rather the very relational mechanism of negation of the type: not-x, not-x*, not-x**, not-x***, (...). This relational mechanism is often followed by romanticisation of the negators themselves, as victims of the law and renegades against the legal strategies and values. This in itself represents a dangerous potential for a rapid escalation of this type of opposition to legitimacy *in principle*. That mechanism, when it is imagined in dramatic proportions, would clearly present an obstacle to successful socialisation and would thus threaten not only legitimacy and legal order, but also the very consensus on the basic values which makes criminal, and every other, law possible. Legality, as a category on which basic social relationships of trust and legitimate mutual expectations are based, would be radically threatened in such a radical perspective. Of course, not every criminality is radical in this sense, nor does the subcultural theory assert that this is the case in a particularly large proportion of societies — the point is that the mechanism of absolute opposition to legitimacy which is present here, as the vital dynamic principle of at least some subculturally determined and organised forms of criminality, is a threat to the *principle of legitimacy* itself.

To some extent, subcultural influences are obvious in nearly all criminal associations, such as gangs. The gang represents a differentiated subculture, or anti-culture, with its own hierarchy, meritocratic values, ideas of rules and normative directions for internal activity, justified mutual expectations and obligations within the gang, desirable personal and character traits. All, or at least most of these elements stand in direct opposition to the respective criteria characteristic of the dominant culture, defined and controlled by the law.

Although one must admit that subcultural influences are obvious in many forms of criminality and criminal organisations, it must also be noted that subcultural theories paint individual agents as entirely deterministic creatures. These theories describe individuals as governed by mechanisms of which they have almost no control, such as the revolt against negative labelling, dissociation from the values and social bonds characteristic of mainstream society, affiliational tendency towards groups with similar behaviour patterns and, above all, a dominant conformism within the subcultural group. This insistence on determinism and conformism within the criminal subculture is explained in subcultural theories by the argument that individuals, when once labelled as deviant, face a continuous and deep rejection by the legitimate social mainstream, which is an additional factor that pushes them even further into the hands of criminal subcultures. However, the assumption of a predominant determinism and conformism in individual behaviour is not in accord with the very assumption that the labelled individuals have fallen out of the domain of the legitimate and legally delineated norms in the first place. Namely, if the main mechanism of their behaviour is conformism and determinism, then one must assume that, in the very beginning of this dialectic, they were equally strongly predisposed to imitate legally prescribed legitimate aspects of social dynamics, legal strategies and law-enforced values, as they were later disposed to imitate their own label and the criminal environment in which they had become entrenched. The latter, in this framework of assumptions, is possible only once they have already actively, and with a great deal of individual initiative, *opposed* the dominant paradigms of legitimacy. If the general assumption is conformism, then the transition between two opposed forms of conformism must be marked by a good deal of initiative and non-conformism on an individual level, and this is certainly the case with the transition from law-abiding lives to criminal lives and careers. The very notion of this self-initiated transition between two forms of conformism, of course, is not entirely in line with the starting assumption of overwhelming conformism and passivity, which characterises the labelling and subcultural theories.

Thus, while labelling and subcultural theories represent a unique, and to a certain extent convincing, explanation of certain *aspects* of criminality, they do not offer the appropriate room for individual initiative, including the initiative in the form of initial rebellion against the dominant values in the form of law-breaking, which they themselves logically *presuppose*. These theories imply that models of reactional dissociation from legitimate values and legal norms must, somehow, be broken, in order to achieve a considerable reduction in criminality by legal means, but at the same time they do not say enough about the way in which this would be possible.[5]

The stigmatisation of deviance has not always been *institutional*; it started as *collective* sanctioning. In early communities deviance was stigmatised and repressed by group or collective opinion and by informal sanctions. In contemporary societies the same function is performed by specialised institutions. They have taken over the function of stigmatisation almost completely, and have turned it into their own *raison d'être*. Institutions have grown in volume and acquired a certain specialised functional autonomy in society, so much so that even citizens' expectations of social control revolve around the expected role of institutions. The citizens' first reaction, in many cases, to a wide variety of deviant phenomena is that institutions, rather than themselves, 'should do something' about a range of social control situations.[6] The initiative for stigmatisation, and thus, partly, for a definition and redefinition of particular forms and perceptions of deviance, in this way increasingly belongs to the institutions, and less so to the informal civil society or public.

In some social contexts, deviance is also used to designate not only those who can be legitimately considered as a threat to social relationships, but also all those who are undesirable for a whole range of other, not necessarily legal, and not necessarily moral, reasons, such as adopting different political positions, a lifestyle which is in sharp contrast to the lifestyle of the rest of the community, as well as priorities and life plans which might disturb the majority and which might be in conflict with their not necessarily legal, and not necessarily obligatory, values. This form of stigmatising labelling can be found in all societies, whichever form of institutional power or political system they might have. To a large extent, that is the reason for the antagonism of the consensual majority towards adherents of communist political positions in western countries, towards individuals who dress provocatively and oddly, towards the homeless, etc. In the most intolerant social environments, deviance is sometimes used as a label for the unemployed members of society, who are seen by the intolerant majority as responsible for their own position, because 'they don't really want to work in the first place'.[7] This is the case in those states of the USA today which are most affected by recession and unemployment, and in which the unemployed, therefore, represent the greatest burden on the public purse. For example, in 1995 the state of Massachusetts presented a blueprint for the reform of the social security system. This involved a dramatic decrease in payments of unemployment benefits and other social security assistance, leading to an increased existential exposure of the unemployed part of the population to the consequences of poverty. The reasoning behind this blueprint, apart from the strictly economic one, was partly moralising, and it implies that the unemployed must somehow be able to help themselves if they have no other choice.[8]

In some other societies, those who do not conform to the dominant sexual morality, including homosexual individuals, are labelled as deviant, and are often separated from the rest of the community and subjected to repressive treatment by the consensual majority. Similarly, in many parts of the contemporary industrialised world, most of the population increasingly tend to label as deviant those individuals who do not possess a certain minimum level of education (often high school education is considered to be the relevant minimum level). These individuals are thus seen as somehow deserving of reproach, even of sanctions. The same applies to those who are dependent on drugs, which does not necessarily have to carry a criminal characterisation. (Furthermore, in many liberal societies the public debate today is not about how to make stricter the sanctions and laws concerning the use and abuse of drugs, but rather about the possible legalisation and decriminalisation not only of consumption, but also of distribution of many soft drugs, such as marijuana.) The point of these examples is not to defend the forms of behaviour qualified by particular communities as deviant, but simply to show that deviance as a social characterisation is by no means limited to those forms of behaviour that are illegal. This then means that social control, whose particular forms can be very repressive, even when they do not include legal punishments, also has a range of uses that reach far beyond the domain of the law, and in its foundations stems from the *de facto* values adopted and choices made by the community as the determinants of its own culture and its own conception of social legitimacy.

The social process leading to the formation of deviance is called deviation. This process includes numerous social factors, the roles of many of which are still insufficiently explained. For example, in the case of criminal deviance, factors often taken as causes of this type of deviation are unemployment, poverty, negative effects of social stratification and restratification, and the so-called 'associational factors' (negative influence of peer group, criminal or excessively tolerant families, etc.).[9] Other possible causes of criminality include extremely competitive and violent cultures of some societies (this is a frequent comment concerning the high crime rates in the USA), lack of adequate social security mechanisms, and a wide range of other social policy problems. According to these assumptions, the process of deviation, which is largely initiated and governed by external (external in relation to the individual) social factors, potentially leads to socially destructive and criminal forms of behaviour. This, of course, does not exclude internal causes of deviance, which are more connected with personal choices and character traits. Assumptions about external causes of deviance, however, suggest some ways in which a reduction in deviance in society can be attempted by social organisation and its institutional order.

Global strategies of social control

Theoretically, there are two global types of plausible strategies for the control of deviance. One is by repressive mechanisms and by the imposition of restrictions intended to discourage and reduce deviant behaviour. The other is by offering alternatives to deviance, founded on insights into its possible causes, as well as into those needs whose social frustration can be seen as a reason for the individual's engagement in deviant, particularly criminal, activities. These two types of strategies also correspond to the dominant characteristics of social systems and social policy frameworks whose parts they are. According to some classifications, all social systems can be systematised into two categories: the so-called 'stabilisation systems', which primarily rely on the elimination and repression of undesirable phenomena, including deviance; and the so-called 'development systems', whose social policy is founded on the concept of cultivation of new and desirable phenomena and on seeking out ways to enable most citizens to engage in such affirmative activities, instead of becoming involved in socially destructive ones.[10] The former type of systems can be conditionally called conservative; the latter, again conditionally, progressive. The predominantly repressive control is more of a social reality in the former, while control through offering alternatives probably plays a more important role in the latter systems.

It is important to point out here that one of the characteristics of the predominantly repressive approach is that its target is the individual motivational structure of the imagined or real typical offender. The target of the approach focusing on the provision of alternatives is the very social structure which is to be changed or adjusted. The latter aims to create a maximum number of possible lifestyles that are functionally equivalent to deviant, and especially criminal, lifestyles (or strategies), in the sense that they lead to socially desirable results and the satisfaction of appropriate social needs in legitimate, rather than in illegitimate, ways.

The repressive strategy — an example

An example of the first, repressive strategy can be found in the popular rationalisation founded on the assumption of the viability of a systematically discouraging penal treatment of the offender — a notion which is the foundation of most existing systems of criminal sanctions. In the contemporary literature, one of the most well known attempts at conceptualisation of this approach comes from the American criminologist Andrew von Hirsch.

In a study entitled *Past or future crimes: Deservedness and dangerousness in the sentencing of criminals*, von Hirsch implicitly assumes that criminality is, to the greatest extent, an expression of individual motivation to acquire illegitimate advantage in the race for the most important social goods. This further implies the assumption that, by attaching certain costs or prices to criminal activities, through penalisation, the motivational structure of offenders can be influenced.[11] The very assumption about the efficacy of deterrent methods of penalisation has been questioned by a large number of criminologists, but in a certain sense it is a logical product of a particular understanding of deviance, and especially of criminality, mainly as the result of individual-motivational, rather than socio-cultural, factors, that is, primarily as a rational, calculated activity.[12]

Von Hirsch thus starts from the assumption that the most efficient mechanism of prevention through penalisation is that policy of penalisation which is based on the idea of *as precise a correspondence between the severity of the penalty and the 'seriousness' of the committed offence as possible.* One of the reasons for this is, of course, the need to avoid unduly severe penalisation of offences for which a less severe penalty would be sufficient for preventative purposes. Another reason, which is more interesting from von Hirsch's point of view, is the assumption that, if there is a precise gradation of penal measures according to the level of seriousness of the offences, it will create a certain two-fold incentive on behalf of the potential offenders. First, the incentive not to commit the offence in the first place, in order to avoid the possibility of being penalised (the standard assumption of deterrence theory), and second, the incentive to commit a less serious, rather than a more serious, offence, once one has already decided to commit one, in order to reduce the probability of being penalised too severely. This two-step ladder of discouragement from committing an offence should thus, ideally, discourage the potential perpetrator of a robbery; however, it should also have a second order effect if the original intention to discourage the offender fails. If the penalties for particular types of robbery are different, depending on the seriousness of the robbery — for example, if the penalty for non-violent robbery is considerably less severe than that for armed robbery — then that means that, according to this assumption, it could be expected that those offenders who decide to commit a robbery will have good reason to engage in a less serious type of robbery, say in a robbery while the owners of the property are away, instead of an armed robbery involving violence or perhaps even murder. Von Hirsch thus starts from the assumption that the specific borderline in the hierarchy of penalties, between those that are not strongly deterrent, and those with a considerable deterrent effect, is marked by the so-called 'in-out line' (meaning 'in and out'of prison).[13] The in-out line marks those levels of seriousness of offences that lead to imprisonment, as opposed to those that are penalised by other, less severe, forms of sanctions.

The method that von Hirsch proposes for determining the places that the in-out line should occupy on the hierarchy of penalties according to the seriousness of offences is the so-called 'sentencing grid'.[14] This grid consists of two axes, the horizontal and the vertical. The horizontal axis includes the parameters having to do with the offender, such as previous sentences, the types of previous offences, in a word what von Hirsch calls the criminal history or career, and what is commonly known as criminal record, while the vertical axis includes the parameters of the seriousness of the offence in a particular case.[15]

If vertical lines are drawn from the various imaginary points on the horizontal axis, and horizontal lines from various imaginary points on the vertical axis, then the points at which these lines meet will mark the levels of severity of penalties for the respective offences, according to the criminal career of the offender (or the absence of such career, in which case the penalty will be less severe). The imaginary line connecting all the points designating the level of severity of penalties that include imprisonment is the in-out line. All offences that, according to the parameters of the seriousness of the offence itself and the criminal career of the offender, can be classified in the part of the grid above the in-out line are punishable by imprisonment. Those offences that are classifiable below this line are punishable by less severe penalties. The implicit line of reasoning here presupposes that, in a certain sense, the in-out line is the fundamental line of deterrence, or line of prevention. It assumes that offenders will do their best to stay out of prison, and that this is the overriding consideration in their decisions whether or not to offend, and if so, how severely.

The sentencing grid therefore does not say which offences should be punishable by imprisonment, and which not; that is in the domain of the law-maker of each particular society. What it says is, in essence, twofold: first, that one and the same offence should be penalised more severely when the offender has an extensive criminal career and a large number of convictions than in cases where it is one's first conviction (this is the case in most existing systems of criminal law), and second, that the in-out line should be well known to the citizens. The assumption here is that deviance, and first of all criminality, is not so much based on deterministically defined, socio-structural factors, but rather on individual-motivational factors which, generally speaking, incite offenders to simply usurp certain types of behaviour which lead to various types of satisfaction and which are illegitimate. From this it follows that there is reason to believe that offenders will try not to transgress that line of seriousness of their offences which, in light of their criminal records, would place them in the area of the grid above the in-out line, should they be so unfortunate as to be caught and charged. (It should be noted that the illegitimate satisfactions which, in this context, are obtained by offending, do not have to be connected with any tangible benefit for the offender — the term 'illegitimate satisfaction' is very wide, and includes not only rational crimes, but also highly irrational crimes, such as many violent crimes are.)[16]

It is clear that the sentencing grid is the structure of reasoning about criminal sanctions which is present in most existing criminal laws, based on the notion of correspondence between the severity of the penalty and the seriousness of the offence. This correspondence is usually understood as an integral part of the concept of justice as 'getting what one deserves', as opposed to mere arbitrary penalisation by the control institutions.[17]

The strategy of 'provision of alternatives' — an example

Unlike the repressive conceptualisation of control, strategies of provision of alternatives advocate changes to socio-political arrangements with a view to reducing deviance and criminality as a specific type of deviance. Thus, unlike the repressive conceptualisation, which has the form of an interpretation of the existing structures of repressive institutions arising from an inherent social conservatism, the strategy of provision of alternatives usually presents itself as a form of political activism. One of the most noteworthy contemporary examples of this approach to control is the so-called 'socialist' or 'left-realist' conceptualisation, which shook the western scholarly public by the mid-1980s. The left-realist conceptualisation of control starts from the presupposition that social and political antagonisms generate criminal deviance, primarily in capitalist societies, and that the only adequate way to reduce deviance is a comprehensive socialist reform of the capitalist form of social organisation.

In 1984, British criminologists John Lea and Jock Young published the now famous book entitled *What is to be done about law and order: Crisis in the eighties*.[18] In the following decade this book became a seminal text for the so-called 'theory of left realism', based on certain political traditions of British socialism. According to Lea and Young, the theory of left realism started as a political platform, or as an appeal to politically left forces in Great Britain in the 1980s to 'take crime seriously', that is to consider criminology not as mere academic theory, but as a reflection of the real life political and social relationships in capitalist society.[19] As a result, the book was reprinted in the following decade, in 1993, with the title: *What is to be done about law and order: Crisis in the nineties*.[20] The whole debate in the context of Lea and Young's conceptualisation revolves around the concept of relative deprivation as the basic factor in increases in crime rates in industrialised capitalist countries in the 1980s and 1990s, and therefore also as the basic cause of criminality more generally in contemporary urban living conditions.

The primary theme of investigation for left-realist theories is street crime. The crime of the powerful or economic crime and various forms of fraud, embezzlement, abuse of official position, etc., are of secondary concern. This type of theory presupposes that the idea of relative deprivation is particularly easily applied to street crime, because that is the type of criminality which to the largest extent engages the poorer layers of the population structure. What is particularly interesting is that the poorer social classes are also the ones most severely affected by street crime. Given that the British, as any other, socialist political tradition and theory place a special emphasis on the poorer, working class, as opposed to the powerful members of the political community, it is natural that the main emphasis of the theory of relative deprivation is on street crime.

During the 1980s and 1990s street crime was the main cause of the overall rise in crime rates in Great Britain. The left-realist theory sees the rising rates of criminality in the numerical sense, and first of all of street crime, as corresponding to the advent of industrial relations and increases in economic efficiency.

The main idea which, in the context of the left-realist theory explains this increase, is the idea of 'relative deprivation'. This idea presupposes that advances in industrial relations in capitalist societies in the 1980s have led to an increase in economic efficiency, and thus to the emergence of structural unemployment of entire classes of the population, to impoverishment and marginalisation which led to a revolt against the existing economic and political systemic characteristics of these societies. The concept of relative deprivation suggests that the main reason why perpetrators of street crimes, who mainly belong to poorer social classes, engage in criminal activities, is not so much the absolute amount of poverty, or the absolute rate of unemployment, as the general perception of unjustified inequalities in society. The perception of one's own marginalisation and exclusion from the race for riches and status, which is so characteristic of capitalism, as well as the perception of marginalisation in relation to legitimate ways for overcoming exclusion, are thus seen as the main causes of criminality.[21]

The phenomenon of relative deprivation, in the interpretation of the left-realist theory, is characteristic of capitalist society, because this is the society that fosters a consumers' culture and values, paradigms of richness and success, as well as the liberal paradigms of equality in access to legitimate ways for attaining wealth and status. At the same time, in reality, the great masses of the population can hardly *ever* attain these ideals. This disparity leads to a justified revolt against the systems which are based on values that, within the systems themselves, only an extraordinarily small proportion of the population has any realistic chance to ever achieve.[22] In their seminal text Lea and Young insist that this phenomenon of relative deprivation, that is, the perception of unjustified inequalities, is not just a marginal phenomenon, but rather an essential element of the dynamics of capitalism, which is aggravated by the fact that the dynamics of industrialised capitalist society indirectly contribute to the breakdown of the more traditional values of the community and the family.[23] As a result of these dynamics, entire subcultures of rebels are formed, those who consider that the difference between the illegitimate and the legitimate opportunities serves only their marginalisation, that the law is not worth obeying because it stems from the interests of an unjustified system which, in the end, leads to an obliteration of the most efficient control mechanisms within the limits of the immediate community. The marginalisation and economic victimisation of entire communities, in a certain sense, turns into structural forms of criminality, into cultures of criminality that are impossible to remove without comprehensive social changes, and a restructuring of the system for the distribution of resources and opportunities.

What is particularly important to note in the theory of relative deprivation is the understanding that criminality, and particularly street crime, as a form of response to the perception of unjustified inequalities, and as an expression of revolt because of that perception, is not to be seen as an individual, illegitimate and strategically calculated activity by which to achieve those things that the individual cannot achieve in legitimate ways. On the contrary, the theory of relative deprivation views street crime primarily as a sensible form of social, and perhaps also class, anti-organisation. This is a strategy that reflects how the marginalised social group perceives the legitimate social group (the majority of the capitalist society) and its laws and criminal and legal institutions as its *enemy*. Enemies are thus also the police, the judiciary, the middle class, even the entire political system. Where on the level of general political theory Marx once insisted on a universal interest of the working class to take over the leadership of society and the means of production in its own hands, and where communism advocated an affirmative strategic activity by which to achieve this goal systematically, British socialist criminology has limited and more pessimistic intentions: it simply imples that, where class and group frustration relating to the dominant social values of the capitalist society are the greatest, deviance and criminality appear as a form of non-affirmative, even anti-affirmative, activities by which the existing system is simply brought into question and animosity is expressed towards its institutions.[24] In this way, relative deprivation leads to the formation of subcultures, which are not only criminal — in the context of the theory of relative deprivation they are also deeply *political*, and their negation of the dominant values thereby assumes a dimension of political activism.

It is clear that this is a romantic presentation of criminality: it is understood primarily as a protest against the political and economic organisation of the capitalist society. The implication is clear, although not explicitly expressed: by changing the capitalist model of production and social organisation, crime rates should also be considerably reduced. This is perhaps true. However, the point where the left-realist theory is not realistic, even when the political theoretical dimensions that it presupposes (and they are not the primary theme here) are disregarded, is that there are many forms of criminality, both street and non-street, which it would be very difficult to explain in class categories. For example, the trafficking of drugs and arms often includes various forms of street crime and violence, even if they themselves are not considered street crime. These forms of criminality present a problem in both capitalist and socialist societies, and their nature is not necessarily in accord with the assumption that their protagonists should necessarily come from the poorest and the most marginalised social classes. Similarly, various types of irrationally motivated violent crimes, such as many murders, even rapes, bear no obvious and necessary relationship with the working class, or with the social status of the group from which their perpetrators come. Many perpetrators of crimes are from the working class, but at the same time most of the working class are not perpetrators of crimes. This probably applies to any other concept of a socially marginalised group or class. Finally, the left-realist theory argues that its principles apply first of all to street crime, but that they can also be applied, if only in a derivative way, to any other type of crime.[25] It is not clear, however, how the concept of relative deprivation could be applied to the explanation of causes of economic crime, embezzlement, price fixing, and similar types of crime, which have the potential to inflict far greater material damages on society than any type of street crime. The perpetrators of these crimes are often members of the most privileged social groups, managers and directors, bankers, members of various highly educated professions who at least apparently have no reason to feel relatively disadvantaged or unequal in the context of relative deprivation.

To point to these limitations of the theory of relative deprivation does not at the same time mean to claim that it does not have considerable advantages in explaining particular types of street crime, in specific social circumstances, committed by specific social groups. Hence, it is neccessary to keep in mind the limitation of domain pertaining to this theory, because it seems that its declaratively universal character, potentially relating to all types of crime, all offenders, and all sorts of capitalist social circumstances, is not sustainable without significant difficulties. Where is the greatest value of this theory? As will become clear in the later discussions, it can make a considerable contribution to the understanding of certain types of criminality predominantly connected with specific parts of the population in specific transitional countries in central-eastern Europe. For example, the systematic inequality of Romanies in many central European countries can, through the theory of relative deprivation, at least partly explain the allegedly high rates of engagement of members of this social group, in some countries, in certain types of street crime, such as pickpocketing. Such alleged or real high rates of crime amongst particular social groups often lead to stereotypical blaming of entire groups and national minorities for crime, and frequently causes various discriminative forms of social policy, particularly so in the domain of social control. This topic will be addressed in greater detail in the comparative part of this book.

What must be noted as a weakness of all strategies of provision of alternatives that are based on expectations of structural changes to social relationships and organisation is that they advocate a sort of social revolution. The theory of relative deprivation does so very openly. This revolution has a meaning and expected concrete results that are determined largely speculatively — it remains unclear, in other words, how the advocated social change would actually create new alternatives. The change that the theory advocates is a change in developed capitalism; the same or similar problems, however, present themselves to central-eastern European societies in transition. The question they are facing is in what way the social restratification, induced by the transition from socialist-communist towards liberal-capitalist features of the social system will, or does, contribute to alternative possibilities for effective, and minimally repressive, social control. This question is one of the main challenges for social policy, especially for crime-control policy in the region.

The role of the community in the constitution of a transitional policy of social control

In democratic societies social policy, and thereby also the policy of social control, to a very large extent depends on public reactions to deviance, in particular to criminality. Social policy is never, however, not even in the most democratic societies, a *complete* reflection of public reactions to the relevant social phenomena, because social policy and the law, by following the moral and cultural sentiments and important interests of society, naturally to some extent fall behind the development of the very sentiments and interests they propose to follow. In addition, social policy and the law have a reverse influence on the formation of public opinion. Social life is wrapped around institutions, media, and other structural and dynamic parts of the social policy itself and of the state apparatus which implements it. Thus public opinion, obviously, is not generated in an entirely free and uncontrolled manner. For the effectiveness of social control as a specific part of social policy it is important that the discrepancy between its determinations of deviance and control strategies on the one hand, and public reactions on the other, is minimal, and that the *trust* of the community in the law and control institutions is maximal. As already discussed, perceptions of deviance and global strategies of social control applied by institutions suggest, even presuppose, that the community is, or can be, divided into a 'right' or 'proper', and a 'wrong' or 'improper' part, where members of this 'improper' part are designated as deviant. When discussing trust in the law and institutions by as large a proportion of the population as possible, as a condition for successful social control, one is discussing both the trust of the 'proper' parts of the community, and the trust of the 'improper' parts of the community. Ideally, the whole community would be expected to obey legal and other social norms because of its trust in the legal system and respect for it because it is justified, and not because of the threat of oppression associated with the institutions. It should be noted here that repression through sanctioning is also a form of oppression, in its ultimate consequences, and in how the offender understands it. Any fine differences in characterising repression as 'deserved', 'proper', etc. are external to the offender, they make sense only to the outsiders, to those who are not subjected to the repressive treatment, and therefore have a merely academic interest in understanding the reality of punishment and its possible effects. As will become clear in the forthcoming discussions, the more procedural questions about the *legitimation* of institutions and systems of social control also suggest this same normative divide within the community, and thus imply unlikely prospects for a successful generation of trust in the system and institutions on both sides of the divide of deviation.

The convergence between legal norms and control strategies of the institutions on the one hand, and perceptions of deviance and legitimate forms of social control by the community on the other, is reflected in a range of subjective and objective indicators. Subjective indicators are, for example, public reactions to specific legislative changes: to an abolition of the death penalty, to a scaling down of maximum prescribed sentences of incarceration, or on the other hand to the bringing forward of more severe penal measures, broadening of the competences of the supervisory bodies, the police, and investigative organisations and agencies, etc. Objective indicators can be seen as, for example, changes in the crime rate in correlation with institutional and legislative changes.

Questions about the legitimacy of specific forms of social control often depend on various presuppositions about the factual state of affairs, primarily on the relationships between citizens and legal institutions. Problems connected with the justification of specific legislative strategies in the changing of criminal justice systems, in the context of changes of political, moral, and other values, depend on the questions of what is considered legitimate in the relevant social order; what was considered legitimate in the previous order; and how the change of orders has come about; whether or not a parallel change of social organisation or a change in members of the community's perceptions of legitimacy has also occurred; and finally, whether or not the community has been conceptually, normatively, value-wise, and emotionally strengthened, or weakened. Questions of procedural legitimation versus moral justification of criminal justice systems are determined by philosophical presuppositions about the conceptual bases of the very ideas of legitimation, rights, community, relationship between consensus, moral and legal obligation, and similar fundamental categories that are always reconstituted when a comprehensive social change occurs. When the socialist revolution in the countries of eatern Europe occurred after the Second World War, a comprehensive and far-reaching redefinition of all fundamental categories of jurisprudence also occurred. The former 'bourgeois' concepts of justice, for example, were changed to a characteristic 'class-based' definition of justice; purely procedural concepts of legitimation of the law and institutions were changed to 'scientific-dialectic' concepts, based on the 'interests of the working class', etc. In the same way, after the 'breakdown of communism' in the late 1980s, a sort of 'revolutionary redefinition' of the concept of social equality as a moral and social category occurred. This was particularly stark in the countries of central Europe. The perspective of static equality of social positions, characteristic of socialism, which implied a suspicion towards any dramatic differences in the accumulation of riches, because of a philosophical preference for equality and harmony within the limits of bearable differences between individual members of the community, was rejected and replaced by the typical capitalist idea of equality of opportunities. The latter idea implies equality in the rules governing the process of competition in the accumulation of wealth, regardless of who is actually the leader in the race for goods, and with no suspicion towards the resulting *large* social differences and inequalities. The class concept of law and legal institutions was changed to a strictly procedural understanding of equality before the law.

Given the comprehensive change in perceptions of the community and its values that has come with the ideological and economic transition, the newly established link between these perceptions and public reactions on the one hand, and the social policy and legal systems that follow them on the other — a link which is a result of democratisation — is under particularly large pressure. The question of trust in the legal system and the control institutions thus includes issues of legitimation and the value basis of legal institutions in the context of socio-political changes. If these questions are clarified, they can create a theoretical framework whereby changes in criminal justice systems in central-eastern Europe can be viewed as a basis for conclusions about the role of social control in the constitution and reconstitution of the conceptions of identity of a political community.

The perspective of democratic legitimation

Whatever the dominant social dimensions of deviance, and in the present context specifically of criminality, and whatever avenue towards a more crime-free society is the best, most theories agree on at least one matter: legal institutions and their control policies must display one common feature in order to be acceptable: they must be *legitimate*. Whether or not social control is based on oppressive (or repressive) strategies, on the provision of alternatives, or, as is usually the case, on both types of strategies, the question of legitimacy of the institutions and policies involved appears insurmountable. Almost invariably, legitimacy is conceived of as a more or less comprehensive accord of control policies with the interests and opinions of the majority of community members. In other words, legitimacy is a political category *par excellence*, because it is usually based on the consensus of a political community.

For control institutions to maintain their function, they must have the necessary operational powers and means to do so, but the existence of those powers and means in itself is insufficient to make their use legitimate. Institutions are usually viewed as legitimate if they enjoy the support and consent of those whom they are supposed to control. What is in the formal sense characteristic of criminal justice systems as a special category of control systems is that those who are the target, or subject of the criminal law, i.e. offenders, are *not* at the same time those who legitimise the use of institutional social control through the criminal law. This special formal character of the criminal law and its institutions in relation to consensual legitimation of social control in general can be illustrated by simple examples. In many areas of social regulation, such as taxation, what is at stake is the imposition of certain burdens on particular members of society. Through taxation, societal arrangements and organisation are financed by community members. In most societies, the amount of the contribution expected from individuals depends on their social positions, meaning that those who have a larger income, and who are in more powerful social positions, are charged more tax and thus carry, in a certain sense, a heavier burden. The subjects or targets of institutional activity in this case are all working citizens, and all of them, on a rational level, supposedly participate in a consensus that societal life is impossible without taxation. The consensus that legitimates the policy of taxation is therefore a consensus of the very same citizens who are burdened by it, or who are its target. The same or similar considerations apply to many other types of social regulation.

On the other hand, criminal policy as a special form of social control is, in an important sense, different. Penal policy and criminal law are normally legitimised through a consensus and the support of the majority. However, the targets or subjects of criminal policy are *not* the majority. Convicted offenders, who are the target of criminal policy, are a minority in any society. Most democratic societies are characterised by the presupposition of the consensual majority that offenders will *not* be found among themselves. Furthermore, those who are seen as the potential target of the criminal law are seen by the consensual majority as a group fundamentally *opposed* to the majority. From the point of view of social policy, this is, of course, a trivial observation, but its formal features play an important role in the moral and legal characterisation of consensual legitimation of criminal justice. The point is simply, that, trivially, unlike in the legitimation of other forms of social regulation, members of the consensual majority do not legitimise institutions of criminal justice through the provision of consensual support to control *themselves directly*, but, on the contrary, to control and punish *someone else*, who is normally *not* expected to be found among them.

This special formal structure of delegation of democratic authority to institutions to apply repressive controls against those who are seen as fundamentally opposed to the majority means that, in a certain sense, the moral justification of crime control is structurally different from the moral justification of other forms of social regulation. It is particularly important to point out at this stage that *the very idea of this procedural legitimation of the criminal justice system suggests a more or less unbridgeable gulf between opposed and mutually confronted social groups.*

The assumption of an 'integrative community'

For the above reasons, the very nature of legitimation of criminal justice in modern political democracies does not support the idea of a completely or predominantly integrated or integrative community. If it is true that a reduction in criminality is most achievable where the community is closely integrated, permeated with trust and mutual bonds, then the very formal structure of democratic legitimation of criminal justice suggests a paucity of reasons for optimism in this regard. The way in which the consensual majority makes political choices and relates to restrictive social control policies suggests a deep awareness of its internal division into the 'good' and 'bad' citizens. While this may not be particularly unusual or surprising, it is important because it implies a low likelihood of any substantial increase in the integration of the 'criminally deviant' into the legitimate community.

Many political theories and theories of criminal justice systems presuppose the possibility of a dominantly integrative community.[26] However, the reality of contemporary political discourse about criminal justice, and especially about penal policy, is often at sharp odds with the assumption of an integrative community. Instead, that discourse often suggests the opposite, '*community of confrontation*'. The traditional rhetoric that once depicted convicts as 'wild beasts', characteristic of the 18th century and especially the 19th century (in some parts of the world even the beginning of the 20th century), seems to have disappeared, but only to give way to phrases such as 'monsters' who 'lurk', waiting for an opportunity to inflict harm, or in the best case 'ill adapted individuals'.[27] The rhetoric of 'paying one's dues', characteristic of the philosophy of early (and not so early) retributivism, increasingly gives way to the rhetoric of 'teaching a lesson', keeping deviant individuals 'where they belong', and increasingly, of 'making sure that they stay there'. This rhetoric, which often serves for the creation of a legitimational field and basis for criminal policy institutions is extremely important for an understanding of the conceptual and value assumptions of that policy.[28]

The question of moral justifiability

Moralising criminological theories of legitimation have repeatedly stressed that, to mobilise sufficient support and consent, and therefore to increase the chances of its effectiveness, crime-control strategies must be not only procedurally legitimate, but also morally justifiable.[29] From the point of view of philosophy of law, there is no doubt that the moral justifiability of, say, penal activity can be discussed sensibly only if the relevant penal policy is subject not only to procedural, political legitimation, but also to specific substantive, moral questioning. On the other hand, one must be very cautious here, because, from a strictly theoretical point of view, the above suggestion that moral justifiability, together with a procedural-political legitimation, are necessary for the *realisation* of an appropriate consensus and political support for the relevant criminal policy is not necessarily correct, and should by all means be subject to separate argument. The reason is relatively simple.

On the one hand, it is certainly correct to assert that, for a control strategy to be able to mobilise an appropriate amount of community support, it must satisfy that degree of moral justifiability which corresponds to its presumed accord with *those* specifically moral values — such as justice or benevolence — that have the greatest *de facto* importance and support in the given community. However, this in itself still does not mean that whatever a community legitimises in the procedural sense, by its support and consent, even by its investment of further trust in the legal institutions, is at the same time morally justified as well. The procedural democratic legitimation of any criminal policy, or any other institutional strategy, is morally justified only so far as the moral integrity of the community can be presumed. Procedural legitimation presupposes only an accord with those moral values that the members of the community accept and introduce into their legitimational deliberations and decisions. Their moral values, their consensus, and their legitimational activity, on the other hand, do not necessarily have to satisfy, on a theoretical level, the demands of an acceptable moral justification.

The amount of moral justification of, for example, a penal system's strategies, will in each case depend on the role that the appropriate moral standards play in the citizens' concepts of the community and rights. In other words, it will depend on the moral integrity of the citizens. There were political communities where the majority were so morally corrupt that the laws that, for example, banned the assembly of more than three members of a certain race or nation in the same place enjoyed popular support. In many isolated and small communities there are still consensual majorities that, for example, condone rape. One should remember the American South before the Civil War, where the consensual majority legitimised the slave system. Finally, can one ever forget the time of Nazism when, at least according to some interpretations, the consensual majority of an entire people legitimised, or at least tolerated, the policy of extermination of Jews and Slavs in concentration camps. In other words, there is nothing in the law that guarantees that a certain control strategy is morally justified just because it is legal. The killing of Jews and Slavs was perhaps 'legal', but this does not mean in any way that it was morally justified. The same applies to any degree of *de facto* consensual support for any type of policy. Democratic legitimation of the law is a political demand, *not* a moral one. It may be justified on grounds of principle, but at the same time it must be separated, on the conceptual level, from the questions of morality of the institutions and the law. This is a distinction that liberal democratic theorists rarely acknowledged, even more rarely discussed as a problem, but that must nevertheless be borne in mind in any consideration of criminal policy, especially penal policy.

In contemporary democratic societies, of course, most of the time the issue does not involve such contrasts between the consensual legitimation and moral justification as the ones that are historically familiar from the period of Nazism or the slave system. However, the principle remains the same. Moreover, in a certain quantitatively more mellow but theoretically even more pronounced way there are reasons to believe that procedural democratic legitimation can be *in principle* at least potentially in conflict with the demands of moral justification. What is at stake here is the fact that civil liberty in the context of at least liberal democracy is to a large extent determined as the liberty to follow one's interest without external coercion, within certain limits, mostly defined on the basis of the reciprocity principle (for example, liberal societies are sometimes described as those which allow the liberty of following one's own interest up to the point where doing so might jeopardise the very same liberty of others — when a conflict of this type occurs, the role of institutions is to resolve the conflict by regulative measures). In that context, the moral values that determine the degree of *moral* justifiability of a certain control strategy are often in principle opposed to the category of *interest*, and often represent certain moral restrictions or compromises on the limits of justifiable pursuit of interests. For example, if it is in the interest of most community members to prevent the arrival of a large number of refugees from other countries, as happens in the USA and some other countries regarding the illegal immigrants from El Salvador, Vietnam, China, and other countries, then the consensual majority and the democratic politics have reasons to support a cruel restrictive treatment of the refugees. Democratic political legitimation, based on the liberal category of interest, presupposes that, from the point of view of consensual legitimation, it is justified to incarcerate people who have fled from the prospect of detainment in concentration camps or seizure of children in camps that are in many aspects worse and more cruel than prisons.[30]

The incarceration of refugees is politically legitimate — it is in accord with the law, and the law enjoys procedural support from the consensual community. At the same time, this illustrates the distinction between the concepts of political legitimation and moral justification, as well as why moral justification is often understood as a set of additional, idealistic *limitations* on the pursuit of politically legitimate interests and strategies.[31] In the context of liberal-democratic determination of liberty primarily through the category of interest, it is, therefore, entirely natural that, in the perspective of consensual legitimation, political legitimation and the insistence on legitimacy often have a priority over questions of moral justifiability, because of the constant pressure of consensually determined strategic goals and daily needs that are reflected in the institutions of democratic authority. This, of course, is not an argument against democracy in an absolute sense, but primarily a methodological consideration of the relevant values and theoretical distinctions that must be borne in mind when discussing socio-political contexts of the moral status of particular forms of control strategies.[32]

Because a satisfactory moral integrity of a particular, moreover of *any* particular, community cannot simply be taken for granted — decidedly immoral political and less formal communities have been known — one can justifiably conclude that it is simply incorrect to assume that any legitimational consensus, that is, its presence in relation to any form of institutional activity, including control policy, in any sense guarantees or logically or procedurally presupposes moral justifiability, or the respect for moral norms. Consensual legitimation is there when institutions in their activity adequately reflect the needs, interests, and worries of the community, whether or not the community itself is dominantly moral or immoral — institutions and institutional strategies that derive from such a consensual support (again in the democratic context) are procedurally legitimate. The wider, and more demanding, question of their moral status is not necessarily, or always, posed.

Historically, legitimacy has been understood in a wide array of meanings, all of which are not necessarily in accordance with the mentioned concept of consensual procedural legitimation. It has been conceived of as arising from categorical moral norms, religious beliefs, or as mundane things as material benefits from particular public policies and activities.[33] The diversity of moral and philosophical paradigms employed to provide the frame of reference for the notion of legitimacy has therefore understandably led to scepticism about the moral dimensions of legitimacy and the feasibility of a reconciliation in principle between procedural legitimation and moral justification. This scepticism is, for example, obvious today in the so-called 'economic theory of law', which argues that the only reasonable legitimational basis for the legal system in democratic societies is the maximisation of welfare, or 'wealth', while categorical, traditionally seen as specifically moral categories, do not really have any sensible meaning or role in such systems. The economic theory thus defines the concept of justice as whatever might contribute to a greater accumulation of wealth, and the judicial process is seen as being governed exclusively by the demands of economic rationalism, as a means for increasing the efficiency of transactions.[34] In the contemporary discourse about legitimation, in the context of jurisprudence and political theory, legitimacy is usually thought of more or less exclusively in its procedural aspect: in its simplest and clearest form, it is identical to the process of popular democratic elections, in which the legitimacy of a political authority is constituted through the legitimacy of the procedure whereby the authority asserts its power, regardless of the substantive considerations of which particular political structure in fact comes to power as a result of that procedure. Political elections are legitimate, even if they lead to an authority that has immoral principles and policies. Similarly, consensual legitimation can, in principle, lead to the formation of legal and socially legitimate forms of criminal policy which, from the point of view of a certain conception of moral justification, are morally unjustifiable. This does not mean that democracy should be replaced by dictatorship, or that the legitimation of criminal policy should be abandoned; what is at stake is that one must always bear in mind that although a certain form of criminal policy may be procedurally legitimate, it by no means guarantees that such form of control is also morally acceptable. Perhaps it is, from the point of view of procedural legitimation, even impossible to reach a full convergence between legitimation and moral justification, but even if this is the case, the theory of criminal policy must take into account this potential deficit of moral justification in any procedural legitimation.

Consequences of procedural legitimation for marginalised groups

This notion of predominantly procedural legitimation of institutions, and in this context primarily of criminal justice institutions, poses the question of marginalised groups and their right to dissensus, because the mathematics of consensual legitimation always give priority to dominant groups. The dominant groups are largely able to generate public consensus regarding the most important values and priorities for any form of social policy. In many central-eastern European countries today, most of the populations often identify the concept of a justified political system with a rather uncritical perception of the liberal capitalist society. The key political and legitimational criterion in this context is viewed as a particular liberal liberty of the citizen, that is, the already mentioned relative liberty from interference by institutions, and the liberty to engage in activities that contribute to the realisation of individual goals and plans, defined mainly in the sense of interest, within the limits of non-interference with the same liberty of others. This concept is largely identical to the famous liberal metaphor of a legitimate social race, that is, a dynamically relatively unlimited social performance stage at which a competition for the limited resources takes place. The resources serve for the satisfaction of needs and interests shared by the majority, and certain structural restrictions in the form of rules of the game apply. This metaphor is often identified with the dynamics of the *market*. Although this metaphor is an accurate reflection of what goes on in modern society, its uncritical acceptance in the transitional societies makes possible a destruction of the principle of social justice and care for the individual as a purpose in itself in the deontic, Kantian sense, as opposed to a mere means for the realisation of the goals of the consensual majority.[35] If the principles of meritocracy and competition are accepted without limitations, then all those individuals whose existence does not fit into the perspective of efficacy of transactions and investments of material and social capital can be legitimately *sacrificed* to the system. This is where the true importance of *categorical* morality lies. According to this morality, certain strategies are absolutely impermissible, and some others are absolutely imperative, *even* when they are contrary to instrumental, progressivist reasons and considerations. That is exactly why in the context of market systems the questions of social justice (for example, of care for those community members who are not able to participate equally in the legitimate social race, such as the structurally unemployed, seriously ill, elderly, and even offenders who are temporarily or permanently deprived of their civil rights) are almost always perceived as *compromises* to the logic of the market system itself. That is also why the traditionally left political formations usually insist on a maximum amount of social justice *despite* the demands of market efficiency of the system, while the traditionally right formations usually insist on *decreasing* the domain of social justice (for example, by scaling down the social security services), while at the same time providing additional incentives and aids for those who contribute to the promotion of the metaphor of the market-place (tax breaks for industry and business, etc.).

Efficiency, social justice, and political culture

The liberal morality of the market, and some philosophers and theorists of jurisprudence consider, not entirely unjustifiedly, that the morality of the market is in its important aspects an anti-morality, is not the only type of morality which makes sense, or which can be discerned as dominant, in central-eastern Europe.[36] In some other parts of the post-communist Europe, in south-eastern European societies, for example, more communitarian concepts probably have a somewhat greater importance than the liberal liberty in the mentioned sense. These concepts by no means exclude liberty — on the contrary, but neither are they based on the market determination of liberty. The concepts of honour and family obligation, respect for tradition and custom as the *sources* of liberty, determined in close connection with the cultural, national, and intellectual identity and integrity, together with a range of similar standards, are probably to a far greater extent the subject of consensus and the main criterion of legitimation in such societies than the metaphor of the market race.

These differences, of course, are not merely political, but primarily cultural. In a communitarian culture the pursuit of individual interests in the sense of liberal liberty may be understood as dishonourable in certain situations, even if, in principle, it does not go as far as to threaten the same rights of others.[37] For example, in the liberal context, the conclusion of a large business contract that brings a large fortune to the individual, but at the same time economically cripples the poor community, in a legitimate and lawful way, is perfectly legitimate, even morally justified, because it is based on the principle of liberty to maximise one's own wealth, within the rules of the game. The individual has, by the conclusion of the contract or by market speculations, taken on a legitimate economic risk and was successful in the final outcome. Conversely, the community has been economically destroyed — a scenario that occurred more than once when market speculators threatened the stability of national currencies.

In the communitarian context, where loyalty to the community is seen as the paramount value, and personal identity is conceptualised as a modus of systematic participation in the communal projects, causing the economic collapse of the community would not only be understood as dishonourable, but might actually lead to stigmatisation, even retribution.

The same disparity can be seen from the liberal perspective. In the liberal context, standing by the tradition of a community could be viewed as irrational, inefficient, and unjustified. If the main liberal moral principle is individual liberty to follow one's own interests within the limits of the law, and if, for example, the refusal of a large number of citizens to follow their individual interests, for communitarian reasons of loyalty to the community, tradition, and specific *mutual* projects and interests, could mean threatening the very status of liberal liberty in the given situation on a more general social level, then it would be conceivable that, from a liberal point of view, such endorsement of the specifically *mutual*, as opposed to *individual*, rights and interests, would be qualifiable as *contrary* to the liberal morality.[38]

These two types of consensus, based on the normative assumptions of individuality and collectivity are diametrically opposed on a semantic level. Still, in every community there are individuals and groups who do not share the values and the consensus endorsed by the majority, or mainstream of the community. Their life in the community may be very difficult. They are often referred to as dissensual elements, and *in practice* there is often only one step from the assertion that they are dissensual and different in their values and attitudes to the assertion that they are deviant. Their different values, their dissensus, are naturally an obstacle to the realisation of consensual legitimation of social policy.

The 'problem' of dissensual minorities

When discussing offenders as a dissensual minority, one must bear in mind that the conception of dissensus here is a fairly uncontroversial one, which derives from the fact that offenders, by definition, do not obey legal and social norms to the same extent as citizens who obey the law. However, on a deeper level, it could be argued that this idea of offenders as participants in any theoretically significant dissensus is in fact unfounded. It could be considered that, for example, offenders abuse the assumption that, in normal circumstances, most community members will obey the law and other rules, and that they thus derive the real opportunity to abuse the rules exactly from the reasonableness of reliance on the assumption that most of the population will *not* do the same. (For example, if everybody in the street was armed and ready for robbery or murder at any moment, then crime as crime would obviously not only be indistinguishable from normal behaviour, but it would also be strategically infeasible: it would be too risky and its benefits would be too small for the amount of risk involved.) Given that all citizens invest a certain amount of trust in others in their everyday life, or a certain amount of social capital, it makes strategic sense to engage in criminal activities, because the probability of success is within the limits of reason and, depending on the circumstances, the potential benefits could be viewed as sufficient to justify the risk.[39] In this context, it could further be argued that offenders in fact *share* the values of the community, and that they are after the same goods and values as the rest of the community, with the difference that they use illegitimate strategies to achieve those goals, whether because of a lack of access to legitimate ones, or simply because they choose to circumvent the obstacles that such legitimate strategies normally involve. Hence, in this context, it could be argued that offenders in fact *participate* in the consensus about values, but that they simply '*usurp*' the right to follow illegitimate avenues towards these goals.[40]

The above remarks acknowledged, it still seems undeniable that the very character, and often the persistence and the structural character of the conflict between such groups and the law mark a dissensus, at least in a formal sense. This dissensus is a *strategic* obstacle, at least on a formal level and at least potentially, for the realisation of consensual social policy. Although the dissensus of minority groups is usually not a *sufficient* obstacle to prevent the realisation of consensual decisions, not infrequently it leads to various types of intervention against the dissensual minority. On a general level this intervention tends to be repressive. In some particularly intolerant communities it can include repression of certain political tendencies, convictions, and values, repression against racial and ethnic minorities, as well as a wide range of less extreme forms of coercive intervention.

At this point the most important difference between democracy and sheer populism becomes obvious: the simplified, mathematical dialectics of the majority is equally potentially oppressive for all forms of dissensus about social policy issues as is a dictatorship of a minority. Democracy, if it is not accompanied by a political culture of tolerance, can be more oppressive than a dictatorship.[41] Thus one of the fundamental questions about the legal legitimation of social policy is how to *protect* dissensual minorities in democracy procedurally. This discussion is a regular subject of jurisprudence and political philosophy, and it is particularly relevant, from the perspective of the morality of application of coercive control measures, in the context of *criminal policy*. Criminal policy, by its very nature, is directed exclusively against the distinctly dissensual minority of those whom the law defines as criminally deviant. The question of protection of the legitimate rights of dissensual minorities, even when they include those who are in conflict with the law, is, or should be, one of the main problems of criminal policy.

The explanatory domain of rights in the legitimation of social control

The domain of the rights of those who are designated as deviant, and especially of criminal offenders, is extremely unclear. The penal responses to their offences result in deprivation and pain that, in an important sense, 'nullify' certain rights. This is clearest in relation to civil rights: prisoners do not have the right to hold a public office or to vote. One of the most obvious nullified rights in incarceratory penalties is the right to freedom of movement and settlement.

Civil and human rights: The traditional distinction and problems of principle

The extent to which the rights of criminal offenders are cancelled by penal measures obviously depends on the seriousness of their crimes, on the nature (such as harshness) of penal norms, and, therefore, on the specific sentences passed on them.[42] On a general level, the discussion of rights usually involves two global types of rights, civil and human. Civil rights can, relatively uncontroversially, be determined as those rights which stem from the structure of a political community. In most democratic societies they are defined through an idea of political participation. In a large number of penal measures civil rights are cancelled.

The human rights of offenders are their *categorical* rights. One of the basic definitions of human rights describes them as those rights without respect for which one could not reasonably claim that the individual is treated as a dignified human being. Even the perpetrators of the most serious crimes, who have been given long prison sentences, may not be killed, physically abused and mistreated, exposed to starvation, systematic humiliation or degradation at least in theory. The murder of a murderer who is serving a prison sentence, by another convict, or anyone else for that matter, is still a murder; the same applies to any unprovoked and unnecessary physical mistreatment and coercion, starvation, or similar treatments. This distinction can therefore be viewed as a fence between those cancellations of rights through penal sanctions that are legitimate, and those that are illegitimate.

However, in practice, and even in theory, the difference between human and civil rights is far from unproblematic. In many cases, as is well known, those rights which, theoretically speaking, would be considered human rights, are severely compromised in the course of penal treatment. It would be very unrealistic to assert that penal systems always respect human rights, anywhere in the world. Cases that occur in British and American prisons, and probably elsewhere, are notorious, and involve frequent physical, and even sexual, abuse of prisoners by other prisoners. Prisoners are subjected to all sorts of degrading treatment and situations in which some of them are literally forced to fight for survival in the cruel environment of a deviant group. Repression often occurs even in supervisory measures such as parole and probation, where an excessively intrusive activity of the supervisory institutions threatens at least some aspects of human rights having to do with privacy and human dignity.[43]

Even in the fundamental sense of human rights, defined as the precondition for treating the individual as a human being, there are serious reasons to doubt that consensually legitimate criminal policy necessarily honours human rights.

One of the main aspects of protection of the rights of those who are the target of criminal policy, and especially of penal policy, is the appropriate supervison and control of those who govern the criminal justice system. In the noise and bustle of democratic political life, concentrated predominantly on the 'good' members of the consensual majority, questions relating to the theoretical and principled dimensions of justice and the need to protect those who are in particularly vulnerable social positions, even when they are offenders, often reduce to the whisper of a silenced conscience, in the daily struggle to remain on the surface of competitive social realities.[44]

In short, although democratic political legitimation has its obvious advantages, and they are quite exhaustively discussed in political philosophy, such legitimation by no means guarantees a moral dimension of justification of the system. The distinction between the good and the bad, consensual and dissensual citizens, which consensual legitimation certainly supports, even if it does not generate, threatens to become an ice wall, on one side of which the increasingly urban democratic societies thunder towards ever greater progress and economic efficiency, while in the silence enveloping everything on the other, dissensual, even deviant side, those moral values that are supposedly the foundation of the very rule of law: justice, benevolence, equality, etc., could easily be lost.

Questions about the role of control institutions: Efficiency and righteousness

Professional and highly coercive criminal justice institutions present special problems of legitimation, as well as of moral justification, because of their wide-ranging discretionary authorisations and their monopoly of coercive power. Discretion is in principle opposed to the principle of checks and supervision of the administration of justice. It is well known that in many countries scandalous abuses of discretion regularly occur. These episodes should not be understood as anecdotal, one-off events; rather they are phenomena arising from difficulties of supervision of the criminal justice system in principle.

Criminal justice revolves around the criteria of supposed professional competence. However, in light of the technological advances made within the system of institutional social control, the question of how to apprehend a dangerous criminal is rarely ever asked today — the way to do that is overwhelmingly a matter of routine. The real question is increasingly what policy to adopt in order to achieve a maximum net result: what communities to target, what sort of policing strategy to use, which offences to prosecute and which ones not to, what sort of evidence to consider admissible in court, etc. In many countries there are very specific policies of targeting. Most industrialised societies consider urban regions inhabited mainly by unemployed younger males as high risk areas for crime and thus make them the target of the bulk of the policing effort.[45] The same applies to various ghettoed groups in large cities. In societies where the absolute number of crimes is so large that the judicial system would be completely congested if all crimes were to be prosecuted in court, a clear selection needs to be made of cases to prosecute and cases to turn a blind eye on. The efficiency of a judicial procedure can depend dramatically on the sort of evidence that is considered admissible in court. This efficiency is the subject of discussion in many contemporary societies, and thus the issue of admissibility of evidence is also a matter of the 'economics' of judicial efficiency, not just of protection of rights and justice.

In Great Britain, for example, the same as in the Czech Republic, in the mid-1990s there were considerable discrepancies in the strategies of policing. The policing based on cooperation with the community (the so-called 'community policing') customarily entails a low level of coercion, an individual approach to potential offenders, and a high degree of interaction with the community and the public. This strategy was predominantly applied in the countryside in both countries, while in the big urban centres there was a predominance of so-called 'military policing'. Military policing includes mass raids, a military organisation of the police in blocking entire suburbs, stop-and-search operations on a mass scale of all passers-by, a high level of coercion, a relatively low level of interaction with the community, a stereotypical approach to potential offenders by targeting entire urban areas in which crime rates are particularly high, etc.[46] Similar differences in strategic approach are seen in the prison systems of many countries. These strategic decisions are made almost exclusively within the framework of the control institution (such as a police organisation or prison system). This illustrates the principle of relative autonomy of control institutions on the basis of a relatively long-term, stable, and wide delegation of authority.

Strategies such as military policing apparently promise quantitatively more complete results in the overall amount than community policing, although at the same time they are subject to a higher risk of victimisation of the innocent than community policing and represent an increased threat to the community. The reason for the skidding towards them is that the economics of institutional social control are seen as increasingly significant. The economics of criminal justice can unnoticeably become more important in the public legitimation of the system than the questions of fairness, individual rights, etc.

In this perspective of economic efficacy there is a distinct danger that the individual might gradually, and unnoticeably, sink into insignificance, and that numbers and statistics might become the only relevant reality for control institutions. This creates a circular track for the criminal justice system. Once that system has become more concerned with the economic logic of results than with the individuals it is supposed to control, the system is in danger of intentionally making itself indispensable. The interest, and often the rights, of the minority of deviants, thus disappear in the clouds of accumulated self-interest, compounded by the discretionary powers and privileges of the professionals. This degrades accountability, and is therefore a serious social policy problem, but more gravely, it is to some extent unavoidable in societies based on majority interest. The perspective thus created hides the interests of 'the bad crop' completely, makes them entirely illegitimate, insignificant, indiscernible, negligible. It makes injustice ordinary and common.

There are further, internal reasons why criminal justice institutions in democracies are inherently problematic. There is the problem of a chronic legitimation deficit which is built into the very nature and constitution of control institutions. Although democratic societies are supposedly open to questioning, transparent, and accountable for the work and functioning of their institutional apparatus, control institutions tend to be highly authoritarian in their internal organisation, opaque, and endowed with a very high degree of coercive power. They tend to be *isolated* from the main dynamics of societal legitimation, and they perform their gruesome functions largely *aside* from those dynamics. In this way, institutionalised social controls, and criminal justice particularly, represent a compromise to democratic principles. Control institutions occupy a highly self-sufficient part in society; their very mechanism of operation is coercion and intolerance of dissent, which is by definition undemocratic. This is of course only a theoretical contradiction, because the compromise to democratic freedom represented by criminal justice appears warranted by the nature of the 'commodity' administered, namely social discipline and respect for the legitimate norms of communal living in a society.

Externally, criminal justice institutions are legitimised through a consensual procedure, but their internal structure is not consensual. Coerced consensus is not a legitimational principle, but simply obedience. In reality, this internal 'consensus', the obedience, is a depressing product of dismay and oppression. Criminal justice institutions, at least in their penal part, contain *secluded pockets of tyranny* within social and political systems of cosmetic liberty and flexibility. Penal institutions especially present themselves as (perhaps unavoidable) dark shadows on the bright surface of progress and economic efficiency, humanity, and human rights. In many contemporary societies there is growing support for increasingly severe and cruel forms of dealing with deviant elements. In 1994 even the previously most liberal American federal state, New York, introduced the death penalty because of public pressures for a more severe system of criminal sanctioning. In central-eastern European countries the public, to a very large extent, supports the widening of discretionary competences and authority of investigative and police organisations, as well as penal systems. The legitimacy deficit on the level of principles, reflected in the incongruity of values and organisational structure of democratic social systems on the one hand, and the systems of coercive social control, particularly penal systems, on the other hand, fades into insignificance on the level of daily politics and their procedural legitimation. This occurs because the *factual* level of consensual support for increasing the role of discretion and making the coercion of deviant minorities more severe is high in most democracies. The penal system is an integral part of every social organisation, including democratic ones, but its authoritarianism and tyranny are particularly glaring in democracies, because they are in such contrast with the very substance of democracy. The unpleasant dialectics of De Tocqueville's tyranny of the majority seem chronic in the theoretical interpretation of social control.[47]

Conclusions

In the forthcoming comparative analyses of control systems in the central-eastern European region, the two perspectives above — (i) the perspective of specifically social characterisations and dimensions of deviance and social control, and (ii) the perspective of procedural democratic legitimation of that control and its institutions, and particularly of criminal policy and criminal justice institutions — play a key role. Socio-political changes that have begun in these countries have led to a significant degree of restructuring of specifically social and, in the context of theory of relative deprivation, political causes and circumstances of criminal deviation. Accordingly, questions about social control increasingly pose themselves in light of various ideas of what particular aspects of the socio-political transition most contribute to the comparatively high rates of criminal deviance. This same transition has simultaneously caused a change in the dominant ideas of legitimation, the importance of democratic decision-making, and the limitations of competences of criminal justice institutions in the interest of protection of democratic values, etc. Changes to criminal laws, strategies of policing, prevention, and other elements of criminal policy and the criminal justice system, fully reflect these two aspects of transition in the context of crime, its socio-political implications, and most of all, the conceptions and strategies of control responses to it. If there is anything to conclude from the previously drawn social dimensions and characterisations of deviance, especially criminality, then it would probably be the following:

(i) *they all imply a fundamental division of society between a consensual majority and a dissensual minority*;

(ii) *the interests and legitimational dynamics of the consensual majority are mainly reflected in the cumulative strategies of social control, based on the economics of input and result, which represents a potential threat to the rights and interests of dissensual minorities*, and

(iii) *if it is true that deviance, and specifically criminality, have fundamental socio-political aspects, even causes, then a purely repressive control strategy, even a preventative strategy based on deterrence, which lacks appropriate alternatives and a positive potential for resocialisation, cannot have any considerable effect on the crime rates. If* the main causes of criminality as a social phenomenon are social, then without social changes, through strategies that exclusively target the individual motivation of the offender, adequate results in prevention and crime reduction cannot be achieved. These are the conclusions that should be kept in mind in the forthcoming discussions, because, as already mentioned, *all* central-eastern European societies are going through changes that lead to a very significant redistribution of burdens and marginalisation, whereby the social picture of criminality is also significantly altered. Similarly, all these societies have passed through changes in ideology, and through changes in the respective conceptions of legitimation of social policy. This means that not only the *social milieu of criminality* has been changed, but also the *political milieu of legitimate forms of crime control.* In some aspects, this new political milieu has led to a higher degree of responsibility and care for the rights of all, including those who are the target of control institutions. In other aspects the results were the opposite, and the changes have caused drifts towards harsher and more marginalising forms of control. The future of the region in the sense of both social control and the establishment of a satisfactory structure of legitimation in the new democracies will depend on the course they take after the tectonic changes of the 1990s. Clearly, to be able to sense that final direction of crystallisation of social policy, one must look closely into the underlying meanings of some of the existing initiatives and events in the central-eastern European countries.

Questions about the social background of criminality and the political background of the legitimational structure of control strategies have reflections in the the realities of the transitional societies of central-eastern Europe and their criminal justice systems. These societies are far too complex for all of them to be examined in this study, given their different circumstances, history, and current perspectives. The aim of the forthcoming analyses is therefore to address three representative countries of the region, where the mentioned problems and questions are reflected in different, and yet for the region typical, ways. The three countries are the Federal Republic of Yugoslavia (FRY), the Czech Republic, and Hungary. They symbolise two contradictory directions of changes in the region. FRY is a leftover and descendant of the former Socialist Federative Republic of Yugoslavia (SFRY), the most advanced of all socialist countries in eastern Europe between the end of the Second World War and the so-called 'post-communist revolutions' in the late 1980s and early 1990s. After these revolutions, or ideological changes, Yugoslavia found itself in the midst of a civil war with immeasurable destructive consequences, its legal and political systems were being eroded, and problems with corruption were constantly growing which were fatal for the economy and social relationships. Because of the civil war and the destruction it has caused, FRY today probably faces the problem of criminality and other problems of social policy to a somewhat greater extent than most other countries of the region. The civil war has produced structural disturbances in society, which suggest that many of these problems, including criminality, are unable to be solved quickly, or particularly efficiently. Because of similar political and institutional circumstances, a similar situation can be found in parts of the former Soviet Union, primarily in the Russian Federation. The perception of a security crisis is clearly present in the entire central-eastern European region.[48] However, this perception is, understandably, more *intensive* in countries that have seen a disintegration of the state, such as Yugoslavia and the states in the territory of the former Soviet Union, particularly the Russian Federation. The impression of the crisis is quantitatively most pronounced in Russia, and least so in the Czech Republic.[49] In Russia, as in Yugoslavia, this perception relates to almost every aspect of life: economic, political, cultural, external security. In other countries of the region the perception of the crisis arises primarily in economic life, but it also relates to aspects of political and social life. In Hungary and Poland the dissatisfaction with the functioning of the political system, especially with the level of political corruption, is very pronounced. In all post-communist countries there is a perception of a sharp rise in the *crime rate*, especially in urban environments.[50] This perception of a crisis appeared early in the transition. In a public opinion survey conducted in central-eastern Europe in 1991 by Penn & Shoen Associates Inc., when asked whether or not they were afraid of 'unrest, chaos and anarchy' in their countries in the near future, 53% of Polish, 46% of Czech, and 65% of Hungarian respondents answered affirmatively.[51] Given that FRY is one of the starkest examples of this type of problem, because of the tragic extent of the destruction of state institutions that has occurred in it, an analysis of its situation with criminality and social control can perhaps throw some light on the general problems of the regions that are in an in principle similar situation with their internal security problems.

The Czech Republic, on the other hand, was one of the most militant and restrictive communist régimes in the region, in the period before the so-called 'Velvet Revolution' of 1989. Since then, foreign investment and socio-political changes have led to important improvements, which may not have been as quick and as radical as was expected at the beginning of the transition, but these changes have certainly been worth the effort and a certain amount of sacrifice. These changes make the Czech Republic a paradigmatic case for the more progressive countries of the region, which have also been luckier with their political and security circumstances in the last ten years. Parallel with its economic recovery and progress, the Czech Republic is also going through comprehensive reforms of its legal system. However, these legal reforms, as will be explained later at more length, have proven far less successful than the specifically economic changes that had been introduced up to the mid-1990s.

Hungary is in a similar situation. Its legislative and criminal justice reform at least appears to have progressed the furthest in the whole region. The reorganisation of the system, legislative changes, and ideological transition by their results also fall behind the specifically economic reforms. As in other countries of the region, many of the problems facing the system of social control in Hungary are of an ideological nature, and their analysis should show how changes in political ideologies influence changes in criminal justice regulation and social control, and how this is reflected in the state of criminality.

In light of the previously mentioned social and theoretical perspectives, the forthcoming considerations will include more detailed analyses of problems of social policy, as well as certain dimensions of the social crisis of the region. This could perhaps suggest a group of conclusions that serve as the point of departure for a further analysis, not only of legal and political changes in central-eastern Europe, but also of possible ways to overcome the general social crisis.

Although the forthcoming discussions will address in detail specific issues of criminality and social control in the former communist part of Europe, a brief overview of some of their most important aspects seems appropriate here. The first phase of reform of criminal policy in most of the countries in the region has led to a certain scaling down of repressive control measures, mainly as a sign of protest and as a reaction to the repression of the previous communist systems. A typical example of this was the abolition of the death penalty in the central European countries (Czech Republic, Slovakia, Poland, and Hungary). In these countries the death penalty was used routinely until the changes that occurred in the late 1980s. Another example is the scaling down of maximum prison sentences, relatively comprehensive acts of abolition of prison sentences, and similar changes.

In many countries of the region, however, laws are still unclear, and their manipulation is made easier by frequent changes to the legislation. For example, the Czech criminal law, enacted in September 1994, states that the longest prison sentence in the Czech Republic is fifteen years, only to add that 'in exceptional circumstances' it can be increased to twenty years. For 'the most serious offences', a life sentence can be passed. Bowing to public pressure, in early 1995 the Czech Parliament introduced amendments to the criminal law increasing the maximum sentences for organised crime *by one-third*, and allowing the pardoning of those who cooperate with the police or reducing their sentences below the limit prescribed by the law for their crimes. The same amendments significantly widened the operational competences of the police, mainly relating to the use of informers. The police are now able to use an informer's services subject to the consent of the public prosecutor, as opposed to the former practice of having to obtain a court's consent. Similar developments have occurred in the legislative activity of the Slovak Republic.

The increasing role of discretionary authorisations is worrying, because of the highly volatile political and social situations in the region. Although the absolute amount of discretion in central European countries is still considerably below that of many western countries, the relative amount of discretion in certain areas has increased considerably in comparison to the former, socialist system. Given the confusion that has been generated in these societies because of systemic and régime changes, the relative lifting of the profile of the role of discretion can cause considerable difficulties.

The newest amendments that provide a widening of operational competences of the police and other parts of the criminal justice system are significant because they reflect a specific negative reaction to the initially emancipating policies of minimally intrusive crime control. This negative reaction can be seen as a true backlash from the public, disappointed by the rise in crime rates. This backlash has led to the direction of changes in criminal policy being reversed, towards tightening the criminal regulation. In the Czech Republic only, about 80% of the population support reintroduction of the death penalty — an even higher percentage than in the USA. In April 1995, there were 19 771 prisoners in Czech prisons, an all-time high in the history of this country, and an extraordinarily high figure in the percentage of imprisoned citizens. In the 10 million strong population, this percentage is dramatically higher than in the European Union countries. Comparative information from Russia and the former Soviet republics is less available, but the rates of imprisonment there might well be even higher, not to mention the regular use of the death penalty in those countries.

By far the greatest problem for legal systems in the former communist world are the traditionally inefficient judiciaries, once notoriously corrupt and politically correct, that still tend to remain under the strong influence of governments. In some of the countries of central-eastern Europe, magistrates and judges simply refuse to issue rulings on cases if they are considered sensitive by the ruling political establishment, important officials, and organisations. Surging unemployment, which accompanied the introduction of the market economy, has led to a sharp rise in property-related crime rates; frustration and confusion, attendant on any major political changes, can partly explain a relatively steep rise in violent and irrationally motivated crimes, not infrequently involving abductions, rapes, and brutal murders, in some countries. The widening of private entrepreneurship invited a new crime for the region — extortion rackets against private businesses by local strongmen, gangs, and even paramilitary criminal organisations. Drug money infiltrates the official financial flow in the region without great obstacles because of the relatively permeable state borders and a lack of appropriate technology for the control of airports, river ports, and rail border crossings. Drug money brings with it a new sort of corruption of police and the judiciary, who are no longer motivated by Party loyalties, but by the cold power of fast and easy gain. As a result, governments often feel insecure, and strive to accumulate as much discretion in their hands as possible in order to deal with a worsening social situation. This conditioned reflex, responding to a security crisis by flexing the authoritarian muscle, regularly falls short of preventing the most damaging crime of the powerful, through which enormous amounts of natural resources and money are syphoned across the borders into the secret bank accounts of the new-old élites, while at the same time alienating the newly democratised parliaments and leading to spectacular shows of authoritarianism versus popular democracy in the streets of eastern European capitals. Right-wing policies gain pre-eminence, increased use of imprisonment becomes politically the safest crime-control policy, and any less punitive alternative strategies tend to be received with extreme suspicion. Even when such alternative policies pass through parliamentary procedures successfully and become the law, they are burdened with such tight restrictions that their real value is dramatically reduced. For example, Czech criminal law allows the use of alternative dispute-settlement procedures between the offender and the victim instead of formal prosecution, subject to *four* conditions. First, the offender must confess the crime. Second, the offender must *compensate* the victim for any damage caused by the crime, *if the victim will accept it*. Third, the offender must make additional '*payments* for the public benefit'. Finally, alternative dispute settlement is possible only for crimes that are punishable by *up to* five years of imprisonment. These conditions obviously exclude all those offenders who cannot afford to pay compensation, much less make payments for the public benefit, and those who commit more serious crimes for which more severe sentences are prescribed. In this way, instead of providing a true alternative to punitive handling of crimes, the value of conflict-settlement procedures is limited to keeping perpetrators of a very narrowly selected group of relatively petty offences out of prison. The latter is certainly a precious little which is not to be dismissed, but its minuteness reflects the suspicions towards non-punitive strategies.

The transitional central-eastern European societies are following the example of 'the West' by making their criminal justice systems harsher, but they are still in many ways considerably more tolerant in using repression than western countries. In 1995, a number of central European governments and parliamentary groups began discussing the possible introduction of the USA-style 'three strikes and out' legislation. The initiative was eventually rejected by all parliamentary groups and governments — only the Slovak government appears to have given up on the idea rather unwillingly. The grounds for rejection were that it would contradict the spirit of the regional criminal laws, which were 'fundamentally educational by nature'.[52] Although it could be argued that there is no such punishment which would be fundamentally educational, that all punishments are trust- and opportunity-degrading for the offender, and therefore in the last instance always debilitating, the insistence on the rehabilitational nature of the criminal laws in central Europe was emancipating in this context. Significantly enough, while the initiative was being debated in central Europe, American states such as Florida and the Australian state of New South Wales put forward new, more 'advanced' proposals for a *one* strike and out legislation. In New South Wales, this was connected with a political change: the conservative state government was replaced by a Labor government. The new premier, drawing on an allegedly large pool of public support, proposed the new legislation, which witnessed a general shift in the public mood towards less tolerant and more traditionally right crime-control policies. This shift towards increasing oppression and repression is not as pronounced in central Europe as it is in many western societies, and it generally follows the trend of public support for the introduction of more severe criminal policies in the West.

One at least seemingly plausible way of addressing the confusion over rising crime rates in the former communist world would probably be to say that the adoption of a new culture, which may seem attractive financially, but which certainly has its dark side, may make it necessary for these countries to adjust to high crime rates as an *inevitable* part of the new political ideology and social order. A daily atmosphere that involves strong competitiveness, a market-based organisation and dynamics of economics and other areas of societal life, naturally lend appeal to uncontrolled and illegitimate applications of essentially the same types of strategies, leading to increased crime, violence, fraud, detachment from the community norms. The result is the ballooning deviance which is an important cause of the current anomie in the region. If this is the case, namely if becoming used to higher levels of deviance is indeed necessary for central-eastern Europeans, then the key parameters that must be monitored are the legislative ones: criminal legislation would have to remain under control and not succumb to public pressure aimed at increasing the oppressiveness of institutional controls.

All these questions and assertions about the true state of affairs will be discussed in the forthcoming chapters in a more detailed and precise way, in order to show the nature of the changes in criminal policy in societies that, in an important sense, are trying to 'start over' and base their criminal policy on new, different principles and norms. Given the essential importance which, in this context, belongs to criminal legislation, that is the essential role that parameters of criminal legislation play in the explanation of the transformation of criminal policy in the transitional circumstances, the forthcoming considerations to a large extent concentrate on the legal aspects of social changes in the region.

Notes

1. See Kvaśniewski, J. (1984), *Society and deviance in communist Poland: Attitudes towards social control*, Berg Publishers Ltd, Leamington Spa, Warwickshire, pp. 25–34.

2. ibid., pp. 15–16.

3. This is the main thesis of the so-called 'labelling theory'. Some of the representatives are Lemert, E.M. (1967), *Human deviance: Social problems and social control*, Prentice-Hall, New York; Tannenbaum, F. (1938), *Crime and the community*, Columbia University Press, New York; Erikson, K.T. (1977), 'Social distance and reaction to criminality', *British Journal of Criminology*, pp. 16–29; Box, S. (1981), *Deviance, reality and society*, Holt, Rinehart & Winston, London.

4. Some of the most important representatives of this subcultural theory are Becker, H.S. (1963), *Outsiders: Studies in the sociology of deviance*, The Free Press, New York; Short, J.F. (1957), 'Differential association and delinquency', *Social Problems*, pp. 233–9; Voss, H.L. (1964), 'Differential association and reported delinquent behaviour: A reapplication', *Social Problems*, pp. 78–85; Jensen, G.F. (1972), 'Parents, peers and delinquent action: A test of the differential association perspective', *American Journal of Sociology*, pp. 562–75; Kandel, D.B. (1973), 'Adolescent marijuana use: Role of parents and peers', *Science*, pp. 1067–70; Krohn, M. (1974), 'An investigation of the effect of parental and peer associations on marijuana use: An empirical test of differential association theory', in Reidel, M. & Thornberry, T.P. (eds), *Crime and delinquency: Dimensions of deviance*, Praeger, New York; Morash, M. (1986), 'Gender, peer

group experiences and seriousness of delinquency', *Journal of Research in Crime and Delinquency*, pp. 43–67.

The theories concentrating on the transmission of technical knowledge about how to engage in deviant actions are called cultural transmission theories. Their representatives, amongst others, include Sutherland, E.H. & Cressey, D.R. (1978), *Criminology*, 10th edn, Lipppincott, New York; Burgess, R. & Akers, R. (1966), 'A differential association-reinforcement theory of criminal behaviour', *Social Problems*, pp. 128–47; Wilson, P.R. & Hernstein, R. (1985), *Crime and human nature*, Simon & Schuster, New York.

5. A wider discussion of the social causes of deviance belongs to the domain of sociology of deviance, which is not the main topic of this book. Relevant information about other theories, such as control theories, theory of structural pressure, can be found in Robertson, I. (1987), *Sociology*, Worth Publishers, New York.

6. Kvaśniewski thus points out that parents often consider that, when their own children behave inadequately at home, the school should do something. This, according to Kvaśniewski, reflects the level of reliance on control institutions in contemporary society, and this includes crime control — see Kvaśniewski, op. cit., pp. 17–18.

7. For some discussions of this problem see Therborn, G. (1986), *Why some people are more unemployed than others*, New Left Books, London.

8. See Larrabee, J. (1995), 'Community braces for lifestyle overhaul', *USA Today*, 14 March.

9. For some discussions of these factors see Becker, H.S. (1973), *Outsiders*, extended edition, The Free Press, New York; Dahrendorf, R. (1985), *Law and order*, Stevens & Son, London; Murray, C. (1984), *Losing ground: American social policy, 1950–1980*, Basic Books, New York.

10. See Kvaśniewski, op. cit., pp. 187–8.

11. Von Hirsch, A. (1985), *Past or future crimes: Deservedness and dangerousness in the sentencing of criminals*, Manchester University Press, Manchester. Similar attitudes can be found in Ashworth, A. (1983), *Sentencing and penal policy*, Weidenfeld & Nicolson, London.

12. Arguments against the thesis that deterrent penalisation has significant constructive effects are present, amongst other authors, in Bottomley, A.K. (1978), 'The failure of penal treatment — Where do we go from here', in Baldwin, J. & Bottomley, A.K. (eds), *Criminal justice*, Martin Robertson, London; Burney, E. (1980), *A chance to change:*

Day care and training for offenders, Howard League for Penal Reform, London; Burney, E. (1985), *Sentencing young people: What went wrong with the Criminal Justice Act 1982*, Gower Publishing Group, Aldershot; Chan, J.B. & Ericson, R.V. (1981), *Decarceration and the economy of penal reform*, Centre of Criminology, University of Toronto, Toronto; Cohen, S. (1979), 'The punitive city: Notes on the dispersal of social control', *Contemporary Crises*, vol. 3, pp. 339–63; Cullen, F. & Gillbert, K. (1982), *Reaffirming rehabilitation*, Anderson, Cincinnati; Cullen, F., Gillbert, K. & Wozniak, J. (1982), 'Fighting the appeal of repression', *Crime and Social Justice*, vol. 18, Winter edition, pp. 23–33; etc.

13. Von Hirsch, op. cit., pp. 77–91.

14. ibid., pp. 19–28, 77–101.

15. ibid., pp. 86–7, 89–90, 94, 97–9.

16. For some discussions see Sadurski, W. (1985), *Giving desert its due: Social justice and legal theory*, Reidel, Dordrecht.

17. In this place it is not possible to enter into the details of a philosophical theory of justice, and thus the argument remains on the familiar notion of justice as getting what one deserves.

18. Lea, J. & Young, J. (1984), *What is to be done about law and order: Crisis in the eighties*, Penguin Books Ltd.

19. 'Left realism originated as a political platform — an injunction to the political left to "take crime seriously" — rather than as an academic theory.' — Lea, J. & Young, J. (1993), *What is to be done about law and order: Crisis in the nineties*, Pluto Press, London & Boulder, Colorado, p. vii.

20. ibid.

21. ibid., p. ix.

22. ibid., pp. 76–105.

23. ibid., p. ix.

24. See ibid., pp. 50–76, 198–226.

25. ibid., pp. vii–ix, 50–76.

26. Examples are the so-called 'communitarianism' and 'abolitionism'. Communitarianism is a type of political philosophy that is usually defined through an opposition to liberalism. Liberal theorists consider that the main value of a political community is constituted through the maximum amount of preservation of individual liberty. Communitarianism, on the other hand, does not insist on individual, discrete rights to differing choices, but rather on the particular character of the community as a convergence of compatible choices and values of its members, who 'cooperate in the project of communal living', and thus create their own historic, cultural, and political identity. Where liberal philosophy insists on the concept of civil liberty, communitarianism often insists on the concept of a 'communal virtue of the good citizen'. One of the most well known attempts to found the philosophy of communitarianism as a special philosophy of civil virtue is Alasdair MacIntyre's book *After virtue*, Duckworth, London, 1981. For other influential works see: Taylor, M. (1976), *Community, anarchy and liberty*, Cambridge University Press, Cambridge; Taylor, M. (1987), *The possibility of cooperation*, Cambridge University Press, Cambridge; Jordan, B. (1989), *The common good: Citizenship, morality and self-interest*, Basil Blackwell, Oxford; etc. The connotations of an integrative community and the significance of the assumption of its possibility in the context of abolitionism are seen in the writings of authors such as Barbara Hudson — see Hudson, B. (1987), *Justice through punishment: A critique of the 'justice' model of corrections*, Macmillan Education, London.

27. The rhetoric from the convict ships which once transported 'criminals', often convicted for petty theft, from Britain to the 'Fatal Shore' in the 19th century, or from prison ships at isolated parts of the British coast that housed offenders in isolation on lower decks, often below water level, was primarily a rhetoric of *blame*, *reproach*, and stigmatisation ('wild beasts'). The dominant rhetoric of today is one of a *fear* of crime in deeply divided and confrontational communities, mainly in industrialised countries. It is enough just to look at what sort of political significance is attached to the 'war against crime' and 'elimination' of those who are designated as 'monstrous' members of the community. The nature of this discourse is obvious from a review of the daily press.

28. This was powerfully shown by Stanley Cohen, in his discussion of dominant visions of values that govern crime control and social control more generally. See Cohen, S. (1990), *Visions of social control*, Cambridge University Press, Cambridge.

29. This perspective, which is extremely important in the discussion of moral justification of punishment, can be discerned in the context of most retributive theories. One of the most readable and consistent discussions of this and other related issues can be found in the writings of Igor Primorac — see Primorac, I. (1978), *Prestup i kazna: rasprave*

o moralnosti kazne, Mladost, Beograd, and Primorac, I. (1989), *Justifying legal punishment*, Humanities Press, New Jersey.

30. In China, it is official government policy to seize children from families who have more than one child and to sterilise the women. This harsh policy of population control is one of the most widespread reasons that refugees from China cite as the main motive for their flight.

31. 'Politically legitimate', in the sense of sufficiently consensually accepted by the community.

32. For some other reasons to doubt the validity of guarantees that the democratic procedure offers, even in the domain of legitimation of institutions of authority, see Zolo, D. (1992), *Democracy and complexity: A realist approach*, Penn State University Press, University Park, Pennsylvania.

33. For a review of these conceptions see Sparks, R. (1994), 'Can prisons be legitimate', *The British Journal of Criminology*, vol. 34, pp. 14–28.

34. The most well known contemporary representative of this line of thought is Richard Posner — see Posner, R. (1981), *The economics of justice*, Harvard University Press, Cambridge, Massachusetts, and Posner, R. (1990), *The problems of jurisprudence*, Harvard University Press, Cambridge, Massachusetts.

35. Kantian ethics, commonly taken as the standard of morality based on treating people as ends in themselves, actually implies that people are never to be treated *merely* as means, but always *also as* ends in themselves — one of the four formulations of the Kantian categorical imperative.

36. At hand here is only one aspect of liberalism — one should keep in mind that there are other aspects of liberal philosophy that are not directly reducible to the mechanism of the market, and that relate, in a more colloquial sense, to the question of the amount of liberty that is at the individual's disposal *in the political sense*. These two questions are not entirely mutually independent, of course, but they have somewhat different connotations and thus the mentioned aspects of the market should not necessarily be understood as the key for the explanation of all liberal philosophies, parties, or political movements. For a philosophical view on the market morality see Khoury, S. (1984), *Speculative markets*, Macmillan, New York; Roth, A. (1985), *Game-theoretic models of bargaining*, Cambridge University Press, Cambridge. Also for some related considerations see Coleman, J. (1988), *Morals, markets and the law*, Cambridge University Press, Cambridge.

37. Some authors trace communitarian political philosophy back to Aristotle — see MacIntyre, A. op. cit.

38. Obviously, what is discussed here are extreme cases, but they reveal problems of principle.

39. This type of analysis, in one of its most influential forms, can be found in the writings of German sociologist and philosopher Niklas Luhmann — see Luhmann, N. (1979), *Vertrauen*, Ferdinand Enke Verlag, Frankfurt.

40. In a certain sense, this is the view adopted by Polish philosopher and lawyer Wojciech Sadurski — see Sadurski, W. (1985), *Giving desert its due: Social justice and legal theory*, Reidel, Dordrecht.

41. This problem is traditionally discussed in jurisprudence and political philosophy as the question of the possibility of tyranny of the majority, and is traditionally associated with Alexis de Tocqueville's classic work, *Democracy in America*, Random House, New York, 1945.

42. At this point the difference between the so-called 'codified' legal systems, characteristic first of all of continental Europe, and the so-called 'common law' or 'precedent-based systems', characteristic of Anglo-American legal systems, is not essential. True, in codified systems penal norm has a more direct meaning, because in such systems offences are correlated to punishments through an explicit system of legal norms, which prescribes specific ranges of sanctions, depending on a variety of circumstances and considerations, for specific offences. In precedent-based systems the main principle is that the interpretation of the law relies on previous cases and rulings on similar cases in similar circumstances, where judges have far greater discretionary authorisations to interpret the legal case and to choose the legal context and the appropriate legal precedent for determing the penal measure. However, in both systems, the term 'legal norm' is correct when used for the purposes of the present argument. Legal norm here means the appropriate mechanism contained in any legal system, whether an explicit penal code, or a norm derived by an argumentative interpretation of the precedent. In this century, however, even the precedent-based systems, because of the need to overcome the arbitrariness in choosing the relevant precedent and to satisfy the demands of as precise a 'measurement of justice' as possible, increasingly rely on codification, and thus an increasing part of the laws consists of enshrined codified legal norms.

43. There are numerous definitions and discussions of human rights. One of the more demanding is the definition describing human rights as the generalised 'right to human dignity'. This is obviously a far more problematic definition, and it raises many questions that otherwise

would not be posed in relation to the less controversial definition of human rights given in the main text. If human rights are determined as the right to human dignity, then, perhaps, one could argue that every penal treatment, or at least a large proportion of such treatments, are a threat to human dignity, and therefore also at least potentially in conflict with the idea of human rights.

44. See, for example, Carlen, P. (1989), 'Crime, inequality and sentencing' in Carlen, P. & Cook, D. (eds), *Paying for crime*, Open University Press, Buckingham, as well as a somewhat more classical text in Bonger, W.A. (1936), *Introduction to criminology*, Methuen, London. For relevant comments also see Box, S. (1987), *Recession, crime and punishment*, Macmillan, London.

45. For some relevant discussions see De Haan, W. (1990), *The politics of redress*, Unwin Hyman, London; Dahrendorf, R. (1985), *Law and order*, Stevens & Son, London; Carlen, P. & Tchaikovsky, C. (1994), 'Women's imprisonment in England at the end of the twentieth century: Legitimacy, realities and utopias', unpublished manuscript, University of Keele; Carlen, P. (1983), *Women's imprisonment*, Routledge & Kegan Paul, London; Carlen, P. (1994), 'Modernisms, poststructuralisms, and miscarriages of justice', paper given at the 64th annual conference of the American Criminological Society in Miami, November; Haln-Rafter, N. (1985), *Partial justice*, Northwestern University Press, Boston; studies of the British Home Office: *Punishment, custody and the community*, Home Office, London, 1988, and *Report of the Holloway Project Committee*, Home Office, London, 1985.

46. Owing to a certain desperation about the real possibilities for successful crime control, the skidding towards military policing has been notorious in the newer British cities (inhabited by a large proportion of unemployed, and particularly a large proportion of unemployed youths) such as Milton Keynes. Military policing was also widely applied in some more traditional urban communities such as Birmingham and some parts of London. In eastern Europe, the Czech capital of Prague became the scene of military policing in 1995, mainly with the rationale of controlling the increased drug trade in the centre of the city, as well as illegal immigration and prostitution. The skid towards military policing in the Czech Republic was so stark that many expatriates wrote letters to their governments protesting against threats to freedom of movement. These aspects of crime-control efforts will be discussed in more detail in the forthcoming text relating more directly to the situation of the Czech Republic. More about military policing can be found in Lea, J. & Young, J., op. cit., pp. 169–97.

47. To criticise democracy for tolerating internal pockets of tyranny and for sometimes yielding tyrannical results for marginalised minorities through a perfectly legitimate democratic procedure is relevant because

democracy is in principle opposed to tyrannic rule. However, that still leaves out of the discussion numerous undemocratic systems that do not even pretend to show respect for human rights recognised in their universal nature.

48. See *Security for Europe project: Initial report*, Center for Foreign Policy Development, Brown University, USA, December 1992, p. 13.

49. ibid.

50. ibid.

51. See *Democracy, economic reform and western assistance in Czechoslovakia, Hungary and Poland: A comparative public opinion survey*, Freedom House, New York, 1991, pp. 21–2.

52. A statement by Czech Prime Minister Václav Klaus in response to a proposal for the 'three strikes and you are out' legislation, in early 1995.

2 Central-eastern Europe: The significance of Yugoslavia and its developments

Although central-eastern Europe was designated as a communist empire, Socialist Federative Republic of Yugoslavia (now commonly referred to as 'the former Yugoslavia') was the glossiest example of a prosperous socialist country, which was not a mere satellite of the Soviet Union, as were most other countries of the region. It combined the most advantageous elements of socialist and social care and services systems with the more efficient semi-capitalist economies in its republics and autonomous provinces. Yugoslavia had a planned economy, but it also had a significant element of market competition of enterprises which brought it half-way to market economy, something that could not be found in the Comecon countries. It had a favourable geo-political position and a good international standing both in the East and in the West. All these combined made possible a society which provided almost unparalleled social services to its citizens (free education, free comprehensive health care, heavily subidised housing and rental prices far below the market value, a living standard considerably above today's living standards in some European Union member countries, such as Portugal). At the same time, this was a society which, unlike almost any other socialist country, gave its citizens a very high level of individual liberty and mobility. While the citizens of the 'Eastern block' countries were severely limited in travelling abroad, Yugoslavs had access to most countries without any administrative difficulties. Political dissidents from neighbouring countries used Yugoslavia as an open road towards the political and geographic west of Europe.

After the disintegration of the Soviet ideological umbrella and the so-called 'anti-communist revolutions' in the late 1980s, Yugoslavia again became the most representative country of the region, this time in the worst sense. Its territories, torn to pieces between secessionist forces, became inflamed by the worst European war since the Second World War, and large parts of it almost bled to death from continuous fighting and political, military, and economic shocks. In both senses, good and bad, Yugoslavia is the epitome of what central-eastern Europe can be, in the sense of prosperity and achievement, and to what depths it can plunge. This alone is sufficient reason to consider Yugoslavia as the first, representative case of the entire region, in a majority of socio-political contexts.

The perception of a security crisis in Yugoslavia has been more dramatic than in most other countries of this part of Europe, because of social and other relevant consequences of the civil war; mechanisms of social control fell short of succeeding in a more dramatic and more obvious way, largely for the same reasons. This state of security affairs is not fully reflected in the official statistics. For example, the total number of criminal prosecutions in Yugoslavia in 1993 was 166 216, leading to 34 855 convictions. Of these 34 855 crimes, the most numerous were offences against property (8231), followed by traffic offences with a criminal character (5782), economic crimes (4861), immediately followed by a close number of crimes against life and limb (4119). There were 8782 offenders imprisoned.[1] The total number of adults sentenced for criminal offences in the whole territory of the former SFRY was 113 803 in 1964, 106 031 in 1974, 113 576 in 1976, 107 398 in 1977, 98 213 in 1981, 107 770 in 1983, 113 655 in 1984, 107 593 in 1985, 110 091 in 1986, 111 604 in 1987, 109 581 in 1988, and 109 049 in 1989. The number of convicted adult offenders during the 1980s was therefore stable around the rough figure of 100 000. If one looks only at Serbia and Montenegro, which today make up the rump of Yugoslavia, in the 1980s the number of convicted adult offenders was between 40 000 and 50 000 annually, or somewhat less than one-half of the entire number of adult convictions in the whole SFRY territory. What is interesting is that in the years in which there was a perception of a large security crisis, socio-political destabilisation, and civil war, years which in the public mind stand out as the years of greatest danger from crime, statistics show an *improvement* in the situation. Thus according to the statistics the total number of convictions of adult offenders in FRY fell from 42 072 in 1990 to 35 756 in 1991. This figure fell further in 1992 to 30 197. There was a slight increase to 34 855 in 1993, with a further increase to 35 269 in 1994.[2] The explanation of this apparent fall in criminality in the year which is perceived as the most critical, lies in the assumption of a dramatic increase in the so-called 'dark figure' of crimes, referring to unreported and uninvestigated crimes, which therefore do not figure in official statistics, but which do contribute to the creation of an impression of a true internal security crisis in the 1990s.

Statistical information therefore does not reveal the full extent of the security problem, given the general impression of a high number of unsolved and insufficiently investigated crimes, which partly contributes to the relatively low percentage of convictions compared with criminal prosecutions. There is also a specific statistical reason for this. The figures from one year show all prosecutions from that year, but not necessarily all of their outcomes, because a significant proportion of prosecutions are taken over into the next year because of the amount of time many judicial cases require, and the use of legal remedy against first-instance court rulings, and the jamming of second-instance courts leading to long delays in reaching the final sentences. These proportions cannot, and need not, be determined completely precisely here. The purpose of these remarks is to point out that statistics in this, as in other aspects of social analysis, should be considered with a certain measure of caution, because there is always a certain disparity between the figures for a particular year and the real amount of crime that occurs in that year. It is therefore important to take into account public reactions to criminality in a particular society, because it can contribute to a more accurate impression of the real state of affairs, where statistics are silent for any of a number of reasons.

In some countries, public reaction to criminality is panicky, and thus unreliable. This is probably not yet the case in the FRY, and public reaction does not relate so much to the general state of criminality as to particular cases that receive high publicity, particular types of crimes that are particularly worrying, or new to the region. It is probably a wise strategy not to pay too much attention to the general attitudes of the population towards criminality, because globally the crime situation in countries such as the USA is very intransparent and largely unequal geographically. In FRY, public reactions to the proliferation of firearms in the streets and the corresponding increase in the number of violent gang show-downs and murders which receive high publicity can represent, to some extent, a guide for global, preliminary impressions that could be useful for a basically socio-political interpretation. In this context, it is particularly important to take into account certain traditionally accepted general truths about the proportion of criminal offences to prosecutions and convictions which, generally speaking, are considered correct for most countries.

The efficiency of prosecutions, in the sense of a numerical proportion of prosecutions to convictions, is generally relatively low. It is usually considered that in most countries not more than *one-half* of committed crimes are ever prosecuted, including both the reported but unsolved or insufficiently investigated crimes and the unreported and unregistered crimes, while the percentage of convictions in only reported and registered crimes usually does not exceed 10%. If one assumes that the same applies to Yugoslavia, then it becomes clear that the number of convictions is almost negligible in comparison with the number of actual crimes committed. This calculation is always and partly inevitably speculative, because it is based on generalisations and certain general presuppositions about the percentage of convictions compared with prosecutions in 'most countries'. However, it reveals an extremely worrying picture: *if* the 'general' proportion of convictions is really below or at the level of 10% of crimes, that would mean that the number of crimes, including the so-called dark figure was probably around 348 550 in 1993. If this hypothesis is correct (and unfortunately there is no precise way of verifying it, because the size of the dark figure is inevitably the subject of speculation), then it means that only about one-half of the real number of crimes (166 216) were prosecuted. As can be seen, this is almost in perfect accord with the general assumptions about the proportion of actual crimes to prosecutions. However, the situation could be considerably worse, given the widespread perception that the dark figure has been dramatically increasing since the beginning of institutional and political disintegration of the state in the early 1990s. This general perception of a security crisis is reinforced by the growing number of spectacular crimes, such as shoot-outs with automatic and other modern military arms, armed robberies, and especially recently, increasingly frequent murders of police officers, which remain largely unsolved, and which in most societies are classified among the most serious crimes.[3]

The fear from outside violence, connected with the civil war, mobilisations, and departures to the battlefields, tends to turn into a fascination with 'careers' marked by violence. The idolisation of criminals as role models for an increasing proportion of the young generation contributes to the crisis of internal security, which complements the external security crisis created by the civil war and its political, geo-strategic, and other consequences. The violence generated by the war in an important sense comes from above, it is carried out in the name of 'higher' purposes and interests, and everybody is its potential victim or perpetrator. Simultaneously, the crime and violence from below, inside the society, have shaken the social psyche and relationships. Because of the interaction between the perspective of legitimate external security crisis connected with the 'higher' interests and the war, and the 'illegitimate', yet in a certain sense romanticised crisis of internal securiy, the perception of criminal figures is gradually turning into idolatry similar to American and Australian *post festum* idolisations of the one-time robbers Bonny and Clyde, or Ned Kelly. The difference, of course, is that in the latter case the romanticising sentiments were created long after the events that inspired them, while in the contemporary Yugoslavia the idolisation is occurring along with the criminal careers of the idols, which has devastating consequences in the sense of mass deviant de-socialisation of the younger generation. This de-socialisation can have catastrophic consequences in criminality and social control for a long time in the future.

Similar trends can be seen in other countries of the region, but the perception of a security crisis is not as pronounced there as it is in Yugoslavia. An exploration of the developments in security and social control policies in Yugoslavia can therefore serve as a micro-example from which one might be able to better understand the true causes of criminality and the true ways and chances for re-establishing an adequate social control policy in the whole central-eastern European region.

In the context of the general perspective generated by the low levels of detection and prosecution of crimes and the low proportion of convictions, there are two basic elements that explain the possibilities for increasing the efficiency of criminal policy. The first element relates to the efficiency of detection and investigation, and it includes organisation of the police and investigative services. Given that the Serbian police force alone numbers around 100 000 which, in light of the size of the population, places Serbia at the top of European countries measured by size of police force, problems with the low level of detection probably stem more from deficiencies in the organisation of criminal policy and the general socio-political climate which contributed to the development and maintenance of high rates of criminal deviance than from any weakness of the enforcement agencies. The other element relates to the efficiency of prosecutions in the limited sense of efficiency of courts (the efficiency of prosecutions more generally also significantly depends on adequate investigative preparation of cases and a high level of correct detection). This problem is not limited to criminal cases. One of the more important problems facing the Yugoslav legal system today is the inefficiency of the courts in civil matters. Civil suits and conflicts routinely spend years waiting to be dealt with. Court inefficiency, therefore, has serious organisational, personnel, and other dimensions which are universal in all aspects of judicial activity today. The low efficiency of social control can also be connected with questions on the procedural, incriminational, and theoretical inconsistency of criminal legislation, the discussion of which is one of the preconditions for a solution to this problem on a general socio-political level.

Questions of legitimation of unequalised criminal legislation, 1989–96

The problem of inconsistency in criminal legislation is particularly relevant in Yugoslav circumstances, because it has political and institutional causes and connotations. It consists in significant discrepancies between the criminal laws of Serbia and Montenegro, as well as between the criminal laws of both republics, and the federal criminal law. These discrepancies are leftovers of the political, organisational, and legal shortcomings in the former Yugoslavia and its institutions. The problems should be solved by the enactment of the new federal criminal law, which has been in the making for a considerable time, and which should supersede the republican criminal legislation. It was initially expected that the new criminal law would be enacted in 1996, but controversies surrounding the proposed abolition of the death penalty, which was included in the draft of the law, as well as the possible replacement penalties for the ultimate punishment, have delayed its enactment. With the political unrest following the Serbian local election on November 3, 1996, which saw the initial election results nullified by the ruling socialist (former communist) government, and with the opposition and hundreds of thousands of citizens besieging the Serbian cities in a mass demonstration for democracy, it remains highly uncertain when the controversies about criminal legislation will be adequately resolved. Such a resolution would necessarily include a comprehensive social consensus and a consistent legal formulation, along with bipartisan support in parliament. Unfortunately, many members of the legal academic community in Yugoslavia have adopted a retrograde position, demanding the retention of the death penalty, and this will result in serious complications and delays which otherwise could have been avoided.

One of the most frequently mentioned and most glaring discrepancies between various criminal legislations in the current system is the paradox that, while the federal Constitution does not allow for the possibility that the federal criminal law prescribes the death penalty for any crime, the harshest punishment exists in the criminal laws of both republics. In other words, penal provisions for the death penalty are directly contradictory in the federal and republican criminal laws. In addition, there are differences between the two republican laws concerning the conditions of application of the death penalty. According to Montenegrin criminal law this form of punishment can be dispensed to an offender who at the time of committing the offence was not eighteen years of age, while in Serbia the death penalty cannot be handed out to an offender who at the time of committing the offence was not twenty-one years of age.[4] The fact that in Montenegro the minimum age for the death penalty is only eighteen is evident of the problem of violent, serious crime in the republic, as well as the considerable proportion of younger offenders who are involved in these types of serious crime. This also reflects the very serious social situation in Montenegro, and is probably to some extent an indication of the conscious implicit acceptance of stereotypes of legitimate violence and violent social regulation.

Similar problems of inconsistency between the two republican criminal laws also exist in the context of conditions of incrimination, of criminalisation (there are offences that are criminalised in Serbian criminal law that are not criminalised in Montenegrin criminal law and vice versa), and in conditions of application of non-penal measures, such as compulsory hospitalisation and treatment. All these discrepancies potentially create possibilities for unfair treatment of the convicted offenders, as well as threatening the principle of citizens' equality. This means that in Yugoslav criminal legislation a major reform and reintegration of its parts is necessary. This requires an overhaul of the Yugoslav federal Constitution, as the divided competences between the federal state and the constituent republics in criminal policy matters were established by Federal Constitutional Amendment no. XXX in 1971, and by the 1974 federal Constitution itself. The current, partly divergent criminal laws came into effect on July 1, 1977.[5] Part of the reason for the long time taken to make this reform are the considerable differences between various parts of the criminal legislation, and in order to prevent the recurrence of the same or similar problems in the new criminal law, considerable time is needed to find adequately equal and fair provisions. The existing inequalities, as well as the way in which they will be addressed in the new federal criminal law, have social, political, and cultural presuppositions, and they are in principle significant when drawing conclusions about the nature of Yugoslav criminal policy and legislation socially, politically, culturally, and legitimationally. In a comparative study of regional problems of social control and criminality, primarily concentrating on their socio-political dimensions, which this study does, a complete legal technical analysis and interpretation of the entire criminal legislation (its genesis, evolution, and the future of its particular provisions) is not feasible. What can be aspired to is a selective analysis of the most important characteristics of the criminal legislation and an interpretation of certain particularly relevant exemplary provisions and their characteristics, to create a basis for wider insights into the nature of the system itself and its connections with the appropriate socio-political context. A comprehensive analysis of the entire criminal legislation, apart from being outside this study, would not be particularly useful in the heuristic sense either, because the laws are relatively frequently amended and the enactment of the new federal criminal law will resolve most of the current legal and technical details and discrepancies. This means that their detailed presentation and analysis in this context would become irrelevant in a relatively short period of time.

From the point of view of criminalisation, or criminal characterisation of actions as criminal offences, Serbian criminal law is more restrictive than Montenegrin law, for it criminalises ten types of actions that are not qualified as crimes in Montenegrin law, namely the criminal offences of violation of management, violation of the right to manage, seduction, serving of alcoholic beverages to underaged persons, unauthorised use of copyright, hiding of cultural goods and items, spreading of false information, gambling, abuse of faith and church for political purposes, and unauthorised conduct of archaeological excavations.[6] The offence of violation of the right to manage is a reminder of the once unique Yugoslav socialist concept of workers' self-management, which in the same form could not be found anywhere else in the world at the time. This organisational ideology of industrial relations was abandoned in practice with the political changes of the late 1980s. Of the ten criminal offences mentioned, four (serving of alcoholic beverages to underaged persons, spreading of false information, gambling, and abuse of faith and church for political purposes) were in Montenegrin criminal law from 1977, but they were deleted from the new law which was enacted in 1993.[7] In other words, a partial decriminalisation occurred in the new Montenegrin criminal law from 1993, for reasons with practical and political connotations. The offence of spreading false information was seen as presenting a danger of criminalisation of the so-called 'delict of opinion', which limits freedom of speech and was characteristic of communist times, and was at odds with the newly emerging socio-political system. Gambling was deleted from the list of crimes because it had already been sanctioned as a civil matter in the Montenegrin law on public order. The offence of abuse of faith and church for political purposes was also deleted for political reasons, given the changing relationship between the government and the church and the need to avoid the possibility of special incriminations which would specifically target the church and citizens involved in church activities.[8] The offence of serving alcoholic beverages to underaged persons was described as the serving of alcohol to persons under sixteen years of age, in quantities which could cause intoxication. This presented serious problems in practice, because it was very difficult to determine whether a person was younger or older than sixteen years, and what quantities could in any particular case cause intoxication. Given these reasons, this offence was rarely prosecuted; it was eventually deleted from the 1993 criminal law.[9]

Questions of decriminalisation in changed political circumstances almost always have presuppositions which reach far beyond the mere domain of criminal policy regulation and into the depth of social relations that are reconstituted where there was previously only state regulation. In Yugoslavia today it is no longer politically correct to view church activities as some sort of at least potential subversion of legitimate social relationships, which it is not possible, or wise, to completely choke by repressive measures, but which, 'just in case', ought to be kept under strict control, and for which repressive criminal policy provisions ought to be kept in store, should the need arise. This was possible in the earlier system, and was one of its ideological characteristics. Similar considerations apply to the so-called 'delict of opinion', or expressing politically incorrect opinions and views in régimes where there is no freedom of expression. In this context there is some controversy over how far the transformation of criminal policy regulations and criminal law will be able to progress in the mentioned direction, as well as whether the mentioned crimes will finally be deleted from the forthcoming federal criminal law.

In another comparison, Montenegrin criminal law contains two criminal offences that are not present in the Serbian criminal law, namely the offences of 'illegal conduct of marriage ceremony', and 'violation of corpse'.[10] There is a reasonable probability that these two types of actions will also be decriminalised in the new federal criminal law. At present the first offence criminalises conduct of a marriage ceremony according to religious rules before the marriage is concluded by the state organ (civil marriage), which is also not in accord with the changed political conditions. This offence has been deleted from the criminal laws of most other countries of the region since the onset of political changes. The offence of violation of corpse has an equivalent in both the Montenegrin and Serbian criminal laws in the criminal offence of 'violation of grave', which means that it can be deleted practically without any loss in the domain of criminal regulation.[11]

Inconsistencies in the Serbian and Montenegrin criminal laws also include technical aspects of provisions of incrimination, such as the descriptive provisions relating to financial fines in Montenegrin criminal law, while the same financial quantities are expressed numerically, not descriptively, in Serbian criminal law. This inconsistency gives rise to a number of technical problems, such as those connected with inflation and the criteria that the court ought to use to determine the equivalent monetary values to those described as 'large' or 'small' benefit, or 'large' or 'small' damage, and similar. In this way, various provisions include, in the Montenegrin law, crimes from the group of crimes against the economy, against property, against public transport, and against the performing of official duty. Descriptions of values are present in Montenegrin criminal law, for example, in the characterisation of the crime of unconscientious performance of business activities in the economy (article 116 of Montenegrin criminal law — descriptive provision of larger material damage in paragraph 1 and large extent material damage), manufacturing and use of false signs for values and financial documents (article 128, paragraph 2 of Montenegrin criminal law — descriptive provision of large value),[12] unauthorised trade (article 131 of Montenegrin criminal law — descriptive provision of larger quantity and larger value in paragraph 1, and large material benefit in paragraph 4), tax fraud (article 133 of Montenegrin law — descriptive provision of large material benefit in paragraph 1 and material benefit of large proportions in paragraph 2). Similar provisions can be found in the characterisations of criminal offences of aggravated theft (article 145 of Montenegrin criminal law), robbery (article 150 of Montengrin criminal law), damage to property (article 152 of Montenegrin criminal law), damage to residential and business premises (article 153 of Montenegrin criminal law), failure to declare income (article 154 of Montenegrin law), petty theft, failure to declare income or fraud (article 155 of Montenegrin criminal law), concealment (article 161 of Montenegrin criminal law), destruction or concealment of archival material (article 162 of Montenegrin criminal law),[13] etc.[14] At least some of the corresponding provisions in Serbian criminal law contain numerical descriptions of values.[15] These and other provisions of incrimination are to a large extent technical problems with which law-makers will deal in their own right.[16]

The most serious differences, however, from the point of view of legitimation, which was mentioned earlier, and from the point of view of moral justification of criminal provisions, lie in differring penal provisions. This is the part of the legislation that must be carefully considered and revised, particularly in the context of the liberalisation of social relations, the establishment of new civil liberties, and the right to equal and fair treatment in the whole territory of the country. Because of the very nature of criminal sanctions, this particularly applies to those provisions which prescribe the death penalty, discrepancies between which have already been mentioned, as well as custodial punishments. These penalties lead to certain moral problems relating to moral justification, and require considerable attention to avoid abuses and arbitrary victimisation.

The relevant differences in custodial penalties between the two republican laws are also present in the provisions that regulate the possibility of meting out fines as alternatives to prison penalties, as well as in the provisions regulating the upper and lower limits of length of imprisonment for punishments prescribed for the same criminal offences. Provisions relating to the changeability of prison penalties for monetary fines are important for judging the harshness of sanctioning of criminality in the two republics. In this context, limited as it is, there are grounds for the impression that the system of sanctioning in Serbian criminal law is harsher than the one in Montenegrin criminal law. Montenegrin criminal law allows for the possibility of handing out a monetary fine as an alternative to a prison penalty in as many as sixteen cases in which this is not allowed by Serbian criminal law. At the same time, Serbian criminal law allows the same in only five cases in which it is not possible according to Montenegrin criminal law.[17] In twelve cases there are differences in the prescribed severity of punishment for the same criminal offence.[18]

Finally, provisions relating to 'disciplinary security measures' (usually custodial educational and disciplinary measures for juvenile offenders) differ in the two republican laws, because Serbian criminal law in some provisions does not *explicitly* mention the foster parent as equal with the guardian and parent in supervision-based measures without detention (compulsory close supervision by foster parent, guardian, or parent), thereby leaving the possibility open that the concept of 'foster parent' is included in the concept of 'guardian'.[19] Montenegrin criminal law does make this explicit statement of equality.[20] There are also differences in the modes of prescription of execution of the penalty of juvenile detention.[21]

If one starts from the assumption that a consistent system of social regulation must be based on the same or consistent values, principles, and strategic intentions, to secure fair treatment of citizens and equality before the law, then it is clear that the above-mentioned cases, like any other similar inconsistencies, lead to serious questions of principle and theory. To what extent these differences can be overcome depends in part on the specific criminality circumstances in various parts of the country. It is also true that, to be able to discuss the legitimational framework for the retention of any differences at all, a theoretical discussion of the nature of the system itself must occur, i.e. a discussion of its ideological, strategic, and value matrix and aspirations. Questions of reconceptualisation and reintegration of provisions of criminalisation, technical aspects of incrimination and penalisation must be left to experts in the area. The reason for the relevancy of this problem, and for its discussion in this study is based on the issue of legitimation: the question of legitimation is always connected with the question of adherence to principle and consistency of any aspect of social policy, and first of all of the system of social control. The legitimacy of criminal legislation constitutes itself in the same way as the legitimacy of any other strategy of social control and social policy in the broader sense: through the democratic standards of consensual support for the law, and for the institutions that execute that law. Given the reconstitution of state institutions in the territory of 'rump' Yugoslavia, and the consequent additional coming together of Serbia and Montenegro, which was partly brought about by their confrontation with secessionist interests of the former Yugoslav republics, the question of their internal synchronisation of social policy and equalisation of standards poses itself with an even greater force. Along with the relative homogenisation of positions and social situations in the two republics, which is the product of their political and social determinations, and which crystallised through the otherwise tragic disintegration of the former state, the demand for a homogenous social policy poses itself as well. This includes the need for a homogenisation of social control from the point of view of a homogenised legitimational and consensual basis of society. In other words, where there was once a relative pluralism of attitudes twoards social policy in the former Yugoslavia, with significant differences between particular republics, a greater disparity between the particular republics' strategies of social control was perhaps legitimate. In the changed conditions, in the socio-politically and culturally homogenised state and institutional cirsumstances, the domain of legitimation also narrows proportionally, thereby demanding a greater degree of harmonisation of social regulation in the two parts of the country than used to be the case in SFRY. The initiative for a harmonisation of criminal legislation through the new federal criminal law is, therefore, a natural expression of this narrowing of the legitimational base of the system of social control.

The distinction in principle between subjective and objective criminal responsibility

Every general conception of criminal law is based on a specific conception of responsibility. Social regulation, which is the main function of criminal justice systems, is structured on the basis of certain culturally, morally, and politically determined forms of ascriptions of responsibility. This means that the structure of responsibility will be understood differently in different cultures, political ideologies, and societies with different forms of morality. In each such society, criminal law will sanction actions in accordance with the main culturally adopted conception of responsibility. However, not every type of responsibility is legal responsibility. Although legal responsibility, and in the context of criminal law specifically criminal responsibility, reflects the dominant conception of responsibility in the given socio-political and cultural context, there are no guarantees that the legal definitions of responsibility in any particular case will capture the relevant mutual concept of responsibility of the given community adequately. The law is imperfect, and there is always the possibility of a discrepancy between its provisions and the moral, cultural, and political ideas of responsibility that dominate the relevant social system.

A full convergence of legal provisions and community norms regarding responsibility is an ideal that is extremely difficult for the law-maker to achieve, for several reasons. First of all, the idea of a 'community morality' is extremely unclear in itself, and it often represents a composite concept consisting of differing and not infrequently mutually contradictory elements, such as is the case in multi-ethnic and multicultural societies, with different understandings of responsibility in different contexts. Perhaps a more important reason for this difficulty is that the concept of a 'community morality' includes in principle different *types* of responsibility, such as, for example, those reflected in the words 'parental', 'human', 'business', and the most general, 'moral responsibility'. Apart from the difficulties connected with the definition of these specific categories of responsibility within 'community morality', and the determination of limits of the respective cultural and moral constructs on which they are based, *not all* these types of responsibility *require, or justify, coercive intervention* by the state. In other words, not all of them are sanctioned by law, and thus not all of them belong to the category of legal responsibility. Some types of behaviour are perceived as entirely illegitimate by the cultural and moral standards adopted by the community, and they often lead to various civil conflicts and torts, because they violate firmly rooted ideas of responsibility. However, many such types of behaviour, despite their illegitimacy, are obviously not criminal offences. Perhaps one of the clearest examples is adultery, which often leads to considerable condemnation by the community in many cultures, and equally frequently results in divorces that end up in the family court. However, adultery is not a legally sanctioned infraction, nor is it a criminal offence. It does not lead to a legal sanction. The specifically criminal responsibility is therefore based on the morality of the community and the dominant perceptions of responsibility, but not on *all* such perceptions in the community, nor on *all* aspects of the community's morality.

It is exactly the need for discrimination between the various types of dominant perceptions of responsibility that represents the hardest task for the law-maker in any society, and especially so for the law-maker whose job it is to define the domain and structure of *criminal* responsibility. It is exactly at this point of discrimination between various types of perceptions of responsibility in the relevant community that the greatest possibility of deviation of legal provisions from the community's views occurs. This aspect of legislation is to the greatest extent the subject of public debate in democratic societies. In other words, at this point there is the highest probability that the criminal law might create a separate, partly self-sufficient, conceptual apparatus that defines criminal responsibility in a way that does not correspond with the community's morality. Jurisprudence of criminal law plays a particularly important role in linking the specifically legal concepts of responsibility and those based on the community's morality at this point.

One of the most widely accepted distinctions in the context of a discussion of responsibility in criminal law is the one based on the division between the so called 'subjective' and 'objective' responsibility. The subjective or *means rea* responsibility presupposes the presence of criminal intent when commiting the offence, that is, the awareness of the criminal nature of the offence, the ability *not* to commit the offence (or the fact that the offender was not merely the casualty of some type of psychological determinism), and a conscious decision and choice to become involved in committing the offence.[22] Objective responsibility implies the responsibility for the consequences of behaviour, whether or not the offender became involved in the offence voluntarily and in a generally *mens rea* criminal manner. Typical examples of application of only the objective criterion of responsibility, without taking into account the subjective responsibility, are usually, but *not exclusively*, non-criminal cases such as breaches of various rules of the so-called 'strict liability', e.g. traffic offences. When parking in a prohibited place or exceeding the road speed limit, whether the offender committed the offence intentionally or unintentionally is not taken into account — the fact that a certain action has been taken *implies* responsibility. Obviously, when judging objective responsibility, not only the physical characteristics of the action are taken into account (such as in parking in a prohibited space), but also the consequences, actual or potential, so that, for example, in many legal systems those breaches of the road speed limit that can be characterised as dangerous driving, *or* those that actually cause a traffic accident with serious consequences are sanctioned more severely. In some societies these offences are often characterised as criminal. Here it becomes clear that objective responsibility, which will be discussed at somewhat greater length in the context of Yugoslav criminal legislation, includes the physical characteristics and circumstances of the action which is characterised as an offence, and the action's consequences, whether they are taken into account in the actual sense (e.g. transgression of speed limit that caused a serious traffic accident), or in the potential sense (e.g. transgression of speed limit that can be classified as 'dangerous driving', although in fact it did not cause an accident).

Objective responsibility is usually (but, as illustrated, not necessarily and not always) *not* applied as the *only* criterion of *criminal* responsibility. Rather, it is used as a *supplementary* criterion for *subjective responsibility*. For example, in some conceptualisations of criminal responsibility, where the conditions of *mens rea* or subjective responsibility are satisfied, guilt is also measured by the severity of possible or actual objective consequences of the action. Thus those actions whose destructive potential or harmfulness are greater are often taken as more serious than those whose destructive potential is smaller, although the subjective dimension of responsibility can be identical in both offences.[23] In this way, subjective and objective responsibility are both present in the characterisations of criminal responsibility in most legal systems, as the presence of criminal responsibility itself is usually judged by the criterion of *mens rea* responsibility, while the seriousness of the offence and guilt in the more general sense are largely judged by the criterion of objective responsibility.

Subjective responsibility and its legal contextualisation: Medical security measures

One of the most important legal contexts for the question of subjective responsibility is the so-called 'medical security measures', handed out for reasons of presence or absence of indicators of reduced accountability of the offender, and the resulting absence or reduced presence of *mens rea* responsibility, as well as for reasons of prevention. These measures are therefore the response to a reduced subjective responsibility, and at the same time they are a response to the full presence of objective responsibility. They are an expression of the almost universally accepted view of moral and legitimational unacceptability of penalisation solely on the basis of objective responsibility for the committed offences, with certain exceptions.[24]

The nature of medical security restrictive measures is preventative: the need for them arises from the awareness that, because of different types of pathological determinism, especially in mental illness, a person may commit a criminal offence unintentionally, in the strict sense of the word at least, while at the same time the full conditions for ascription of criminal responsibility are not, or at least not uncontroversially, fulfilled. Here one should note that the standard condition for ascription of full criminal responsibility *in the subjective sense* is usually considered to be the so-called 'McNaughten Rules' criterion, which was first introduced in the Upper House of the British Parliament in 1843. According to McNaughten Rules, for an offender to be considered fully subjectively criminally responsible, one must have 'known that what one was doing was wrong and prohibited' at the time of committing the offence. This is therefore an essentially *cognitive* criterion. Apart from the cognitive criterion, most contemporary conceptions of full criminal responsibility also include the 'volitional' criterion, according to which the offender must also be able to resist the temptation to commit a forbidden action, from the *volitional* point of view, on the level of psychological functions and integrity. The satisfaction of both these conditions, cognitive and volitional, establishes *mens rea* or subjective criminal responsibility. Insufficient satisfaction of either condition opens room for ascription of *reduced responsibility*, and it is exactly in these cases that the question of possible use of medical restrictive measures arises. In Yugoslav criminal legislation, criminal responsibility is in accord with this contemporary conceptualisation for two reasons. First, criminal responsibility consists of (i) *accountability*, and (ii) *intent* or *neglect*. Thus, article 11 paragraph 1 of the federal Yugoslav criminal law reads: 'Criminally responsible is that offender who is accountable and who has committed the offence with intent or out of neglect.' Article 13 of the federal criminal law describes intent in the following way: 'A criminal offence is committed with intent when the offender was aware of his actions and wanted their execution; or when one was aware that due to his actions or inactions a prohibited consequence might occur, but one still agreed to its occurrence.'[25] Article 14 of the federal criminal law describes neglect by emphasising the difference between the offender's *de facto* awareness of the ensuing consequence of his or her actions, or of the absence of a relevant consequence, on the one hand, and his or her duty to be aware of the possible consequences, according to the circumstances and his or her personal characteristics and abilities. This article thus reads: 'A criminal offence was committed out of neglect when the offender was aware that due to his actions or inactions a prohibited consequence may ensue, but he negligently believed that he would be able to prevent the consequence from occurring or that it will not occur, although according to the circumstances and his personal characteristics he was obliged to be aware of the possibility that the consequence might occur.'

Accountability is, therefore, a condition for criminal responsibility. Apart from that, responsibility is *defined* in accordance with the two conditions mentioned (the McNaughten Rules and the volitional criterion), so article 12, paragraph 1 of the federal criminal law prescribes that: 'The offender who at the time of commission of the offence could not understand the meaning of his actions,[26] or could not govern his actions,[27] due to a long-lasting or temporary mental illness, temporary mental disturbance or disturbed psychological development (unaccountability), is not accountable'. Paragraph 2 of the same article reads: 'The perpetrator of a criminal offence whose ability to understand the meaning of his actions or to govern his actions was *significantly reduced* due to an illness or disturbance from paragraph 1 of this article may be punished less severely' [significantly reduced accountability].[28] Clearly the federal criminal law leaves no room for a dilemma here, because it first defines criminal responsibility on the basis of the principle of accountability, that is in the context of subjective responsibility,[29] and then it points out that for assessments of criminal responsibility the degree of accountability is also relevant, not only its presence or absence, meaning that reduced accountability leads to reduced criminal responsibility.

Medical restrictive measures have a special weight in any system of criminal sanctions, because they are aimed at offenders whose psychological or physical integrity is impaired, whose legal liability is a controversial issue, and who, once convicted and sentenced, have a demonstrated need for medical treatment, not just penalisation. Considerable debate has taken place many times in the history of penal policy on the appropriateness and moral justifiability of penalisation in such cases, but most existing legal systems retain both elements: treatment and punishment.[30] The balancing of these two elements and the special weight that is attached to each of them in any particular system reflect various theoretical and legal views on these specific, medical cases. Some systems emphasise the penal component, while others give prominence to the treatment component. The Yugoslav system, in which these measures were mentioned for the first time in 1929, is designated as a dual system, because the restrictive procedures which it prescribes, in the relevant cases, generally distinguish between the *penal* component and the *treatment* component. In other words, the penal measures and medical restrictive measures can be prescribed as separate measures, which then means that in cases of reduced responsibility on the basis of reduced accountability, a part of the penal measure may be changed to a medical restrictive measure, so that the medical restrictive measures itself, and the modality of its application, partly depend on a corresponding penal measure.[31] In practice, however, in the immediate post-Second World War period, criminal policy was based mainly on penal treatment, while medical treatment, in the context of the idea of reformation, was more or less a derivative or secondary function in the process of criminal penalisation. Thus the 1947 criminal law does not explicitly mention medical restrictive measures at all as security measures, but qualifies them instead as *criminal sanctions*. These criminal sanctions, for example, involved confinement to a mental hospital by court order.[32] This was a dangerous conceptual situation in criminal legislation, because if confinement to mental hospital for compulsory treatment is defined not as a medical security measure, but as a criminal sanction, then this opens up the possibility of a real use of this measure for penalisation, which is contrary to the very meaning of medical treatment and borders on abuse of medicine, especially in the context of mental illness. The characterisation of medical security measures as criminal sanctions also opens up the possibility that hospital patients might be subjected to a prison-like penal treatment, which would threaten their human rights, regardless of whether or not they are convicted offenders. Penalisation is not reconcilable with the concept of treatment and healing. Such use of medical institutions, which is at least conceptually and potentially facilitated by the mentioned characterisation of medical measures, would lead to a corruption of the very idea of the right to treatment and care by the medical system and personnel, and could lead to additional stigmatisation, especially of the mentally ill. Penal treatment could easily become usual practice in the hospitals that often house offenders committed to compulsory medical treatment by court order. For these reasons, it is of fundamental importance in every system conceptually and legally to separate medical security measures from penal ones.

Probably to some extent because of these reasons, medical security measures are mentioned again in the 1951 criminal law, as well as in the 1971 version, whose provisions relating to these measures are still valid today.[33] In today's use of medical security measures the primary role belongs to medical treatment, and only afterwards to penal treatment, which is in accord with the logic of curing and care of the ill.

In cases of reduced subjective responsibility, moral questions of justifiability of penalisation in the usual way pose themselves because full responsibility cannot be uncontroversially established, and there is an obvious need for the use of preventative measures for the protection of other community members, as well as the offender. It is thus considered the best and most acceptable approach to this problem to commit such offenders to compulsory medical treatment, which usually takes place in special institutions.

The so-called 'general provisions' of the federal criminal law contain three different types of medical security measures, including: (1) compulsory psychiatric treatment and confinement to a hospital, (2) compulsory psychiatric treatment without confinement, and (3) compulsory treatment of alcoholics and drug addicts.[34]

The application of these measures, and particularly the one cited under (1) above, is subject to a high degree of discretion on behalf of the court. The court is empowered to decide entirely about the expert testimony (including the question of which expert witness is to offer a professional assessment of the offender), about the mental state of the offender at the time of committing the offence (taking into account the opinion of the expert witness), about the appropriateness of the use of medical restrictive measures instead of penalties, and to a large extent also about the duration and conditions of their application. The court also decides whether or not a medical restrictive measure may be revoked or its application interrupted, whether or not the offender can be sent to serve the rest of the sentence in a penal institution, or whether or not the offender can be released on the basis of assessment of sufficient recovery, which guarantees that the offender no longer represents a social danger because of mental illness. For example, article 63, paragraph 2 of the federal criminal law qualifies the use of the measure of compulsory psychiatric treatment and confinement to a hospital in the following way: 'The court will interrupt the measure prescribed by paragraph 1 of this article [compulsory psychiatric treatment and confinement to a hospital] where it establishes that the need for compulsory treatment and confinement of the offender to hospital has ceased.' The court therefore decides on the time when this need has ceased, on the basis of discretionary authorisations, taking into account the relevant medical opinions. If the length of treatment is shorter than the length of the sentence (for example, a prison penalty whose initial part is spent in a closed psychiatric ward), then paragraph 3 of this same article states that 'the court may determine that the offender be sent to ... serve the remainder of the penalty or to be released on parole', thereby taking into account the relevant circumstances, such as the time spent on treatment, the length of the remainder of the sentence, and the health status of the offender. Article 64 contains similar discretionary authorisations relating to the measure of compulsory psychiatric treatment without confinement, where the court may, in certain circumstances, decide to send the offender to serve the remainder of the sentence under the measure of compulsory psychiatric treatment with confinement to a hospital.

In the above context, it is difficult to imagine any reasonable alternative to discretionary decisions of the type mentioned, given the nature of the problem under consideration and the need for prevention. However, such wide use of discretion obviously opens up questions of legitimation and those relating to checks of the ways in which it is used, as well as questions about how often and how carefully the court considers the progress of treatment of particular mentally ill offenders and how fair are the decisions it makes on the basis of such considerations. Obviously, if offenders are committed to compulsory treatment in closed institutions, and if the court forgets about them, and their fate almost completely depends on judicial discretion, it is easy to imagine to what sort of conflicts with the principles of fair treatment and protection of human rights such practice and regulation can lead. This problem with discretion is particularly difficult in the context of authorisations that the staff of relevant institutions have in relation to the patients/offenders, given the importance of their recommendations for the release of particular offenders. For example, article 63, paragraph 3 of the federal criminal law provides that, when making a decision to release an offender fom compulsory treatment and confinement to a hospital on parole, the court will particularly take into account the success of the treatment, the offender's health condition, etc. It is obvious that in these assessments the court's decision must largely depend on the recommendations and opinions of the medical staff of the institutions conducting the treatment and confinement, which, from a formal point of view, widens the domain of influence of discretionary decisions. The possibility of mistakes or abuse is thereby also increased.

Although the role of discretionary decisions of courts is apparently unequal in the context of all three medical security measures, in essence its absolute amount is very worrying. The measure of compulsory psychiatric treatment and confinement to a hospital is a measure whose duration, because of its very nature, is potentially unlimited, and depends on the assessment and decision of the court, which means that the role of the court's discretion is largest here. That role is somewhat smaller in the context of compulsory psychiatric treatment without confinement, because the length of this measure is limited by law to two years.[35] However, when this measure expires, the court is empowered to use the option of committing the offender to compulsory treatment and confinement to a hospital, if the offender's medical condition has not improved sufficiently or has worsened. In other words, *on the level of application of the measure* of compulsory psychiatric treatment without confinement, the court's discretion is relatively limited, but the full measure of discretion comes back after the expiration of the measure, *through the right to use another measure.* The problematic status of the legitimational basis and the possibility of adequate checks of the applications of such far-reaching discretionary authorisations are extremely important in every system.

The 'dual' character of treatment of offenders suffering from various types of mental disturbances is particularly clearly reflected in the measure of compulsory treatment for alcoholics and drug addicts. The conceptual distinction between penal and medical treatment is present in the specification of three conditions that must be satisfied for the application of this measure:
(i) there must be a clear causal connection between the drug or alcohol dependency and the criminal offence itself,[36]
(ii) there must be a clear danger that the offender, because of the dependency, will continue to commit similar offences,[37] and
(iii) the offender must have been convicted of a criminal offence and must have been sentenced to an actual or probationary penalty.[38]

These conditions also show that medical security measures are meted out partly as an alternative to penal measures in cases of mental disturbance and illnesses of addiction. They can therefore be transformed into an actual penalty, or into a probation, depending on their duration in relation to the ordered penal measure. In the context of the measure of compulsory treatment of alcoholics and drug addicts, it is important to point out that those offenders who are, for example, alcohol- or drug-dependent, but who have been convicted of criminal offences in the commission of which *no clear causal relation* between their addiction and the offence itself was present, will be subjected to penal, and not medical, treatment. At the same time, it should be noted that, when those offenders who have been committed to compulsory treatment of alcoholism or drug dependency are concerned, the assessment of their *accountability* plays a *secondary* role, unlike the measure of compulsory psychiatric treatment and confinement to a hospital. The primary role in the context of application of measures of compulsory treatment of alcoholics and drug addicts belongs to *the causal connection* between their illness of addiction and the offence, and not necessarily their accountability. There is a significant difference here that can be illustrated by an example. If a drug addict breaks into a pharmacy, in a perfectly normal, calculated and accountable way, thereby satisfying both the criteria of the McNaughten Rules and the volitional criterion of *mens rea* responsibility, to prevent running out of an already depleted personal stock of drugs on which he or she is dependent, then on a conceptual level it could be argued that the provision cited above under (i) means that such an offender should be treated medically, and not merely penalised. From a formal point of view, *mens rea* reponsibility is present in such a situation, but the very fact of dependency and the probable motives for the break-in, which are directly connected to the dependency, represent a certain basis for the argument that a medical measure should be applied, and not a strictly penal treatment. At the same time, the dual nature of the law facilitates a situation in which the *mens rea* character of the offence leads to a conviction and sentencing, which then, in light of the circumstances, is completely or partly transformed into a medical measure or at least overlaps with one. *The modus of application* of the medical measure is also partly determined by the character of the penal measure that has been meted out: if the offender has been sentenced to probation, then as a rule the medical measure will not be applied along with confinement to a hospital, in which case it cannot last for longer than two years.[39] If the penal measure is a prison sentence, then the medical measure will be applied along with confinement to a hospital. As with the measure of compulsory psychiatric treatment without confinement, the compulsory treatment of alcoholics and drug addicts without confinement and along with a sentence to probation may be transformed into a confinement to a hospital and revocation of the probation, depending on the court's judgment and the discretionary decisions that it is empowered to make.[40]

One of the special challenges for any social system, and thus also for the Yugoslav system, is what to do with juvenile offenders who are impaired in their mental development. This type of regulation is absent from the federal criminal law, but it is present in both the Serbian (article 30) and the Montenegrin criminal laws (article 22). The republican laws provide that in such cases a measure of committal to a *special institution for juveniles* will be applied, instead of the measure of compulsory psychiatric treatment with confinement to a hospital. The problem with the application of this measure lies in the lack of an appropriate institution for such juvenile offenders, which means that, practically, they must be housed with other offenders. This practice obviously has serious weaknesses, because it exposes the juvenile to the influence, even the dangers, of accommodation and treatment with adult offenders. Given that juvenile offenders require a greater amount of care and medical treatment, the establishment of institutions that would be less restrictive, while specialising in the treatment of juveniles, could have beneficial results in possibly bringing down the rates of recidivism in this category of offenders, as well as avoiding the repression and the sort of régime that are sometimes unavoidable in the institutions that house adult offenders with the same type of mental health or mental development problems.

What is important to emphasise is that all these problems represent general legitimational, even strategic, problems for every system, not only the Yugoslav system. It could be argued that in the Yugoslav system they are treated with at least the same degree of consistency and constructive approach of the law-maker as in any other country of central-eastern or western Europe. Discretion simply cannot be avoided in the application of preventative measures when what is at stake are mentally ill or disturbed offenders. At the same time, a pronounced role of discretion is a problem in principle, and the use of discretion must always be seen as requiring frequent checks in order to minimise or avoid the injustices that could stem from mistakes in it being exercised. The integrity of the judiciary, the criminal law, the police organisation, and the perspectives of democratic supervision by the public of the activity of social control institutions, all depend on a certain number of factors that are systematically affected by the political changes through which Yugoslavia, together with other countries of the region, is now passing. These changes represent an opportunity for the establishment of a more stable basis for a legitimate, strategically and socio-politically more solid social control, but they also represent systematic obstacles that can be understood only in the context of the internal security situation as reflected in the amount of criminality, and the relevant ideological, socio-political, and other circumstances.

Elements of discretion in the Yugoslav system, similar to the systems of other central-eastern European countries, are aimed at achieving the maximum degree of *prevention*. It was mentioned before that this discretion goes in a direction that is inherently worrying, because it gives the courts the right to decide the application of measures that include deprivation of liberty and incarceration of citizens in a fairly unlimited way, and that such measures are often made available in the law as *mutual alternatives* and *additions*. At the same time, however, there are theoretical and conceptual elements of the Yugoslav criminal legislation that go *in the opposite direction*, and constructively place certain *additional restrictions* on the ascription of criminal responsibility, penalisation, and criminalisation of actions. One of the most important conceptual and regulative, liberating characteristics of the system is the so-called 'objective condition of incrimination'.

Objective responsibility and the objective condition of incrimination

In the previous discussions it was suggested that to some extent the insistence on subjective responsibility contributes to the avoidance of penalisation of all those offenders who are objectively responsible but do not fulfil the conditions of *mens rea* responsibility. However, objective responsibility can also serve as a restriction on the penalisation of all those offenders who *fulfil* the conditions of *mens rea* responsibility, but whose offences do not have a sufficient objectively destructive dimension, whether in the potential or in the actual sense. If one looks primarily at the *potential* character of the social danger or damage that an action produces, then the condition of objective responsibility would be that the offender must have committed an offence which could have certain destructive consequences. If, on the other hand, one looks primarily at the *actual* character of this damage, then the objective responsibility would be present only where (i) a dangerous and destructive action was committed and (ii) certain harmful or dangerous consequences have actually occurred, whereby the domain of incrimination on the basis of both subjective and objective responsibility is considerably *narrowed*. The latter interpretation of objective responsibility is therefore more liberating. It is, in an important sense, the interpretation in the Yugoslav criminal legislation, so far as the so-called 'objective condition of incrimination' is concerned.[41]

Incriminations in criminal legislation are typically based on *subjective* responsibility, which constitutes the very criminal essence of the criminal offence, but Yugoslav criminal legislation, in certain cases, contains additional provisions that further *limit* incrimination based on the essence of an offence alone. This limitation is connected with the requirement of the presence of certain *additional*, *objective* elements, which constitute a sufficient legal basis for criminal prosecution.[42] This category of objective condition of incrimination largely reflects the role of theoretical concepts of guilt and 'just desert' in the everyday practice of criminal justice, and particularly so in the judicial practice as one of the most controversial elements of social control, given that what is at stake is punishment and the application of repressive measures. The objective condition of incrimination presupposes that, to be considered criminally responsible in particular cases, the offender must (i) be *factually* responsible for the offence, (ii) fulfil the criteria of subjective responsibility, and (iii) in connection with the offence, certain *objective* consequences must have occurred, which confer the status of a criminal offence on the action, although the essence of the action might be undoubtedly criminal, even with no such objective consequences occurring. In a formal sense, this means that certain criminal offences are determined not only as descriptions of certain *physical actions* of which they consist, but also as descriptions of certain *factual events* which have occurred as a result of these actions and which, in themselves, do not have to be included in the *intentions* of the offender. These objective events bestow a criminal status on the relevant actions. For example, Yugoslav criminal legislation sanctions participation in a street brawl, but for this to assume the character and status of a crime, the objective condition of incrimination must be fulfilled according to which, because of one's participation in a street brawl, another person must have been killed or seriously injured. Article 55 of Serbian criminal law thus reads: 'An offender who participates in a brawl in which someone is killed of life or another person suffers serious bodily harm, will be punished for the participation in the brawl itself by imprisonment from three months to three years.' Here the very formulation of this article of the law is highly ambiguous. On the one hand, the article requires that a serious consequence has occurred (death or serious bodily harm to another person), but in the continuation of the same sentence it states that the punishment will be meted out 'for the participation in the brawl itself', which obviously represents the essence of the criminal offence and thus suggests that the basis of responsibility is subjective, that is the intention to participate in the brawl itself. Article 38 of Montenegrin criminal law has an identical text.[43]

These formulations suggest that, if someone has participated in a physical confrontation, which could include all elements of *mens rea* responsibility, and if, entirely accidentally, such a brawl has not produced any serious consequences in the form of someone's serious bodily harm or death, then a criminal prosecution is unlikely. If, however, serious consequences have resulted, criminal prosecution is a certainty. Many actions which formally belong to the category of criminal offences are treated as infractions, unless they are followed by objective conditions of incrimination.[44]

The whole post-Second War evolution of the Yugoslav criminal legislation reveals a certain direction of *reduced restrictiveness*. Numerous offences, which had once been the subject of criminal prosecution on the basis of their criminal essence alone, meaning without a need for the realisation of any objective condition of incrimination, were later added to the list of *latent* criminal offences.[45] Factually, this has led to significant decriminalisation, because a considerable number of actions which, according to their essence, represent criminal offences, have been relieved of active criminal attributes. This means that the activity of the criminal justice system has in a certain sense been reduced as well, namely in the sense of the number of active criminal offences that are prosecuted as such, and a greater amount of deviant or delinquent behaviour is treated in a more lenient way, as infractions. While once, for example, the very failure to execute an order issued by a superior officer in the armed forces, or a refusal of it, led to court martial, today, if there are no serious consequences for the service, the restrictive consequences are far more lenient, because disobediance is treated as a *disciplinary infraction*, and is sanctioned by disciplinary measures imposed by the unit commander.[46] These are extremely important aspects of the evolution of the criminal justice system, because they open the way for a more reconciliatory and less confrontational way of control of deviance and dissensus in principle.[47] As was already mentioned, the introduction of objective responsibility as an additional restriction on the application of repressive measures that are otherwise based on the criterion of subjective responsibility is a liberating characteristic of the Yugoslav criminal legislation, because it *narrows* the domain of criminal incrimination.

More theoretically, however, the principle of objective responsibility and its presence in Yugoslav criminal legislation in the form of the objective condition of incrimination also has *negative* sides. Although this type of responsibility can be seen as a liberalising element of the legislation, as a road towards partial decriminalisation, it also potentially widens the very concept of criminal responsibility on the basis of events that do not have to depend on the agent, and of which the perpetrator may not even be aware, nor does the perpetrator have to be aware of his or her role in the definition of incrimination — in some cases, even in the determination of severity of sanctions pertaining to the offence. The consequences of a criminal offence, as captured by the category of objective condition of incrimination, play a role in the kind of treatment the offence will receive (whether criminal or non-criminal) on the basis of their *presence or absence* in principle. They also play a certain quantitative role entailing an influence of the relevant consequences on the *severity of sanctioning* of the offence based on the *degree* in which the relevant harmful or dangerous consequences have actually occurred.[48] Thus some authors consider that the objective condition of incrimination potentially *threatens* the principle of subjective responsibility in criminal law, because it introduces as elements of responsibility the consequences that do not have to be part of the perpetrator's intentions. For example, one may engage in a street brawl with no intention of causing the death of another person whatsoever, and yet some person might unintentionally be killed. Similarly, one who refuses an order issued by a higher ranking officer in the Yugoslav Army may have the best intentions regarding the service, and may have no intention of inflicting any damage on the service, and yet such damage might occur. It can even occur in circumstances where, in a particular case, the offender might have had good reason to believe that the damage would *not* occur, that is in circumstances where the offender 'was not aware nor was due to be aware nor could be aware' that any harmful consequences would occur. Thus, for example, a leading Yugoslav criminal lawyer, Dragoljub Atanacković, argues that the objective condition of incrimination is an inherent threat to the principle of subjective responsibility and that in the new criminal law a clear distinction should be made between the consequences of a criminal offence that constitute a part of the essence of the offence, and those that do not. He argues that the role of objective condition of incrimination should be limited to those consequences of which the offender was aware, or should have been aware.[49]

This proposition is certainly useful, and it is in accord with the considerations of subjective and objective responsibility in principle that were touched on earlier. An explicit characterisation of the offender's *duty* to be aware of possible consequences that might play the role of objective condition of incrimination would advance the conceptualisation and formulation of subjective and objective responsibility in the Yugoslav system of criminal justice. However, again in the context of what has been said earlier about subjective and objective responsibility in principle, perhaps the existing legal characterisation of subjective and objective responsibility can to some extent be *defended* against the charge that it allows threats to the principle of subjective responsibility by the objective condition of incrimination.

To attempt such a defence, one ought to take a step back and note, first of all, that objective responsibility is present in the objective condition of incrimination only *in a limited sense*, because what is at stake is the responsibility for the consequences of an action for which *action* the offender is *subjectively* responsible. This is a very important qualification. It means, for example, that one is responsible for the death of another person which was the result of a physical confrontation in which one had participated, and for which *participation* one is *subjectively* responsible. This limited sense of objective responsibility, therefore, does not include an *absolute* application of objective responsibility which would be based entirely on the fact that a certain harmful or dangerous consequence has occurred. If, while cleaning a firearm, in a situation where one *could not* reasonably know that the weapon was loaded, nor could one reasonably expect that another person would be in the vicinity, the weapon accidentally discharges and thus causes the death of another person, then in such a situation the conditions for ascription of objective responsibility would be present in an abstract, absolute sense, because the person who was cleaning the firearm would have, strictly speaking, caused the death of another person. However, such objective responsibility is *not* part of the objective condition of incrimination, given that in its context objective responsibility is present only where *subjective* responsibility already exists, and where the initial action itself (independently of the consequences) is qualifiable as a latent criminal offence. The cleaning of a firearm which one does not reasonably know is loaded and in a location which is reasonably believed to be secure is not a latent criminal offence, and thus the harmful and dangerous consequences that this action might produce, in the described circumstances, do not constitute an objective condition of incrimination. On the other hand, the involvement in a street brawl *is* a latent criminal offence, and the offender is *expected*, even without an explicit formulation of this expectation in the law, to be aware of the possible harmful and dangerous consequences, and to *refrain* from becoming engaged in this action, to a large extent *exactly because* of its potential harmfulness and dangerousness.

Involvement in a street brawl is proscribed by criminal law first of all *because* of its destructive potential which, when actualised, is captured by the objective condition of incrimination. In other words, this action is proscribed exactly *because* of the possibility that in a brawl someone might be seriously hurt or killed. It is therefore not unreasonable to ascribe a limited *objective* responsibility to this offence. The point of this ascription of responsibility is exactly in *the meaning of the criminal characterisation*, in *the reason for the proscription* of the action of participation in a brawl, that is in the *potential consequences* of which the offender *ought to be aware*. The fact that this action is treated as an infraction where the relevant consequences do not occur is an expression of lenient treatment of the offence by the criminal justice system. This *does not mean* that the more severe, criminal treatment of the action is unjustified only because it includes elements of objective responsibility, nor does it mean that the objective condition of incrimination in such a case in any way broadens the domain of subjective responsibility. Objective responsibility is not separable here from subjective responsibility, and what is at stake is not an abstract, absolute objective responsibility; rather it is the responsibility for a *relevant type* of consequences of the action, which represent part of the reasoning behind the criminal characterisation of the action in the first place and of which the offender, by assumption, was aware or had to be aware when engaging in the action. One certainly ought to agree with Atanacković's proposal, however, that it is a shortcoming of the current legislation that this legitimate expectation that the offender must be aware of the meaning of the criminal characterisation, the reasons for it, and thereby also the relevant consquences of engaging in the action, is not *explicitly* present in the legal characterisation of the objective condition of incrimination.

The question of objective responsibility is, therefore, not posed in cases where there is no intentional, conscious breach of the relevant norm. It is of fundamental importance that a part of this norm, a part of its social meaning, consists in the possible consequences that are defined as the objective condition of incrimination. Non-compliance with a superior officer's order in the Yugoslav Army is proscribed *exactly because* of the possible erosive consequences for discipline in the armed forces, that is for the damage that could harm the service. Non-penalisation of non-compliance with the order when such harmful consequences do not in fact occur is an expression of lenience, which again does not mean that the treatment of non-compliance with the order as a criminal offence where it actually does cause significant damage to the service, is unjustified, nor that it broadens the conceptual domain of criminal responsibility by introducing objective *instead of* subjective responsibility. The domain covered by objective responsibility in such cases represents *a part of the domain* covered by subjective responsibility, given the *inherent* relevance of the consequences that constitute the objective condition of incrimination for the meaning of that very norm for the violation of which the action is characterised as a 'latent' criminal offence in the first place, and for which subjective responsibility is required first of all.

From this it can be argued that the existing conceptualisation of the objective condition of incrimination, at least in *some* cases and in relation to the characterisations of *some* criminal offences, still to a significant extent *honours* the principle of subjective responsibility even in the context of the objective condition of incrimination. The danger of threatening the primary significance of subjective responsibility in criminal law is therefore, at least in some cases, more a technical danger than one of principle, given that it arises from the absence of an appropriate explicit provision alone.

However, there are other cases where the objective condition of incrimination endangers the *fair and equal treatment* of all offenders who fulfil the subjective conditions of responsibility for the same criminal offence. It is important to point out that this would be the case even *if there was an explicit characterisation* of the relevant consequences for the objective condition of incrimination as those consequences of which the offender could be aware or should have been aware. In the text above it was argued in favour of the position that the consequences that constitute the objective condition of incrimination, at least in the context of offences that were taken as examples, belong to those consequences of which the offender is reasonably expected to be aware, and therefore ascriptions of *objective* responsibility in that context are in a certain sense covered by the domain of *subjective* responsibility. The question of *fair treatment* of all offenders who satisfy the conditions of subjective responsibility is very similar, but the perspective from which it is posed is somewhat different. That perspective is not so much one of the relationship between subjective and objective responsibility in a system of incriminations, as it is a perspective of the *mutual relationship between the rights of particular offenders* in the situations arising from their offences. This perspective deserves a somewhat more detailed discussion.

It was mentioned earlier that in a case such as a street brawl or non-compliance with a superior officer's order, or any other case where the consequences that constitute the objective condition of incrimination represent the underlying meaning of the criminal characterisation of the action itself, the objective condition of incrimination does not lead to a widening of criminal responsibility beyond the domain of subjective responsibility. However, it does lead to a threat to the principle of *fair and equal treatment* of all offenders who have committed the same offence under the same circumstances, which is also part of the very meaning of subjective responsibility. This meaning lies in the principle that it is *unfair* to ascribe a lesser responsibility, or to mete out a less severe sanction, to someone who is equally subjectively responsible as someone else who has committed the same offence under the same circumstances, on the basis of the single fact that the actions of the former offender *did not in fact cause* certain relevant consequences, while the actions of the latter, incidentally, *did* so.

For example, imagine a situation where two soldiers systematically undermine the hierarchy of their (different) army units by disobeying orders, with the intention of damaging the service and causing harm. If one of the soldiers succeeds in causing a disturbance in the service because of poor discipline in the unit, while the other soldier, because of strong discipline in the other unit, does not cause any severe consequences, then, from the point of view of subjective responsibility, it would be inconsistent with the principle of fair and equal treatment to treat the behaviour of the former as a criminal offence, and the behaviour of the latter as a disciplinary infraction. From the point of view of their intentions and the physical description of their actions, both soldiers were *equally* subjectively responsible — the occurrence or absence of the desired consequences (in this case, damage to the service) is not something that would have been entirely under their control. The fact that, owing to circumstances beyond the control of the offenders, one of them has in fact succeeded in producing the desired harm, while the other has not, does not mean that the latter is any *less* responsible than the former, from the point of view of subjective responsibility. The objective condition of incrimination therefore really widens the domain of responsibility beyond the domain of subjective responsibility in this context, and it does so whether the consequences that constitute the objective condition of incrimination are *explicitly* characterised in the law as those consequences of which the offender was aware or had to be aware, or not. Both soldiers in the example were, by assumption, more than aware of the possible harmful consequences; moreover, both had specific intentions and planned to produce such consequences. One has succeeded, for entirely external reasons, while the other has not, for the same type of external reasons. The former ended up in a court martial, while the other was sanctioned by a disciplinary measure imposed by the unit commander. The difference between the two cases is based exclusively on objective responsibility, or more precisely on what was earlier mentioned as abstract, absolute objective responsibility. Such cases suggest that the offender can have an extremely destructive intention, can be maximally subjectively responsible, and yet whether or not one will be prosecuted or merely subjected to a less severe disciplinary measure can depend only on whether or not one has succeeded in one's destructive intention.

The same principle relates to numerous other examples. Two offenders participate in a street brawl with a clear intention to kill someone. One succeeds, and the other one, entirely accidentally, does not, because the victim manages to escape before any serious injuries or death have occurred. These two offenders can also be treated in dramatically different ways, and also exclusively so on the basis of the criterion of purely objective responsibility. Thus, from the point of view of fair and equal treatment, what was previously referred to as a sign of lenient treatment of criminal deviance by the system may be the cause of unjustified imposition of objective over subjective responsibility.

These two perspectives are very different. The first mentioned critique of the objective condition of incrimination suggests that the fact that the offender did not know or perhaps was not, within the explicit provisions of the criminal law, 'necessarily due to know' that certain consequences could ensue from his or her actions, implies that one could be punished too severely, on the basis of ascriptions of responsibility for a consequence which was not a part of one's *psychological relationship* with the action itself, and therefore also not part of one's *intention* when committing the action. Thus the first critique targets the upper domain of objective responsibility (or the supposed danger that ascriptions of objective responsibility through the objective condition of incrimination might lead to criminal prosecution instead of a sanction for an infraction) of those offenders who did not intend to produce the consequences that normally lead to the more severe treatment. In other words, the first critique objects to the possible *excessive use of repression* on the basis of ascriptions of this type of objective responsibility. The second critique is based on the potentially destructive influence of the objective condition of incrimination on the fair and equal treatment of the accused, and it thus relates more to the lower domain of the restrictive function of the system, that is, it questions the justifiability of the *less severe* treatment of those offenders who are equally subjectively responsible as some other offenders who have in fact caused the relevant danger or harm. In other words, the latter critique objects to the less severe treatment which is based exclusively on the contingent fact that the offender did not *succeed* in producing the intended harm or damage.

These two critiques also differ in principle. The former, as was already mentioned, can be the subject of an argument to the effect that consciousness of the possible consequences of actions is a legitimate requirement in the context of criminal law, even without an explicit determination specifying what particular types of consequences the offender must have been aware of. The reason for this, it could be argued, is simply that at least in some mentioned cases of application of the objective condition of incrimination, arguably the relevant consequences represent the reason for the criminalisation of the relevant actions itself, and they are a part of the meaning of the criminal characterisation. Therefore, it would be a reasonable expectation that the offender should or could have been aware of them. As was already mentioned, this is not necessarily a conclusive argument because it depends on *the way* the relationship between the essence of a criminal offence and its consequences is characterised, namely on how the belonging of the consequences to the essence of a criminal offence is defined. The latter critique, based on the principle of fair and equal treatment of all offenders, which is part of the meaning of *subjective responsibility* in principle, is not liable to the above argumentation, because the fact that one offender might not have succeeded in achieving the relevant dangerous or harmful consequences because of external circumstances, and despite his or her intentions, while another offender might have succeeded in doing so, does not open up room for questions of whether the offenders could be legitimately expected to have been aware of the consequences. Rather what is at stake here is that the offenders in these examples, by assumption, *were* aware of the consequences *and* they intended to cause them, but because of strictly objective circumstances, some succeeded in doing so, and some did not, which then represents a basis for ascriptions of varying degrees of guilt and of different statuses to their actions, which results in their different treatment by the criminal justice system.

What can be concluded from these discussions? The objective condition of incrimination and the objective responsibility that is, at least to some extent, implied by the objective condition of incrimination, potentially threaten the principle of fair and equal treatment in the lower domain, that is the possibility of an unjustified *less severe* treatment of offenders from the point of view of subjective responsibility. This implies that the criminal legislation is unprincipled, but that is by no means the same as to say that it involves unjustified repression. This critique implies only that, in a strictly speaking 'unfair' way, the criminal legislation allows the luckier offender (the one whose actions did not in fact cause certain destructive consequences), to get away with a less severe treatment than some other offender who was in this sense less lucky. In other words, the argument here goes back to the point of a *partial decriminalisation* which the objective condition of incrimination implies as compared to a situation where only the principle of *subjective responsibility* would be applied. In this sense, it would certainly be useful to introduce an explicit enumeration of those types of consequences that may constitute the objective condition of incrimination, in the law. These consequences would be qualified as those that the offender was able to predict or should have been aware of, which is Atanacković's proposal (in accord with his proposal, this can be achieved simply by introducing an explicit determination of culpability, which is otherwise described in article 13 of the Yugoslav federal criminal law, that is a formulation requiring the offender to have been aware that because of one's action or inaction a prohibited consequence might occur, and to have accepted the likelihood or possibility of its occurrence). The dilemma that the second critique of the objective condition of incrimination really implies here is whether the benefit in the reduction of the amount of state repression is worth the sacrifice of the theoretical principle of fair treatment. Perhaps the answer to this question, however odd it might seem, is affirmative, because, and this ought to be pointed out once again, *if the above two conditions are fulfilled* what would be at stake would not be any unfair treatment in the upper domain of penalisation, that is a more severe treatment than warranted by the subjective responsibility. What would be at stake instead would be an 'unfair' treatment that, in some cases, implies a less severe treatment of some offenders than is warranted by their subjective responsibility. Perhaps in this sense the term 'unfair' ought to be used only conditionally, because it is usually associated with unfairly excessively severe penalties, rather than unfairly less severe than warranted penalties. Clearly, both cases involve a violation of the principle of equal treatment of equal cases from the point of view of subjective responsibility, but it is equally clear that this is a far more benevolent type of unfairness than extreme penalisation, which would be a violation of the principle of fair treatment in the upper domain.

The family, kinship, and criminal legislation

Onc of the more interesting characteristics of the Yugoslav criminal legislation, more precisely of the Serbian and Montenegrin criminal laws, which could be retained in the new federal criminal law, is the extremely important role attached to the family and kinship in the context of ascriptions of criminal responsibility. In the Yugoslav system, the importance of loyalty to the family, in some cases above the loyalty to the broader social community and the law, probably goes beyond that of many other systems. Loyalty to the family in most systems usually includes provisions relating to the proof of guilt, mainly those relating to the use of evidence in court. Thus the rules regulating the use of evidence in Anglo-American common law systems recognise the so-called 'marital privilege', ensuring that private details of marital and family life are inadmissible as evidence in court. The rules of evidence thereby provide a certain insurance against the use of so-called 'pillow talk' in the court room.

In Serbian and Montenegrin laws, however, the equivalents of marital privilege (or more precisely, what could be called 'family privilege') extend far beyond this. They are present in the provisions regulating the treatment of crimes of non-reporting of a criminal offence and aiding and abetting the perpetrator, in the group of criminal offences against the judicial system. Article 202, paragraph 1 of Serbian criminal law and article 178, paragraph 1 of Montenegrin criminal law sanction the non-reporting of the preparation of a criminal offence which is known to the person, where the law prescribes a penalty of five years of imprisonment or more for the unreported crime, *and* the offence is attempted or committed. The sanction for non-reporting here is imprisonment for up to one year. Article 202, paragraph 2 of Serbian criminal law and article 178, paragraph 2 of Montenegrin criminal law sanction the non-reporting of a crime punishable by the death penalty, with the penalty of imprisonment from six months to five years. But paragraph 3 of both these articles exempts from the penalty for non-reporting the spouse of the perpetrator, a person with whom the offender lives in a permanent extra-marital relationship (de facto), next of kin, brother or sister, adopting parent or an adopted child, as well as the spouse of any of these exempted persons, or a person living with any of the exempted persons in a permanent de facto relationship.

The same exemption from culpability for the same categories of persons applies for the criminal offence of aiding and abetting the offender *after* the commission of the offence (article 204 of Serbian criminal law and article 180 of Montenegrin criminal law). Both these articles sanction the hiding of the perpetrator, assisting one in avoiding detection by hiding the means or traces related to the offence, or in some other way, as well as assisting in evading the execution of a penalty, security, or disciplinary measure. Obviously these offences are depicted in the law as serious, because they are sanctionable by imprisonment for up to one year (article 204, paragraph 2 of Serbian criminal law and article 180, paragraph 2 of Montenegrin criminal law). The severity of the sanction for aiding and abetting depends on the gravity of the offence committed by the perpetrator who is being aided. The exemptions from penalties for aiding and abetting for the perpetrator's family members are therefore not allowed on the basis of a low level of seriousness of the offence; rather they stem from the fact that loyalty to the family is understood by the law-maker as potentially, and importantly, to some extent *legitimately*, *opposed* to the loyalty to society, even in the most serious of cases.

An identical exemption from culpability also applies to the legal attorney, physician, or priest who has heard the offender's confession.[50]

These provisions are of extreme importance for a cultural and value interpretation of Yugoslav criminal legislation and the system of social control, because they reflect a *priority* placed on the value of *family obligation* compared to *social obligation* and the obligation to the legal system. They also clearly reflect the cultural characteristics of the Serbian and Montenegrin societies, which are highly determined by customary values and a long-standing social history. Hiding the offender is depicted as an offence in itself; but if the offender is next of kin, the spouse, or spouse's next of kin, then hiding one is in a certain sense understood as a normal reaction by a family member, and not a crime. Similar principles relate to questions of honour, defamation, and privacy.[51] In this sense, Serbian and Montenegrin criminal laws can be understood as paradigmatic cases for a possible, and possibly desirable, revival of the role of traditional values in modern legal systems.

Defamation, honour, and criminal law

Traditional values are also reflected in the criminal provisions regulating exemptions from penalties for criminal offences against honour and reputation.[52] Offences enumerated in this group of criminal offences include defamation (article 92 of Serbian criminal law and article 786 of Montenegrin criminal law), insult (article 93 of Serbian criminal law and article 77 of Montenegrin criminal law), unauthorised public exposure of personal and family circumstances (article 94 of Serbian criminal law and article 78 of Montenegrin criminal law), insult by unfounded accusation of a criminal offence (article 95 of Serbian criminal law and article 79 of Montenegrin criminal law), as well as crimes against the reputation of the Republic of Serbia and Republic of Montenegro (article 98 of Serbian criminal law and article 82 of Montenegrin criminal law), and insult of the nations and national minorities of FRY (article 100 of Serbian criminal law and article 83 of Montenegrin criminal law). The greatest proportion of these offences are prosecuted by private legal action. Only the last two (crimes against the reputation of the two republics and insult of the nations and national minorities) are prosecuted by the state. Offences of defamation and those committed 'against a territorial unit, state organ, or public or army officer in the execution of their duties or functions' are prosecuted by official duty.[53] Although most of these offences are prosecuted by private legal action, it is interesting that for each of them imprisonment is a possible outcome. In the case of a defamation committed by using the media, the court may also publish the verdict at the expense of the convicted offender.[54]

From the point of view of traditional values, the most interesting characteristic of these determinations of offences against honour and reputation are the conditions for excuses from penalties, that is for issuing a judicial caution rather than a penalty. A caution may be passed instead of a penalty for defamation, insult, unauthorised public exposure of personal and family circumstances, and unfounded accusation of a crime, in the following cases:

(i) where the offender 'was provoked by indecent or offensive behaviour of the victim', or

(ii) where the offender has 'declared before the court readiness to *apologise* to the victim'.[55]

In a case of defamation, insult, or unauthorised public exposure of personal and family circumstances, a caution may also be issued instead of a penalty if the offender has 'retracted the offensive statement in the court'.[56]

In the case of an insult, if the offender has retracted the insult, the court may penalise one or both parties less severely, or excuse one or both of them from penalty.[57]

These provisions reveal that the dialectic of treatment of the particularly personal offences against honour and reputation (defamation, insult, unauthorised public exposure of personal and family circumstances, and insult by unfounded accusation of a crime) is to a large extent based on mechanisms characteristic of a more informal community — there, insult, defamation, or similar actions are no longer seen as offences or infractions of community relationships and norms if the offender has apologised to the victim, or if the offender has withdrawn or retracted the offensive statement. In this type of situation, the court is shown in a role similar to that of the so-called 'mediation tribunals' for conflict-resolution.[58] The relevant difference between courts and mediation tribunals here is that if the offender is extremely uncooperative and unwilling to compromise, to apologise and retract the insult, defamation, untrue statement, or rumour which constitutes the offence, and especially if the offence has caused serious consequences for the victim, the court is empowered to pass a penalty, while a tribunal, in normal circumstances, cannot do so. The presence of relatively severe penal provisions (possible imprisonment for up to three years)[59] to some extent serves the purpose of inspiring the offender to make an effort in attempting to resolve the conflict by an apology, retraction of the offence or statement, etc. The very mechanism of conflict-resolution in these provisions is essentially the same one that is visible in an uninstitutional group or community. In some social control systems today there are significant initiatives for increasing the role of such forms of conflict-settlement *instead of* penalisation of as many offences as possible, part of the reason being quite pragmatic, namely the congested judicial systems and the resulting inability to prosecute petty crimes. The presence of these mechanisms in the Yugoslav criminal legislation is therefore, in this context, to be seen as encouraging and positive, because they can serve as the basis for further decriminalisation and deformalisation of the treatment of particular offences, and thereby also a further reduction in the repressive potential of the crime control system in the future.

The law and sexual morality

The description of crimes 'against personal dignity and morality' in both republican criminal laws also has considerable cultural significance.[60] Crimes in this group include rape,[61] coerced or unnatural intercourse,[62] forced intercourse or unnatural intercourse forced with a defenceless person,[63] intercourse or unnatural intercourse with a person less than fourteen years of age,[64] intercourse or unnatural intercourse forced by abuse of official position,[65] prostitution,[66] unnatural sexual prostitution,[67] and solicitation or facilitation of prostitution.[68] The Serbian criminal law also contains, as was already mentioned, a provision relating to the crime of seduction, which includes persuasion of a juvenile female person who is fourteen years of age or older to engage in intercourse by a false promise of marriage, whereas Montenegrin criminal law does not criminalise this type of action.[69]

The very enumeration of the *names* of these offences suggests a strong anti-homosexual orientation of the criminal legislation. The fact that unnatural sexual behaviour is criminalised in both republican laws reflects this orientation. This is probably a real underlying moral position of the law-maker, with one additional qualification: the name of the offence, i.e. 'unnatural intercourse' in itself does not fully reveal the real nature of this criminal characterisation, because in the text of the relevant articles, in both criminal laws, only *coerced* unnatural intercourse is mentioned. Apart from that, the provision relating to unnatural intercourse does not only refer to homosexual behaviour, but also, at least semantically, to any other type of unnatural sexual behaviour, which can also be heterosexual. The fact that the law criminalises only coerced unnatural intercourse, however, is an expression of considerable lenience of the law-maker regarding the question of sexual morality of dissensual groups. Given that the criminal law does not allow the oppressive treatment of homosexual behaviour in general, the underlying moral position *against* such behaviour must be seen as a cultural and moral position, and one that certainly generates a considerable consensus amongst the population, while at the same time the letter of the law precludes it from facilitating institutional repression.

The provisions relating to intercourse or unnatural intercourse with a person who is less than fourteen years of age (or with 'a juvenile person', according to Montenegrin criminal law)[70] refers to a female person less than fourteen years of age. This reflects the traditional and probably well-founded position that most crimes of this type are committed by male perpetrators against female victims, although contemporary circumstances and situations in some other countries suggest that it may be desirable to introduce a more gender-neutral provision in the new federal criminal law regarding the sex of the perpetrator and the victim of this crime, whereby the possibility of intercourse or unnatural intercourse committed by a female person against a male juvenile victim could be legally acknowledged.[71]

Serbian criminal law contains, as already mentioned, a provision that criminalises seduction, and sanctions it by imprisonment from three months to three years. This provision does not exist in Montenegrin criminal law. A similar provision, however, exists in both republican laws in the group of criminal offences 'against marriage and family',[72] namely the crime of extramarital relationship with a juvenile person.[73] Serbian criminal law sanctions this offence considerably more severely than Montenegrin law, because the former provides imprisonment from three months to three years for the 'basic' form of this offence,[74] while the latter prescribes imprisonment from three months to one year for the same form of the offence.[75] If this crime is committed for material benefit, Serbian criminal law prescribes imprisonment from one to five years,[76] while Montenegrin law prescribes imprisonment from six months to three years.[77] The criminalisation of this offence does not relate only to the supposedly male person who forms an extramarital or de facto relationship with a juvenile female person, but also to a parent, foster or adopting parent, or legal guardian, who has allowed the juvenile female person to enter into an extramarital relationship. The penalty prescribed for a parent, foster or adopting parent, or legal guardian, is the same as the penalty for the person who lives in the extramarital relationship with the juvenile female person, in the 'basic' form of this offence, that is, the penalty of imprisonment from three months to three years according to Serbian criminal law, or from three months to one year according to Montenegrin criminal law.[78] It is interesting to note that both laws provide that 'if a marriage is concluded, the prosecution will not take place, and if it has commenced, it will cease'.[79]

The mentioned desirability of introduction of more gender-neutral provisions relating to the sex of the offender in the context of rape,[80] coerced intercourse or unnatural intercourse,[81] and intercourse or unnatural intercourse with a defenceless person,[82] is not the subject of debate at the moment, which probably means that the probability of the introduction of such changes in the main text of the new federal criminal law is low.[83] These discussions do not imply that there is any urgent need for changes in this particular regard; what is intended is to illustrate the domain of the role of traditional values in the relevant part of criminal legislation.

Conclusion

In the discussion of objective responsibility and the objective condition of incrimination it was mentioned that the Yugoslav criminal justice system treats certain offences as infractions if certain dangerous or harmful consequences, which constitute the objective condition of incrimination, have not occurred. In deciding whether to treat an action as an infraction or a criminal offence, and how severe a sanction to attach to it on the basis of the gravity of its consequences, the emphasis is on the consequences themselves and their effects on society. This fact alone reflects the predominantly *preventative* character of the criminal legislation. Crime prevention is often conceived as being more or less identifiable with general deterrence. This is supposedly achieved through a system of criminal sanctions. The sentencing grid, discussed in the first chapter, was one example of conceptualisation of prevention as deterrence. In the Yugoslav criminal legislation the emphasis is *not* on sanctions as the basis of deterrence, but rather on an understanding of sanctions as a special 'social prophylaxis', that is, on their understanding as a form of treatment which leads to a *reformation* and *resocialisation* of the deviant individuals. This is another and equally historically common depiction of prevention. Article 33 of the federal criminal law thus determines the goals of penalisation within the criminal justice system as: (1) prevention of the perpetrator from reoffending and his or her re-education, (2) exertion of educational influence on others not to offend, and (3) strengthening of public morality and influence on the development of citizens' responsibility. The very definition of a crime suggests that the social control system is preventative, for article 8 of the federal criminal law says that a criminal offence is first of all a *socially dangerous action*. This article goes one step further, and in paragraph 2 it determines that an action which contains the legally determined characteristics of a criminal offence is not to be considered a crime if it entails only an insignificant danger to society, 'because of the small significance or absence of its destructive consequences'.

The preventative character of the legislation is to be emphasised by the proposed deletion of the death penalty from the new federal criminal law — a matter which is still the subject of heated debate. Article 38 of the current 1992 federal criminal law determines the conditions for the use of imprisonment, which cannot be shorter than fifteen days, nor longer than fifteen years, and in the most serious cases, up to twenty years. The same article prescribes that the convict who has served a half, and in special circumstances, a third of the original sentence, may be released on parole for the rest of the sentence. Apart from being conceived as the replacement for the death penalty, twenty years of imprisonment are also prescribed as the penalty for a *qualified* form of an offence for whose basic form fifteen years of imprisonment are prescribed, and where aggravating circumstances apply. Given the terminal character of the death penalty, it is obviously incapable of serving any socio-prophylactic purposes as far as the offender is concerned. The only preventative connotation of the death penalty is general deterrence, and its deletion from the federal law would reinforce the reformatory philosophy adopted in the 1992 federal criminal law.

The explanation of the absence of the death penalty from the federal legislation, which is to be found in the Yugoslav federal Constitution, also clearly reflects this reformatory philosophy, as well as the *values* adopted by the law-maker. Article 21 of the Constitution thus reads: 'Human life is inviolable. The death penalty cannot be prescribed for criminal offences that are regulated by federal law.' However, there is a certain semantic incongruence between the two sentences themselves, mainly stemming from their scope. If human life, according to the Constitution, is inviolable, if it is the supreme value for society, then that value choice surely implies that human life is the supreme value and inviolable *in the whole territory* of FRY. It is inconsistent to assert the inviolability and supreme value of life, only to proceed, in the following sentence, to limit the *upholding* of that value only to the domain regulated by the federal law. Human life in a legal system is either inviolable, or it is not, it is either the supreme value, or it is not; there is no consistent meaning in ascribing some type of administratively limited or jurisdictionally conditioned 'inviolability' and value to human life.

One of the indicators for assessing the future directions of the development of the Yugoslav criminal legislation will certainly be the outcome of the current debate on the abolition or retention of the death penalty in the new federal law. If the high rates of violent crime and political pressures from conservative stake holders force a retention of the 'ultimate sanction', then that would clearly violate the value choices and the reformatory, socio-prophylactic philosophy in the current Yugoslav Constitution and the federal criminal law. One ought to remember here the limitations of criminal sanctions as a means of crime control where the reasons for the rise in crime rates are first of all social.[84]

Modern currents of social regulation concerning the death penalty are clear — it is not considered an acceptable form of repressive social regulation in any country of the European Union, and that is probably the main reason why the countries of central-eastern Europe have already abolished this penalty at the beginning of the region's political transition. If FRY intends to become included in the European integrative currents in the foreseeable future, the death penalty will have to be removed from its criminal legislation.

A separate problem concerning the death penalty, both in Serbia and in Montenegro, is that, unlike many other European, and especially western European, countries, in Yugoslavia the death penalty and its execution do not lead to a pronounced *public debate*, they are not a subject of discussions and questions about the legitimacy of particular executions and the ultimate penalty in principle. Such a debate could contribute to a change in the social atmosphere and the final abolition of this type of punishment. At the moment, the death penalty usually passes almost unnoticed by the public. The power of the institutions, and their autonomous position in society, have a truly frightening profile if these institutions can conduct executions of convicted citizens without at the same time subjecting that practice to wide public debate.[85] By surrounding the death penalty with silence, the degree of public supervision over the institutions is reduced, and that represents a threat to democratic order in itself. Citizens' freedom must be defended not only by ideological concepts, but first of all by a democratic society's struggle against silence, especially when it surrounds the most problematic and morally most worrying aspects of social policy. Social policy of social control by the use of the death penalty is a worrying problem *par excellence.*

Certain methodological difficulties were mentioned earlier concerning the procedural democratic legitimation of the criminal justice system, and any other aspect or institutional arm of social control. It was mentioned that democratic-procedural legitimation is a necessary, but not always a sufficient, condition for the moral justifiability of a repressive social control policy. However, when the most severe criminal sanctions that are surrounded by a wall of silence are at stake, even the very standard of procedural consensual legitimation is threatened. There can be no consensual legitimation where the public is uninformed about the use of particular drastic forms of social control. Consensual legitimation is the basis from which one must start in order to be able to discuss the legitimacy of the system. Only in that sense is it a necessary condition for the system's moral justification. In societies where the question of legitimation of drastic penalties is largely ignored, and where such penalties are executed without the presence of witnesses, there can be no question about the moral justification of the control systems themselves. It is well known that even in the USA, which is a country notorious for its security crisis and high crime rates, as well as frequent use of the death penalty, no execution is conducted without the presence of witnesses. This is an important element, because the presence of public representatives contributes to the formation of an accurate picture of the true nature and cruelty of the death penalty, especially the procedural aspects of its execution, which is arguably the cruellest in the whole ordeal for the offender. In the long term, the presence of witnesses can contribute to the formation of well-informed attitudes about the use of this type of penalty. In other words, if there is a considerable proportion of community members who have been present at an execution, other citizens will find out from them what the real nature of the death penalty is, and will be able to take positions in the public debate about the death penalty from a perspective that is closer to the reality of what they support or oppose. They may support the use of the death penalty, which is the case in most American federal states, but then that support for the most severe sanction has a certain legitimational force, which it would not have if the public did not have access to the executions.

The question of democratic legitimation and moral justification of criminal sanctions is posed with a special force and starkness in the context of the death penalty, because of its extreme character. The same or similar problems relating to democratic legitimation also apply to other, less controversial, and therefore less noticeable, elements of the social control apparatus. The death penalty is a *heuristically* convenient theme, because it throws light on general theoretical problems of political legitimation that are less noticeable, albeit in principle equally present, in less radical forms of social control.

The testing of the limits of repression by public debate appears to be a necessary *first step* towards a more solid moral, and legitimational, basis for the system itself. The question of supervision and public control of repressive institutions and their policies is part of this first step. For example, the Yugoslav Constitution guarantees the inviolability of human physical and psychological integrity, including privacy and personal rights, personal dignity, and security.[86] The Constitution also determines that any 'violence against a person under arrest, or under supervision, and any extortion of confessions and statements' is prohibited and sanctionable.[87] There are doubts about the extent to which the police and prison authorities live up to these principles in certain circumstances. There is a widespread perception amongst the public that physical violence is a regular occurrence in police stations and prisons, and similar evidence is found in journalistic writing about particular cases.[88] In spite of that, public debate and public supervision of these aspects of the practice of social control are still gravely lacking. It would therefore be a necessary first step to establish an independent ombudsman who would be empowered to conduct and maintain close control of police practices, prison organisation, and related parts of the social control system.

Generally speaking, the problems facing Yugoslav society today are not so much the result of a lack of appropriate legal regulation, but more a lack of respect for the law. Legal regulation and its integration and harmonisation are not insignificant at this time. They are of fundamental importance, because the reform of criminal legislation can contribute to the beginning of a reconstruction of civil and legal institutions and relationships, based on the rule of law, on trust and on other values which are a precondition for the appropriate functioning of a well-organised society. The reintegration of criminal legislation will be an initiative for a broader institutional reintegration, including not only institutions of repression and control, but also those for the implementation of other aspects of social policy and for the maintenance of standards of social justice. In this sense, if the new federal criminal law, as the supreme instrument of social control, is sufficiently progressive and if it fully takes into account the social and legitimational aspects of criminal deviance, it could fulfil an educational, regenerative, even motivational role for other parts of the legislation, for the institutions and civil society, all of which are now in a process of reawakening.

Notes

1. *Godišnjak Saveznog zavoda za statistiku* (*Federal Bureau of Statistics Yearbook*), Beograd, 1994.

2. ibid., 1985–95.

3. Of the more spectacular murders, several can be mentioned, including the murder of Branislav Matić Beli, one of the more well known members of the Belgrade underground, on August 3, 1991, by fire from an automatic rifle; the murder of the most famous gangster of the 'younger' generation, Aleksandar Knežević 'Knele', on October 28, 1992, in the New Belgrade Hyatt hotel; the murder of one of the most well known businesspeople in Serbia, Radojica Nikčević, Director of the 'Šumadija' enterprise, on Ocober 7, 1993; the murder of another well-known member of the underground, Goran Vuković, on December 12, 1994; the murder of the Belgrade boxer, Mihajlo Divac, after a shoot-out with automatic rifles in the New Belgrade Putnik hotel, on February 12, 1995. To these and other spectacular murders add a series of murders of police officers and security guards, including, amongst other cases, the murder of one and wounding of another police officer on March 16, 1995; the murder of two security guards of the postal service during an armed robbery of a money delivery van, on April 1, 1995 in Belgrade. Other more widely publicised cases include, for example, the robbery of a jewellery store in the Proleterskih brigada Street in Belgrade, on July 23, 1992 and the murder of the shop assistant Borjanka Tatić with a handgun; break-in into an apartment in 33 Pohorska Street in Belgrade and the brutal murder ot Vera Žigić and her son Davor by two assailants, also by firearms. For these and other examples, as well as the relevant anecdotal and journalistic evidence see Knežević, A. & Tufegdžić, V. (1995), *Kriminal koji je izmenio Srbiju* (*Crime that changed Serbia*), Radio B-92, Beograd.

4. Article 3a, paragraph 2 of Montenegrin criminal law, and article 2a, paragraph 2 of Serbian criminal law.

5. See paper by Montenegrin Minister of the Interior, Filip Vujanović (1995), 'Različite inkriminacije u KZ Srbije i KZ Crne Gore i pitanje jedinstvenog krivičnog zakona' ('Different incriminations in Serbian and Montenegrin criminal legislation and the question of a unique criminal law'), in the collection *Problemi reintegracije i reforme jugoslovenskog krivičnog zakonodavstva*, Institute of Criminological and Sociological Research, Belgrade.

6. Articles 86a, 86b, 109, 132, 183a, 184b, 218, 232, 238, 240a of Serbian criminal law.

7. Vujanović, op. cit., p. 19.

8. Vujanović, op. cit.

9. Also see Vujanović, op. cit., pp. 19–20. Serving of alcohol to persons under sixteen, and even eighteen years of age is also characterised as an infraction in other parts of the world, but in these countries the documentary checking of the identity of potential customers who could be under the age limit is also obligatory. Given that in Yugoslavia only the police and other investigative agencies normally have the right to check citizens' identification documents, this was an additional reason for the practical inapplicability of this criminal characterisation.

10. Articles 212 and 215 of Montenegrin criminal law.

11. Article 241 of Serbian criminal law and article 214 of Montenegrin criminal law. Also see Vujanović, op. cit., p. 22.

12. In this case, there is also a descriptive provision in Serbian criminal law, in the equivalent article 144, paragraph 2 (descriptive provision of larger value).

13. In relation to the last offence, Serbian criminal law also contains a descriptive provision, in the equivalent article 184a, paragraph 2 (descriptive provision 'large importance' or 'large value').

14. See also articles 172, paragraphs 1 and 2 (violation of public traffic rules); 173, paragraphs 1 and 2 (violation of public traffic rules by a dangerous action or means); 216, paragraphs 2 and 3 (abuse of official position); 217, paragraphs 2 and 3 (embezzlement); 218, paragraphs 2 and 3 (fraud in the performance of public office); 226, paragraph 2 (illegal usurpation of property during the execution of a search of premises or of a warrant) of Montenegrin criminal law, as well as the equivalent articles which mention numerical depictions of values in Serbian criminal law.

15. See, for example, article 136 (unconscientious business dealings); article 153 (incorrect measurements of merchandise), article 147 (unauthorised trade); article 154 (tax fraud); article 166 (aggravated theft); article 168 (robbery); article 171 (fraud); article 176 (damage to property); article 170 (concealment); article 173 (petty theft, concealment or fraud), and elsewhere. Once again, given the relatively frequent changes in criminal provisions, there would be little point in citing a full list of all the differences here, because the probability that they remain unchanged over any considerable period of time is not very high.

16. Other important types of differences in incriminations in the two republican legislatures are present in articles 64, 71a, 80, 84, 91, 142, 166, and 189 of Serbian criminal law and articles 46, 56, 60, 65, 75, 134, 145, and 157 of Montenegrin criminal law. For a more extensive discussion also see Vujanović, op. cit., pp. 23–4.

17. See Vujanović, op. cit., p. 25.

18. Vujanović, op. cit.

19. For example, see article 17 of Serbian criminal law.

20. For example, article 16 of Montenegrin criminal law.

21. Serbian criminal law prescribes the execution of juvenile detention penalties, while in Montenegro the execution of this penalty is regulated by a separate law on the execution of criminal sanctions — see article 38 of Serbian criminal law and article 69 of Montenegrin law on the execution of criminal sanctions. Also see Vujanović, op. cit., p. 24.

22. In a somewhat more complex form, this systematisation can be found in Kleinig, J. (1973), *Punishment and desert*, Martinus Nijhoff, The Hague. Some of the more influential discussions of this problem originated from Hart, H.L.A. (1968), *Punishment and responsibility*, Clarendon Press, Oxford, and in an especially concise form in his article 'Legal responsibility and excuses', in Kipnis, K. (ed.) (1977), *Philosophical issues in law: Cases and materials*, Prentice-Hall, Englewood Cliffs. Other relevant discussions in the area of forensic psychiatry can be found in Morić-Petrović, S. (1987), *Psihijatrija*, Medicinska knjiga, Beograd and Zagreb, and Sadoff, R.L. (1988), *Forensic psychiatry: A practical guide for lawyer and psychiatrist*, Thomas, Springfield; Gunn, J. & Taylor, P. (1983), *Forensic psychiatry: Clinical, legal and ethical issues*, Butterworth-Heinemann, Oxford. Finally, one of the newest and most interesting attempts at an explanation of criminal responsibility, in a somewhat narrower context of subjective responsibility of psychopaths, can be found in Elliot, K. (1994), 'Puppetmasters and personality disorders: Wittgenstein,

mechanism and moral responsibility', *Philosophy, Psychiatry & Psychology*, vol. 1, pp. 91–100.

23. This reasoning is present in the conceptualisation of crime control based on the sentencing grid, advocated by people such as Andrew von Hirsch, Andrew Ashworth, and other adherents of the repressive strategy of crime control, which was discussed in the first chapter.

24. The exceptions relate to the mentioned cases where ascriptions of 'strict liability' at least appear to be unavoidable for effective prevention.

25. For a brief discussion of some problems connected with this description of intent see Đorđević, M. (1995), 'Osnovna pitanja u vezi sa donošenjem krivičnog zakonika SR Jugoslavije' ('Key issues relating to the introduction of a new federal criminal law of FR Yugoslavia'), *Problemi reintegracije i reforme jugoslovenskog krivičnog zakonodavstva, (Problems of reintegration and reform of the Yugoslav criminal legislation)*, Institute of Criminological and Sociological Research, Beograd, p. 12.

26. Or 'did not know that what he was doing was wrong, criminal, and prohibited', that is, the McNaughten Rules.

27. Or was not necessarily able not to commit the crime from the point of view of specifically volitional psychological functions and integrity, that is, the 'volitional' criterion.

28. Author's emphasis.

29. It ought to be pointed out here that in the context of discussion of criminal responsibility what is usually discussed is subjective responsibility in the light of psychological accountability. In broader philosophical contexts, it is possible to discuss a lack of subjective responsibility in situations where any form of psychological unaccountability is out of the question, such as situations where one cannot be considered subjectively responsible for the success or lack of success of particular actions and strategies which completely or to a considerable extent depend on others, and not on the individual under consideration, etc. In the context of criminal responsibility, such conceptions of subjective responsibility or the lack of it are irrelevant, because criminal law describes crimes as those actions which in the relevant sense depend on the individual (perpetrator), meaning that the only directly relevant type of questions to be asked here relate to whether or not the offender knew that he was committing a criminal offence, whether or not the offender was aware of the nature of his or her actions, whether or not the offender had sufficient control over his or her own actions, etc. Of course, there are complicated cases of coercion where the individual concerned (the perpetrator) may not be the

only relevant actor, and where the relevant actions might not be so obviously under the complete influence of the individual concerned, but these are questions that pose themselves mainly in the sphere of investigation and which, although undoubtedly important, are not conceptually directly relevant to a discussion of ascriptions of responsibility in the present context.

30. Some of the earliest discussions were by the adherents of the positivist theory of criminal sanctions, who argued for a change of paradigms of penalisation for paradigms of reformation and rehabilitation. One of the best known representatives was Enrico Ferri — see Ferri, E. (1968), *The positive school of criminology*, University of Pittsburgh Press, Pittsburgh. An equally large influence in the evolution of this debate belongs to the version of reformatory theory that attempts to change paradigms of justice and institutional sanctions for *medical* paradigms. This theory is usually connected in its genesis to the name of Lady Barbara Wootton — see Wootton, B. (1963), *Crime and the criminal law*, Stevens & Son Ltd., London.

31. See Stevanović, Z. (1995), 'Pravno regulisanje mera bezbednosti medicinskog karaktera i problemi njihovog izvršenja' ('Legal regulation of medical security measures and problems of their implementation'), in *Problemi reintegracije i reforme jugoslovenskog krivičnog zakonodavstva (Problems of reintegration and reform of the Yugoslav criminal legislation)*, Institute of Criminological and Sociological Research, Beograd, p. 44.

32. ibid.

33. ibid., p. 44.

34. Article 16 of the federal law.

35. Article 64, paragraph 4 of the federal criminal law.

36. Article 65, paragraph 1 of the federal criminal law.

37. Also article 65, paragraph 1 of the federal criminal law.

38. Article 62, paragraph 4 of the federal criminal law. Alternatively a disciplinary measure must have been ordered for a 'young adult' offender (all offenders between eighteen and twenty-one years of age).

39. Article 65, paragraph 4 of the federal criminal law.

40. Article 65, paragraph 3 of the federal criminal law.

41. In some other aspects, Yugoslav criminal legislation also implies objective responsibility in the sense of the potential danger or damage which could be caused by the action. For example, articles sanctioning the criminal offences of defamation (article 92 of Serbian criminal law and article 76 of Montenegrin criminal law) and unauthorised exposure of one's personal and family circumstances (article 94 of Serbian criminal law and article 78 of Montenegrin criminal law) from the group of criminal offences against honour and reputation, in both republican laws, contain such provisions. Here one finds the provision that 'if what was publicly exposed was of such significance that it has led, *or could lead*, to serious consequences for the victim of this offence', the offender will be punished more severely [emphasis by the author]. What is at stake here are clearly the potential as well as the actual consequences, and in that sense the domain of objective responsibility is broader than in the case of the objective condition of incrimination.

42. For an extremely useful discussion of some aspects of the objective condition of incrimination see Atanacković, D. (1995), 'Objektivni uslov inkriminacije i njegovo razgraničenje od posledice krivičnog dela' ('The objective condition of incrimination and its distinction from the consequence of a criminal offence'), in *Problemi reintegracije i reforme jugoslovenskog krivičnog zakonodavstva (Problems of reintegration and reform of the Yugoslav criminal legislation)*, Institute of Criminological and Sociological Research, Beograd.

43. ibid., p. 54.

44. ibid.

45. ibid., p. 54.

46. ibid.

47. The strategy of control of deviance, from the state's point of view, is often similar to the strategy of control of dissensus. Legally and morally, however, this does not necessarily have to be understood as though the categories of deviance and dissensus can be reduced to each other, or in any way be seen as identical on a general level. This was discussed to some extent in the previous chapter.

48. With some offences, more severe consequences (of the sort that normally constitute the objective condition of incrimination), lead to a more severe sanctioning of the offence than where the objective condition of incrimination is not fulfilled. For example, see article 210, paragraph 1 and paragraph 2 of the Yugoslav federal criminal law, as well as Atanacković, op. cit., p. 57.

49. ibid., pp. 63–4.

50. Article 203 of Serbian criminal law and article 179 of Montenegrin criminal law.

51. See the next section, 'Defamation, honour, and criminal law'.

52. Chapter 11 of Serbian criminal law and chapter 9 of Montenegrin criminal law.

53. Article 101, paragraph 2 of Serbian criminal law and article 84, paragraph 1 of Montenegrin criminal law.

54. Article 102 of Serbian criminal law and article 85 of Montenegrin criminal law.

55. Emphasis by the author.

56. Article 97 of Serbian criminal law and article 81, paragraph 1 of Montenegrin criminal law.

57. Article 93, paragraph 3 of Serbian criminal law and article 81, paragraph 2 of Montenegrin criminal law.

58. For some arguments in favour of conflict-resolution, see for example Christie, N. (1981), *Limits to pain*, Norwegian University Press, Oslo; Burton, J. & Dukes, F. (1990), *Conflict: Practices in management, settlement and resolution*, St. Martin's Press, New York; Burton, J. & Dukes, F. (eds) (1990), *Conflict: Readings in management and resolution*, Macmillan, London; Burton, J. (1990), *Conflict: Resolution and provention*, Macmillan, London.

59. For example, article 92, paragraph 3 of Serbian criminal law and article 76, paragraph 3 of Montenegrin criminal law; article 94, paragraph 3 of Serbian criminal law and article 78, paragraph 3 of Montenegrin criminal law.

60. Chapter 12 of Serbian criminal law and chapter 19 of Montenegrin criminal law.

61. Article 103 of Serbian criminal law and article 86 of Montenegrin criminal law.

62. Article 104 of Serbian criminal law and article 87 of Montenegrin criminal law.

63. Article 105 of Serbian criminal law and article 88 of Montenegrin criminal law.

64. Article 106 of Serbian criminal law and article 89 of Montenegrin criminal law (Montenegrin criminal law mentions 'intercourse or unnatural intercourse with a juvenile person').

65. Article 107 of Serbian criminal law and article 90 of Montenegrin criminal law.

66. Article 108 of Serbian criminal law and article 92 of Montenegrin criminal law.

67. Article 110 of Serbian criminal law and article 91 of Montenegrin criminal law.

68. Article 111 of Serbian criminal law and article 93 of Montenegrin criminal law.

69. Article 109 of Serbian criminal law.

70. Article 106 of Serbian criminal law and article 89 of Montenegrin criminal law.

71. Episodes where sexual abuse of male juvenile persons by female perpetrators are not a rarity in countries such as the USA. There is no logical reason why this possibility should be excluded from the characterisation of this criminal offence.

72. Chapter 13 of Serbian criminal law and chapter 11 of Montenegrin criminal law.

73. Article 115 of Serbian criminal law and article 97 of Montenegrin criminal law.

74. Article 115 paragraph 1 of Serbian criminal law.

75. Article 97, paragraph 1 of Montenegrin criminal law.

76. Article 115, paragraph 3 of Serbian criminal law.

77. Article 97, paragraph 3 of Montenegrin criminal law.

78. In this context, Serbian criminal law and Montenegrin criminal law equalise the position of a foster or adopting parent and legal guardian with the position of a parent, but they do so in the context of incrimination.

79. Article 115, paragraph 4 of Serbian criminal law and article 97, paragraph 4 of Montenegrin criminal law.

80. Article 103 of Serbian criminal law and article 86 of Montenegrin criminal law.

81. Article 194 of Serbian criminal law and article 87 of Montenegrin criminal law.

82. Article 105 of Serbian criminal law and article 88 of Montenegrin criminal law.

83. Serbian criminal law contains a specific provision relating to the female person as the 'victim', in the context of the criminal offence of forced intercourse or unnatural intercourse by abuse of official position (article 107 of Serbian criminal law), while the characterisation of the same offence in Montenegrin criminal law is neutral in relation to the sex of the victim (article 90 of Montenegrin criminal law).

84. It was already mentioned that, when a rise in crime rates is discussed, what is really at stake is primarily a fairly widespread *perception* of a rise in criminality.

85. The role of the media here is extremely problematic as well.

86. Article 22 of the Yugoslav federal Constitution.

87. Article 25 of the Yugoslav federal Constitution.

88. For one of the most recent sources see Knežević, & Tufegdžić, op. cit., especially pp. 95–6, where the treatment of Ilija Vujić and Darko Lončarić in Belgrade's Central Prison is discussed.

3 The Czech Republic and its 'Revolution'

In countries such as Yugoslavia in the 1990s, crime is largely a product of disintegration of the state, which in turn is a product of ideological disintegration. The demise of SFRY meant the disappearance of organised systems of loyalties that would be sufficiently attractive for the political élites of the former republics. The former imposed socialist-communist unitarism, which was also to some extent a universalism, thus gave way to an ideological particularism. This *particularism* is not the same as political *pluralism*, although it contains some of its elements. The ideological particularism that appeared in the late 1980s in Yugoslavia led to the crystallisation of a model of political leadership that is capable of changing ideological directions with almost no substantive restrictions whatsoever, while at the same time retaining its leading role. This has led to a certain separation of the population's loyalty systems from the former substantive standards, and a restructuring of loyalties *away* from that to an ideology and ideological principles (and these principles were unitary in the former system) *towards* loyalty to a political leadership, regardless of the changes in ideological and political values that the leadership introduces from time to time. This clearly presents a danger of crystallisation of a *static* loyalty to the political élite, a loyalty that threatens to become unconditional, which would be in an obvious contradiction with democracy. The departure from the loyalty to substantive standards has in fact led to a crisis of civil values. Civil values characterise the civil society as to some extent *independent* of the political system. In other words, the phenomenon of restructuring of loyalties away from the substantive ideology and towards the political leadership has caused a certain 'suction' of civil society by the political system. In the resulting partial vacuum of civil values, which have been systematically marginalised by the political system since the mid-1980s, the general political and economic collapse has occurred even more quickly and more dramatically. Thus Yugoslavia of the late 1990s is the most obvious example of a country in central-eastern Europe experiencing high crime rates with specifically political causes.

According to most analyses (economic, criminological, and political), if there is an opposite example, one embodying the parameters of growth and political stability which should normally be expected to contribute to comparatively low crime rates, then that example would probably be the Czech Republic. This is one of the countries that have prospered economically and whose institutions have been strengthened after the end of communist rule. The Czech Republic's National Bank's foreign currency reserves rose from around US$400 million at the beginning of 1993 to around US$8.5 billion at the end of April 1995. When the existing reserves of commercial banks were taken into account, the total figure was around US$10.5 billion in April 1995, thereby ensuring extraordinary economic stability for the system in central-eastern European circumstances. In addition, the Czech community was characterised by a high level of consensus on the initial anti-communist forms of social policy. This consensus has led to a certain strengthening of civil relationships. However, in spite of all these formal, favourable circumstances, crime rates in the Czech Republic have risen substantially since 1989, both in the strictly quantitative sense, in the number of particular types of crimes committed annually, and in a qualitative sense, meaning that some sorts of crime which had been practically unknown during communism have become prevalent. The rise in criminality was particularly rapid in the first years following the political changes. Subsequently it has slowed down somewhat, but the amount of criminality overall has remained high.[1]

The 'internal security crisis' and political changes

The Czech Republic is often described as a country that has experienced extraordinary continuity of reform in this decade, and a consistent shift towards a liberal society. Its overall economic and social circumstances have improved steadily, but this has been followed by an equally steady rise in the crime rate. It has been rising substantially every year since 1989, with the lowest such jump being *16%* in 1993. This figure would normally be considered an extraordinary aggravation of the social control situation in any society. Between 1989 and 1995, the crime rate in the Czech Republic at least *tripled* for most types of crime. What once used to be a safe though undemocratic country with low crime rates is experiencing a virtual explosion of economic crimes, such as embezzlement, tax evasion, and all types of fraud, along with an equally fast increase in organised crime, the narcotics trade, and individual violent crimes.[2] This has happened along with the recent establishment of mechanisms for citizen-participation in major decision-making processes, a large influx of foreign investment, an opening of the borders, and a re-affirmation of private ownership and capitalist values.

The rise in crime rates has been perceived as a true crisis of law and order, and has caused shock and apprehension among the population. Part of the problem with economic crimes has been connected with the way in which the political reforms have been designed and implemented. This particularly concerns the privatisation and restitution policies. Many individuals and groups who once participated in the communist decision-making processes, and who were therefore able to use considerable connections and personal relationships established under the former system, were able to obtain property and assets of high value in what would not be considered a fair competition. Many state enterprises were privatised in extremely dubious ways. In 1994, the head of the state privatisation service, Jarosláv Lizner, was arrested in a Prague nightclub with a suitcase full of money. Lizner was accused of corruption in the conduct of privatisation. The following year he was acquitted because of a lack of evidence, but was sacked from his former position. Such developments in privatisation have increased the lack of faith of large sections of the population in the new institutions.

Czech government agencies and officials, and especially the police, are often quick to point out that, generally speaking, the Czech crime rate is still considerably lower than those of most western European countries, and that in this sense there is really no tangible crisis of law and order in the country yet. That argument may indeed be largely correct. However, the rise in the crime rate after the post-communist changes naturally leads to questions about the ability of the new economic and political arrangements, as well as the current government, to provide effective social control services. There is a widespread perception in the population that the social control system is inefficient and partly inadequate for the changed social circumstances. This perception leads to questions about the domain and role of the criminal justice system as a subsystem of social control. There is a combination of factors that make this subsystem inefficient. Some of them are simply the remaining consequences of the former political régime, which was almost entirely unconcerned about types of crime that at the time were rare in the Czech Republic, and that are today seen as negative consequences of the liberalisation. This particularly concerns the emergence of organised crime. Other factors relate more to the changed social circumstances themselves. In all newly liberalised systems the amount of enthropious tendency usually increases rapidly in the first period after the political and social changes. After this period of adaptation is over, enthropious tendencies tend to lose strength. The dynamics of the increases in deviance thus decrease, but the cumulative amount of deviance remains large in the long term. This assumption partly explains why crime rates in liberal societies are higher than in societies where the dominant policy of governance is one of strict control and supervision. Communism was an example of the latter.

For the above reasons it is not surprising that, along with the post-communist changes comes the danger of high crime rates. The most important question here is whether or not the governments and the communities in transitional circumstances will be able to devise alternative crime-control mechanisms sufficiently quickly to minimise the destructive consequences of increases in deviation. For the answer to this question to be affirmative, the newly liberalised societies must pay attention primarily to the *structure* of the crime rate, that is to the *types* of crime that are most prevalent and whose numbers are rising most dramatically, and to draw conclusions therefrom about the possible social *causes* of these types of crime. Once these causes have been determined, and gradually changed, crime rates could become more controllable, and in any case more stable. In all likelihood, given the existing high correlation between the liberalisation of a political system and the increase in delinquency in it, even thus stabilised crime rates would still be at a considerably higher level than they were in authoritarian social circumstances.

Most concerns about crime in the Czech Republic today are centred on the city of Prague. At the crossroads of international travel throughout Europe, Prague glitters on the map of organised crime as 'the drug capital' of Europe, with the lowest street prices for narcotics in the world, and with fairly poorly adapted social control mechanisms for coping with the problem. It is a major transitory point for drug-trafficking into other European countries. It is also the part of the Czech Republic with by far the highest concentration of criminality. Although just 10% of the Czech Republic's population live in Prague, it accounts for around 25% of the total number of some types of crime.[3]

A more recent phenomenon of organised crime, also frequently occurring in Prague, has been the smuggling of stolen radioactive material, mainly the enriched uranium from the former Soviet nuclear power plants and experimental facilities, which is suitable for use in the production of nuclear weapons. Some of this material originates from the local, Czech powerplants and similar facilities, and the smuggling operations usually include both foreign and Czech nationals in a smuggling chain. This makes detection even more difficult and complex.

With the new liberal legislation regulating foreign investment, the very large increase in the number of foreign firms, corporations, and private businesses in the Czech Republic, and especially in Prague, has led to a rise in extortion rackets. A number of gangs specialise in this criminal area. Their detection is extremely complex because of their very elaborate organisation and the general reluctance of businesspeople to report incidents to the police for fear of further victimisation by other members of the criminal organisation. With the socio-political changes there was also a dramatic increase in the smuggling of refugees from the most economically disadvantaged parts of Europe into western Europe via the Czech Republic. White-collar crime has also sky-rocketed, with tax evasion and illegal infringement of contracts topping the list. Holes in some parts of the legislation and a lack of enforcement mechanisms for contractual matters mean that at this moment in the Czech Republic it is practically impossible to count on the respect for contracts and agreements and to avoid more than occasional victimisation by contract-breakers.[4]

Exclusivism and criminality

A rising crime rate and the apparent inability of control institutions to stop it have aggravated some of the already bad consequences of the political transition on the domestic front. One of the more notorious negative consequences of the collapse of communism in central-eastern Europe has been the emergence, or revival, of various exclusivist attitudes in the population, first of all of nationalistic exclusivism. Like the rest of eastern Europe, the Czech Republic has not been spared this development. The Skinhead movement is gaining prominence fast, and has already been responsible for a wide range of mainly violent crimes. Skinheads particularly target the Romany minority, which has traditionally been the quiet victim of nationalism in Europe, and which is still on the receiving end of much of the public debate about crime. The high incidence of crime is often attributed to 'the Gypsies' and 'the foreigners' in the Czech Republic. The stereotypical blaming of particular nationalities and ethnic minorities is a strong incentive for the population psychologically to link the presence of those minorities in the country with the high crime rates, especially for some types of crime. There are highly developed and detailed stereotypes in this area. Thus drug-trafficking is colloquially attributed almost exclusively to Arab ethnic groups, the smuggling of uranium and other radioactive materials to 'the Russians', extortion rackets to 'Yugoslavs' and 'Bulgarians'; the same applies to a wide range of other types of crime. As a rule, petty thefts and pickpocketing are attributed more or less exclusively to members of the Romany ethnic group.

In this way, the anger of the general population, their frustration with the high and rising crime rates, is used for two purposes: for the creation of an even more monolithic racist core within the society, both urban and rural; and for diverting the direction of collective aggression (in the positive sense, in which it requires social change and improvement in living conditions) away from generating a constructive social critique of social policy, and thus having a political impact on the Czech government. Instead, by encouraging, or at least tolerating, racist prejudices, this aggression is diverted towards a stereotypical blaming of racially targeted groups, which ultimately really begs the real questions arising from the social crisis. If a true political impact of the population's anger over the social crisis were achieved, instead of racial and especially anti-Romany discrimination, it could conceivably systematically contribute to policies that would gradually reduce deviance in the Czech society. However, such a political impact would almost certainly be a destabilising factor in the current political establishment, which still rides high on ideological promises and the sentiments aroused by the end of communism.

In spite of the racist explanation of rising crime rates, statistics clearly show that ethnic Czechs are responsible for nearly all types of crimes, with the Romany minority members often accused of petty theft and pickpocketing, crimes which can be directly explained by their subdued social predicament and the corresponding lack of participation in the positive economic results of the transitional process. The unwillingness of most of the population to look at the real face of the real problems of social crisis more openly and directly arises partly from a fascination with market-based reforms and socio-political transition, coupled with a perception of a certain *corresponding worsening* of the specifically *social* situation. Could it be that the security crisis arising from high crime rates is somehow a result of the liberal political reform? If so, then this is certainly not what most supporters of the conservative government want to believe. In other words, the Czech Republic may be paying a price for its political liberalisation through its internal security crisis, and it may have to pay an even greater price in the future. This possibility, unwanted as it is by 'true supporters' of the spirit of liberal capitalism, can, at least seemingly, be done away with easily, if one simply assumes that all the perils connected with crime and deviance arise not from social circumstances, but from the presence of people with a different colour of skin, or at least of passport.

It could be argued that the connection between political changes and changes in the internal security situation is obvious. The former Czechoslovak society was once thoroughly equalised, with a planned economy and a systematic way of addressing the citizens' key living needs and problems. This was an authoritarian way, but one that led to almost full employment and at least a seeming absence of homelessness, in accordance with the communist ideology and the iron fist of the communist social policy. Today the Czech society is passing through the rapid process of delayed social stratification. The negative side of this delayed stratification results in a progressive marginalisation of an increasing number of citizens. In other words, the once almost entirely equalised society is facing a rapidly growing amount of freedom and opportunity for advancement. At the same time, it is facing an equally fast-growing, and often existentially coloured, crisis of financial, political, and social inequality. This phenomenon was partly caused by the rapid privatisation of state-owned industrial complexes and other economic assets. Such a rapid privatisation process naturally favoured those who were already well organised and connected through the old communist networks of power and privilege. Many former communist 'apparatchiks', who had benefited from corruption in the previous system, have been able to generate far more wealth and political influence for themselves than most other citizens, who had also been marginalised in the former system, though perhaps in somewhat different ways. By using their often illegitimately acquired assets and connections, these 'new rich' have occupied the driver's seat of the new economic system. In the course of doing so, many of them have been accused of fraud, embezzlement, and other economic crimes. This economic dialectic of transition has also, naturally, *antagonised* those on the receiving end of the transitional social restratification, prompting many of them, in turn, to engage in other, perhaps more petty, types of economic and other crime. Property-related crime has ballooned, from burglary of apartments and offices, which presents a very serious problem in Czech cities, to tax evasion and theft. It ought to be noted here, so far as the rise in economic crime can be attributed to fast privatisation, that the Czech example of privatisation is considered as perhaps the most successful and well conducted in the whole of central-eastern Europe. Privatisation in countries such as Russia was many times faster and less controlled. It is thus not difficult to imagine just how devastating the economic consequences of privatisation were in the region.

The phenomenon of the rise of petty thefts and economic crimes referred to above can be explained by the theory of relative deprivation, presented briefly in the first chapter. The feeling of being abused, of a continuing inferiority of the majority to many who are perceived as former beneficiaries of ideological services of the communist régime, at the expense of their compatriots, can be seen as a partial cause, especially for engaging in street crime. This feeling is coupled with that of growing social injustice and a lack of legitimate opportunities, while at the same time the familiar minority from past times continue to enjoy the economic and political rewards of their continuing high social profile, which was almost automatically taken over from the previous régime. The disenchantment thus created prompts an increasing number of those who feel marginalised to become involved in various socially 'erosive' activities. The feeling of relative deprivation thus becomes a specifically socio-political cause of criminality.

The newly created atmosphere of openness and freedom to pursue individual choices and opportunities has also had its dark side. It unleashed the sentiments long-tamed by the strong hand of communism. Rates of racially motivated crimes have thus risen dramatically after the 1989 reforms. Bashings of Romanies, break-ins into their houses and flats, molestation, murder, and arson are increasingly frequently attributed to the Skinhead movement, which is systematically trying, and not without success, to gain a considerable political voice. Many times in the past few years Skinhead movement members were involved in the molestation, killing, and house-burning of Czech citizens of Romany ethnicity. The movement operates relatively undisturbed in many parts of the country, and has enlisted the support of, or at least is tolerated by, a number of town mayors in the countryside, especially in North Bohemia.

An even more worrying perception is conveyed by the public opinion polls that suggest a far more widespread presence of racial intolerance. Some polls show that as many as 80%, even 90%, of all ethnic Czechs harbour racial and ethnic prejudices towards various ethnicities, and overwhelmingly so towards Romanies. This to some extent explains why the government is practically hampered from fighting racism effectively, given that any decisive anti-racist policies could carry an inherent risk of antagonising a large part of the electorate.

The new Czech law on the acquisition and loss of citizenship, introduced by the Czech National Council on December 29, 1992, has drawn accusations of racism from the Council of Europe and international human rights organisations. The controversial provision of the law is the requirement that any person applying for Czech citizenship must have had a clear criminal record in the five years preceding the application.[5] There is a crucially important political context for understanding the mentioned provision. After the disintegration of Czechoslovakia, *all* citizens living in the territory of the Czech Republic had to *apply* formally for Czech citizenship. The relatively large numbers of Romanies, who have some sort of a criminal record, usually for petty theft, were thus the most direct target for exclusion by the new law, which could turn them into stateless persons.

There are also more general grounds for criticising the new citizenship law. It could be argued that the existence of a clear criminal record is not supposed to have any influence on a person's citizenship in the land where the person was born. True, many of the people now living in the Czech Republic were born in a country that at the time was called Czechoslovakia, but in real terms that was the same land and the same nation where they live now, and there is no justification for conditioning their citizenship on any behavioural consideration. The penalisation of criminal behaviour by revocation of citizenship, even if this penalisation is only indirect, is a breach of human rights. This applies with even greater force to the penalisation of the very existence of previous convictions for which the offender has already been penalised or excused. The Czech government was not responsive to this criticism at all, and it made no move to reverse or amend the controversial legislation. The controversy gradually died away, but the fundamental problems of racial discrimination have of course survived and still play an important role in Czech society.

Racist sentiments, however, should not be taken as a final argument against the current form of organisation of Czech society. Racism is to a far greater extent present in many other countries of the 'liberal West', and is by no means a problem that is in any way specific to central-eastern Europe. The racist sentiments in the Czech Republic are important because they further inflame the already burning issue of crime and social control, and by focusing public attention on the wrong target, allow crime rates to increase at a pace entirely unacceptable for the social mainstream, even in the context of fast socio-political changes. Racism can indeed be seen as a major obstacle to successful social control in Czech society today.

The racist explanation of criminality, which is largely traditional in the Czech lands, has its own unwanted effects in actually promoting racially motivated crimes. As attacks on darker skinned foreigners became more frequent in the Czech capital in 1993 and 1994, the perception of an internal security crisis also increased. Increased publicity surrounding the rise in racially motivated crimes, which threatened to jeopardise the country's reputation and to have an adverse effect on its tourist industry, eventually forced Prime Minister Václav Klaus to announce a major set of new anti-racist policies in 1994. The new policies generally entail a harsher treatment of perpetrators of racially motivated crimes, and greater obligations for state agencies to prosecute them. However, the real impact of such policies may not be as great as hoped for, because of a possible unwillingness of state agencies and officials to implement them fully for the above-mentioned electoral considerations. Not implementing the law has always been the main problem of criminal justice systems in central-eastern Europe, despite the fact that the legislation itself has never been any less advanced and progressive than in most 'western' countries.

Those wishing to implement the new policies are likely to face resistance from many quarters, especially in the countryside. Many officials there have their own deeply entrenched views. Some of them perceive legal reform as not-too-serious a matter that will fade away with time — a view that is unacceptable in a modernised and liberalised society. Local officials and magistrates often pay more attention to their towns' and municipalities' public reactions to the treatment of perpetrators of racially motivated crimes than to the country's official policy. In many regions the majority harbour strong racist sentiments, which means that public officials' reliance on local popular support can hardly lead to an anti-racist system of social control, at least not in the short to medium term.

General characteristics of the Czech crime-control system

In some aspects, the crime-control system in the Czech Republic is proportionally considerably harsher than the systems of western European countries. The proportion of Czech citizens who are in prison or on remand on an average day is very high, while the proportion of convicted offenders who are placed on parole is very low. Prison sentences are quite usual and are regularly applied, partly because of a general lack of confidence in more liberal, parole-type sentences. With a population of around ten million, the Czech Republic has about 20 000 prisoners on an average day, which means that *one in every 500* citizens is in prison. This figure is very close to that of the USA which, with approximately one in 450 citizens in prison on an average day, is considered *extreme* in the application of custodial measures world-wide. The Czech internal security crisis is certainly nowhere near that of the USA or many other western countries, and a use of imprisonment comparable with such crime-ridden societies therefore does not seem justifiable in any respect.

The high rates of imprisonment and remand suggest that the courts are used to a routine application of custodial measures as a crime-control instrument which, under the previous régime, did not yield such a high rate of incarceration, because crime rates, and thus also the absolute number of crimes, was considerably lower. In the changed social environment, the continuation of the same policies highlights new elements and features of the society that could be a cause for some worry. Only slightly more than one-half of the 20 000 people incarcerated in Czech prisons and gaols on an average day are actual, convicted prisoners. Slightly less than 10 000 of them are yet to be charged, or charged but awaiting trial. Many have been in custody, awaiting trial or charges, for considerably longer periods than the law allows, which signals a violation of human rights. Czech parliamentarians, however, appear aware of this problem and one would hope that new legislation making this type of practice more unlikely and more difficult will be forthcoming. It is quite another matter whether or not, and how fast, any such legislative regulation would be implemented in reality.

One must note here that the courts' adherence to old habits is not always bad. This is illustrated by the very low rate of sentences to life imprisonment. Communist régimes did not like or encourage life sentences, partly because, according to their ideology, prisons were supposed to serve reformatory and rehabilitative purposes. It was thus thought that life sentences, which mean permanent punitive isolation, but certainly not rehabilitation, were beside the point, and were therefore comparatively rarely used. Most communist régimes did not hesitate to impose the death sentence, which has its own ethical and other problems. The ideological position that limited the use of life sentences in communist societies is at odds with the practice of the use of such sentences in some contemporary western liberal democracies, where life sentences are used regularly. Among the 20 000 inmates in the Czech Republic, only six are serving life sentences. In Great Britain, by comparison, this number was 100 000 in 1995. A further overcrowding of prison facilities in 1996, signalling the continuing policies of mass incarceration supported by the conservative government, has even led to a reintroduction of the eighteenth-century policy of using prison ships, which was implemented in March 1997.

The Czech criminal justice system is declared to be reintegrative, educational, and reformatory, at least as much as the Yugoslav system. Similar to the Yugoslav system, the main problems in the Czech Republic arise from disobedience of the law and lack of implementation of its control provisions. The form of the Czech legal system has been considerably improved over the past few years, but the souls behind the levers of justice and social control are much the same as before. This is a general problem for all ideologically transformed societies, and one for which it is difficult to find a quick solution. It means that practical compromises to the letter of the Czech criminal law must be seen in perspective. The ongoing social transformation of the Czech Republic may mean that more time is needed for a full achievement of the rule of law and the particular legal, cultural, and ideological goals of the law-makers.

Czech criminal legislation and its political controversies

Controversies about the death penalty

Following the general political and constitutional changes, the Czechoslovak Parliament abolished the death penalty in 1990, immediately before the disintegration of the country. After the subsequent separation of the Czech and Slovak Republics, each state retained the legislation ruling out the death penalty. Public debate about the possible reintroduction of the ultimate sanction continues, however, sparked by the perceived internal security crisis. The current Czech criminal law, enacted in 1994, initially promised to be a true liberation from the restrictive communist past. However, rising crime rates have led both Czech and Slovak parliamentarians to reopen the death penalty debate, especially during the second half of 1994 and the first half of 1995. The main argument in favour of the death penalty seemed to be that some crimes, particularly violent and sexually motivated assaults and murders, appear so wicked that there can hardly be any hope for the offenders' reintegration into mainstream society, or for their reformation and recovery. Given the perceived need to protect 'decent citizens', or society at large, the death penalty has been thought deserving of renewed attention.

The Czech and Slovak internal situations in this respect are, however, somewhat different. Czech Prime Minister Václav Klaus and all members of the main parliamentary groups opposed any reintroduction of the death penalty, though for quite pragmatic political reasons. The Czech Republic is hoping to join the European Union in the near future, and is thus striving to streamline its legislation, including criminal law, with the legislation of EU member countries. These countries do not allow the death penalty in their legal systems, and the Czech leadership fears that any reintroduction of this form of punishment could block the country's joining the Union. This argument is confirmed by the fact that the recent admission of the Russian Federation to the Council of Europe was conditional on a speedy abolition of the death penalty in Russia, among other factors. The wish to join the EU and other European institutions, perceived as a 'return to the West' where the Czech Republic has allegedly belonged from time immemorial, is widely shared by the population. That was the main reason why Prime Minister Klaus was able to oppose the pro-death penalty initiative so decisively, despite wide public support for the penalty as a social policy measure. The very linking of a possible reintroduction of the final penalty with possible obstacles on the road of a 'return to the West' was sufficient to divert any serious pressures aimed at reintroducing the death penalty into the criminal law.

The Slovak Republic, on the other hand, has a government somewhat less keen to join the European common institutions and market formally, and more so to capitalise on Slovakia's 'unique' position as a 'bridge between the East and the West'. This includes a significant strengthening of ties between Slovakia and the Russian Federation. Slovak Prime Minister Vladimir Mečiar has promised that he would support the reinstatement of the death penalty if the Parliament approved the initiative. The pro-death penalty initiative made it to the bill stage, but the Parliament did not approve it, perhaps partly because of a desire to remain within a common general legal framework with the Czech Republic. Slovak parliamentarians are surely aware that after the abolition of the death penalty in 1990 crime rates *fell* sharply in the whole of the former Czechoslovakia. This was particularly the case with the rates of violent crimes, and it contradicted the very rationale for a possible reinstatement of the death penalty, namely the assumption that it would help to reduce crime. The calls for reinstatement of the death penalty arise from panicky reactions to the rising rates of serial murders and other extremely violent crimes. However, the obvious *negative* correlation between the death penalty and effective crime control has been so clearly present in recent Czechoslovak history that no politician or political party, in either the Czech or the Slovak Republic, is really able to ignore it completely.

The reformatory nature of the penal system

The allegedly reformatory and educatory functions of punishment in Czech criminal legislation are extremely important for an understanding of the newest developments in this country's criminal justice policy. This feature of the system came to the fore particularly clearly with the March 1995 initiative of the Christian Democratic People's Party (Křesťansko-demokratická strana) for the introduction of an American-style 'three strikes and out' policy. This policy prescribes that all repeat offenders who are convicted of the third crime in a sequence are to be given a *mandatory and irrevocable life sentence*. This provision, introduced in some of the American states since the end of 1993 and the beginning of 1994, has been widely criticised as a Draconian measure, which deliberately ignores the large differences between different types of offences, and which allows for a mandatory life sentence to be passed even on the most petty third-time offenders, for offences such as petty theft or pickpocketing.

Although there was great concern about criminal recidivism in the Czech Republic, the political parties' awareness of the declaratively reformatory nature of Czech criminal law was sufficiently strong to enable them to reject the proposed 'three strikes and out' amendment, on the grounds that it contradicted the very spirit of the criminal legislation and the country's philosophy of social control. In his 1990 New Year speech to the nation, President Václav Havel announced an extensive presidential pardon of prison sentences, and appealed to the population to allow the released prisoners to resume their normal and legitimate roles and positions in society, and not to make their lives difficult. This speech marked a whole new era in the country's political life, but it also reflected an awareness of the ineffectiveness and personally devastating consequences of custodial penalties for offenders. Many of the convicts who were released by this presidential pardon have since reoffended and found themselves in prison again. But the words and ideas expressed in that speech still ring in the progressive decisions made by the Czech parliamentarians on new criminal justice policy initiatives. One such progressive decision was certainly their striking down of the 'three strikes and out' proposal.

Criminal legislation and penal provisions

Evidently the 'toughening' of Czech Republic's criminal legislation has not proceeded by the most Draconian route, which is characteristic of some western countries, namely by swelling the volume of Draconian punishments such as the death penalty and life imprisonment. The high proportion of imprisoned and remanded citizens is not a result of general changes in the criminal legislation, but rather of the changed social situation and rising crime rates which fill prisons through the legal mechanisms that are no more severe, and are in many aspects less so than were those of the former communist system. However *some* penal provisions have been made more severe, and the investigative and other operational competences of the law enforcement agencies have been broadened. These changes were caused by a growing concern with crime, and the belief that the tightening of investigative and operational control measures is more in accord with the general reformatory philosophy of the whole system than would be the sole pursuit of more severe *penal* measures.

On March 8, 1994, the Czech government introduced into Parliament a set of amendments to the criminal law. These included, among others, provisions increasing sentences for offences committed 'in an organised way' by one-third of the upper limit of imprisonment (officially this limit is fifteen years), to target organised crime. Offenders who serve as informants and generally cooperate with the police would be given special excuses, and these would often lead to sentences *below the lower limit* of legally prescribed sentences for their crimes. The police were given additional operational powers, a greater discretion in investigation, including the right of search and arrest *without a court warrant* in a number of sensitive situations (such as entering the suspect's home). Most democratic countries normally prohibit police from entering a private home to search and arrest its occupants without a court warrant.

When Czech criminal law is compared with Yugoslav legislation, especially with Yugoslav federal criminal law, it appears considerably more severe. The minimum age for full criminal culpability and liability to penalisation according to Czech law is fifteen years (as opposed to sixteen in Yugoslav law, where it applies to the so-called 'older juveniles', between sixteen and eighteen years of age). Czech provisions regulating the granting of 'mental' excuses from culpability are practically identical to the Yugoslav provisions, and they require the presence of both the cognitive element of awareness of the meaning and likely consequences of one's actions, and the volitional element of one's actual ability to influence and control one's actions.[6]

Czech criminal law includes a number of provisions that suggest a strong similarity in its strategic orientation to the Yugoslav legislation. For example, this involves the provisions sanctioning 'necessary defence' (article 9 of Yugoslav federal criminal law and article 13 of Czech criminal law), and 'ultimate need' (article 10 of Yugoslav federal criminal law and article 14 of Czech criminal law). Both laws determine that necessary defence does not imply criminal responsibility, except if the amount of force used for self-defence obviously exceeds the needs of necessary self-defence arising from the specific situation. Thus article 9 of the Yugoslav federal criminal law reads:

(1) An action taken in necessary defence is not a criminal offence.

(2) Necessary defence is that defence which is necessary in order to defend oneself or another against an immediate assault.

(3) The offender who has transgressed the limits of necessary defence can be penalised less severely, and if the excessive use of force has occurred due to strong aggravation or fear caused by the assault, the penalty can be waived.

Czech criminal law summarises the same provision in its article 13, in the following way:

An action which would otherwise be considered a criminal offence, and whereby one defends oneself against an imminent or actual assault which is sanctioned through this law, is not a criminal offence. Necessary defence is not that defence which is obviously inappropriate to the way in which the assault was intended or attempted.[7]

The same applies to the provisions of ultimate need and many other provisions that are based and determined in almost identical ways in the two laws. This convergence of the philosophies of prevention that determine the nature of the two criminal laws is also reflected in the mechanism of synchronisation of the relevant legal provisions with the time of committing the offence — a mechanism which is, again, identical in the two laws. This mechanism reflects the demands of benevolence and minimal restrictiveness towards the offender, as well as the demands of reformation, when it determines that every criminal offence is to be treated in accordance with that criminal law which was in force at the time of committing the offence, *except* in cases where a subsequently changed law facilitates a more lenient treatment of the offender.[8]

Although the two laws are largely identical in shape, Czech criminal law, even after the 1989 changes, contains a number of criminal sanctions that are reminiscent of former communist times. This relates particularly clearly to the punishment by seizure of property. Article 27 of Czech criminal law enumerates all forms of criminal sanctions available under the law in the following way:

(1) imprisonment, or 'denial of freedom' (odněti svobody),

(2) cancellation of honorary titles and medals (ztrátu čestných títulu a vyznamenáni),

(3) cancellation of military ranks (ztrátu vojenské hodnosti),

(4) ban on engaging in various activities (zákaz činnosti)

(5) seizure of property (propadnutí majetku),

(6) fines (peněžitý trest),

(7) seizure of particular items (propadnuti věci),
(8) banishment (vyhoštění), and
(9) deportation, or prohibition of stay in the country (zákaz pobytu).

Some of the penalties are especially interesting, such as seizure of property, banishment, and the so-called 'exceptional' custodial punishments.

Seizure of property is a sanction aimed at expressing community reproach and reprimand to the offender, and it specifically targets offences motivated by the desire to acquire illegitimate *material* gain. The rationale behind attaching a special weight of blame to offences motivated by illegitimate acquisition of material benefit reflects a remnant of communist and communitarian values, whereby acquiring illegitimate benefit was perceived as particularly dishonourable, in some cases more so than violent crimes.

In this context, it could be argued that the meaning of seizure of property as a criminal sanction is to inflict a financial blow to the offender who has betrayed this special social philosophy adopted by the system. Of course, the former communist régime in Czechoslovakia, which was extremely militant, often applied this strategy to target all activities, especially economic crimes, that could be considered as leading to an extreme accumulation of wealth.[9]

Financial penalties play a similar role to that of confiscation or 'seizure' of property. Article 53 thus explicitly determines that fines, ranging from 2000 to 5 000 000 Czech crowns, are to be imposed only for offences committed in the pursuit of illegal financial gain.[10] The penalty by seizure of property excludes from seizure those items or parts of property that are necessary for the offender's existence, or for the support and welfare of those who are dependent on the offender and for whom the offender is legally responsible.[11]

Expulsion, or deportation, can be imposed only on a foreigner, or on a person who has neither a foreign citizenship, nor a refugee status in the Czech Republic, and who represents a danger to the public or public property, or whose presence in the country 'is contrary to public interest', generally speaking.[12] Although the formulation of this article, which allows expulsion of a person on the basis of an unexplained assertion that their 'presence in the country is contrary to public interest', leaves considerable room for worrying that it may be used to justify and legitimise abuses and expulsions without good reason, similar provisions do exist in the legislation of many other countries.

It is interesting, however, that Czech criminal law contains a highly controversial criminal sanction, namely banishment from a part of the country or region.[13] This provision determines that a person cannot be banished from the region or municipality where that person possesses a legal permanent residency permit, but only from some other region of the country. The duration of this sanction ranges from one to five years. It is imposed if it is seen as necessary given the offender's previous way of life, the question of whether a person's presence in a particular place or region is a threat to 'public order, family and family relations, health, morality, or property'.[14]

The criminal sanction of banishment has had a long history in early societies, and it is one of the alternative, extremely controversial, possibilities for change to the current criminal legislation in many western countries. At present this sanction is somewhat of a subject of public debate in the USA, where in 1994 a case was widely publicised where a judge -re-affirmed a sentence of *banishment* for two Indian offenders, which was initially handed out by their tribal elders, *instead of* the equivalent western (and legal) sanction (which would have included imprisonment). The debate surrounding the case was fierce, precisely because this type of sanctioning of criminality was so far removed from the 'mainstream' of modern criminal justice systems that the very thought of it was somewhat of a challenge to the imagination. In Czech criminal law, banishment is a legitimate part of the very mainstream system of social control, and this fact is not widely known.

Imprisonment in Czech criminal law is limited to fifteen years, 'under normal circumstances'.[15] Life imprisonment may be imposed for 'qualified' (aggravated) murder,[16] grand treason under aggravating circumstances,[17] terrorism,[18] causing of danger to the public,[19] and genocide.[20]

It has been mentioned that in 1995 there were only six offenders sentenced to life imprisonment in the Czech Republic. The number of offenders sentenced to 'exceptional' penalties (from fifteen to twenty-five years) changes from one year to another, and there is a certain measure of unwillingness on the part of the administrative services and Prison Service to make current information about these sentences readily available. The characterisation of the offences that can be penalised by 'exceptional' penalties in itself leaves a great deal of discretion to the courts to decide what particular offences are to be considered 'extremely dangerous to society', and which offenders 'do not have a chance' to be successfully 'rehabilitated' and 'reformed'. The amount of discretion in the application of prison penalties from fifteen to twenty-five years is far greater than the amount of discretion involved in the application of life sentences, because the latter type of 'exceptional' penalties can be applied only for specifically enumerated and described crimes, under specifically determined aggravating circumstances, in accordance with article 29 of Czech criminal law.

The existence of 'exceptional' penalties in Czech criminal legislation brings that legislation in line with the more severe penal codes in Europe, and compromises the initial impression of its 'liberal' nature, which is based on the penalty provisions defined as applying under 'normal' circumstances. Given the crucial role of discretionary decisions in the application of 'exceptional' sanctions, it is clear that political pressures could easily play a deciding role in penal policy. In this way, the demands of fairness and justice could be compromised by the mood of the electorate. The population whose reactions to criminality are in this sense relevant varies: sometimes it can be determined as narrowly as the prosecutor's electoral unit, or the judge's neighbourhood or municipality. The reactions of the electorate in the immediate social 'environment' of those individuals who are in charge of penal policy — and these reactions are largely emotional, can have a strong influence on the application of 'exceptional' measures. There are reasons to suspect that many judges and magistrates in the Czech Republic may be under such local pressure in the performance of their duties. This phenomenon became obvious in some cases during 1993 and 1994, when perpetrators of racist attacks and other racially motivated crimes were treated with a great deal of tolerance, while those who had committed violent offences against members of militant racist groups were penalised severely. This is not a general accusation, because most judges in the Czech Republic perform their duties properly. Those who do allow political pressures to compromise their decisions can thus not be taken as typical of the entire system. However, the emergence of compromises to the control policy because of such pressures in itself means that certain aspects of the current situation in crime control, and some aspects of the tradition, do not suggest any good consequences of increases in the role of courts' discretion in handing out 'exceptional' prison sentences, apart from life sentences, whose application is precisely and explicitly regulated in the law.

Immediate perspectives for control policy

Despite the problems with the high degree of discretion in decision-making, it is clear that legislative reform in the Czech Republic is proceeding, and its direction is likely to continue to be towards granting greater discretionary and operational competences to the courts, police, and other law-enforcement agencies. This trend of an increased role of discretion hides numerous dangers, because it does not make it clear how these competences will be used in particular cases and circumstances, and in the service of which values. The Czech Republic's central position in Europe, and its opening towards the western part of the Continent, mean that after the changes in the late 1980s many smuggling routes and avenues for organised international crime have been diverted to go through Czech lands. The importance of the Czech lands on the world map of international crime has been dictated by the closure of alternative routes and markets, the increasing number of Mafia-type organisations in the former Soviet territory, the Balkan wars which made it more difficult and dangerous to run criminal operations through the Balkan Peninsula, etc. Along with the economic changes in central-eastern Europe, the demand for drugs and all sorts of other commodities and services typically provided by criminal organisations has increased rapidly. This has created a tension between high demand and high profits on the still underregulated and fairly fresh criminal markets in the region on the one hand, and the socio-political disturbances and problems in the region that make access to consumers and organised activity much more difficult on the other hand.

The changed political and security situation in the region has also created new commodities, which were previously not available on the market, such as powerful assault weapons, military equipment, and nuclear materials. The stakes have thus risen for all criminal organisations, and central-eastern Europe is now one of the most attractive areas in the world for organised crime. In such circumstances, it was predictable that Prague and other regional capitals would see an explosion of heroin-trafficking, uranium and plutonium smuggling, smuggling of refugees, extortion rackets, organised motor vehicle theft, etc. But this situation does not mean that an increased use of discretion will necessarily be the solution. High crime rates in the region today are largely a result of greater demands being placed on regional law enforcement than ever before, and the lagging shortcomings of legal systems that were not designed for the control effort which is required of them today. In societies that are underregulated in comparison with western countries, the solution is not necessarily in a proliferation of regulations and a compromising of public policy by allowing it to become a matter of discretion that is influenced by public mood. Both perils are obvious in western countries, where they have led to an enormous alienation of large sections of the population, higher crime rates, use of stereotypically geared methods of control with stereotypical target groups (such as military policing), and ultimately a division of society into an ever-decreasing consensual majority and an ever-increasing dissensual minority. The same phenomena have led to extremely bureaucratic, overregulated investigative organisations with large discretionary and intrusive powers in many countries today.

Legislation to control the new crime wave is only starting in the Czech lands, but some restraint is needed to prevent the swelling of the police force beyond reasonable limits, and the overregulation of a still attractive and spontaneous society towards uncritically accepted paradigms characteristic of western countries, mainly the European Union and the USA. This concerns all aspects of crime control, but especially policing. Czech police were used increasingly for military policing in 1993 and 1994. This practice continued in 1995, and the police officials stated several times that they intended to continue with the same policy. Massive stop and search operations, large-scale, highly visible raids on small offenders and street dealers, and similar operations, are geared to score political points with a population increasingly worried about internal security. However, these are inefficient, highly intimidating, and intrusive ways of policing a modern society. They are policing strategies that have been employed in countries that represent an almost complete failure of crime control, such as the USA and Great Britain. In these countries military policing has proven ineffective as well.

The Czech police are still underequipped and undertrained to fight major international Mafia figures and their organisations. These difficulties appear especially clearly in the most demanding part of police work, namely in *investigation and detection*. Compromises and shortcomings in investigative and detective policing cannot be disguised for long, much less overcome, by an increased use of military policing, and especially not in the midst of the worsening situation of criminality and deviance that the Czech Republic is facing today. If the current trends of military law enforcement continue, as is likely to be the case, they may further antagonise the stereotyped groups that are typically targeted by military policing. This is likely to produce a division within Czech society, an underclass which could become its greatest economic and moral ballast, and its greatest challenge. It is here that many modern capitalist societies would wish that they had acted differently in the past, to avoid the creation of this social division. It is here that social control, and first of all crime control, is an indicator of where society is heading, and where that development falls short of productive social and political reform, as opposed to deeply divisive and disintegrative socio-political change.

The ideological dimension of social control and the system of criminal law in the Czech Republic

The Czech ideological scene in the 1990s

In every society that is between fundamentally different socio-political régimes and forms of organisation, there is a certain degree of tension between those who are in favour of a return to the old and familiar arrangements, and those who see promises and opportunities at the end of the road to a different future. In the Czech Republic today, a battle is going on between *three* distinct types of political ideologies: the liberal conservatives, the communists and former communists, and the Social Democrats.

The first, and for the moment the strongest ideological force, are the hard-line liberals, led by Prime Minister Václav Klaus. They are extremely conservative in their political and economic outlook, and believe that the laws of market and conservative European political values, such as those once advocated by the former British Prime Minister, Margaret Thatcher, are the most important directions for the countries of central Europe. They also tend to insist on a fairly sharp conceptual distinction between 'central' and 'eastern' Europe, whereby eastern Europe is considered as a less progressive and 'western' region than central Europe.

The conservative ideology therefore views central and eastern Europe as two very different political and cultural entities. Its exponents often state that, in central Europe, the Czech Republic is the most advanced and 'the most European' country. Their social and economic policies are motivated by the idea of a rapid transformation of the Czech Republic into a 'western' country by the same path as the one which is known from history as the evolution of capitalism in Europe. This course obviously leads through the troublesome waters of the early phases of capitalism, sometimes referred to as 'Manchester capitalism'. For conservative liberals, such a transformation of the industrial and social system, though sure to inflict painful consequences on the population, and especially on those who are in the socially and economically weakest positions, would promise the Czech Republic a historically familiar course of development which was characteristic of the western democracies on the Continent. This is seen as implying that, in good time, the Czech Republic would become identical to the most developed European countries. This vision presupposes that questions of social justice, continuity of the culture and political awareness, and other related issues of continuity, should be largely ignored, if that proves unavoidable in the context of the country's thorough westernisation. This ideology implies that the fifty years spent under communist rule should be forgotten as though they had never happened, and that, as far as the political mind set of the modern policy-makers is concerned, history should in a certain sense be wound back to a point before communism. It is an ideological school that capitalises on the sentiments of many of the Czech people, who were traumatised by the legacy of intrusive communist rule. Conservative liberals control the country's political institutions today. Since the beginning of 1993, however, they have lost a lot of political ground, because of the economic and social difficulties inflicted on large sections of the population through the application of such drastic market reforms which would be considered harsh even in societies with a long tradition of capitalist economy.

Despite its strong policy of market-based liberalisation of the economy, the Klaus government shied away from abolishing rental subsidies for council flats overnight and introducing industrial legislation aimed at bringing workers' salaries more into line with the higher prices and changed economic circumstances. The reasons for this were simple: any abolition of council flat rents overnight, in one of the most expensive accommodation and real estate markets in Europe, and at the same time a country with one of the lower average incomes in the central European region, would have surely led to a crisis of government. The proportion of the urban population that was completely, existentially dependent on various forms of state subsidies for rents was probably about 90% at the beginning of the political reforms in 1990 and 1991. That proportion was still above 70% in 1994. Today it is probably still at or around at least 40% of the entire urban population.

The same considerations apply to the widely publicised achievements of the Czech government in maintaining a low unemployment rate. A low unemployment level is one of the conditions of political stability in the Czech Republic, which under communist rule had almost no unemployment. Inflicting a shock on the population with a sudden surge in unemployment, which, it could be argued, would have fully corresponded to the social, economic and ideological changes, would have certainly meant major political sacrifices. The unemployment rate is maintained at a low level simply because salaries are so low that a large proportion of the employed population is forced to maintain *two parallel full-time jobs* in order to earn enough for basic living needs. In the Czech Republic there has not been a large increase in salaries since the period of communism, although the prices of many consumer items are comparable with the prices in the neighbouring, western European countries. This is not a realistic situation in the long term, but it leads to a rosy picture of unemployment when it is presented in statistical terms.

Low unemployment is not a great solution if workers cannot cover their costs from one full time job, and if consequently many of them hold two full-time jobs. This means that workplace discipline and productivity cannot be high, because it is not possible to do two full-time jobs in a satisfactory way if they are done at the same time, given that working hours are likely to coincide. In addition to this situation, Czech industrial legislation allows Czech citizens to be employed in foreign firms on the same jobs as foreign, mainly western, and mainly American, immigrants, with the same qualifications, for a *much lower* salary than that of their western colleagues. This issue has not been addressed with any degree of success by Czech workers' unions either.

There are many other inconsistencies in the Czech Republic which compromise certain normative presuppositions of modern capitalism. Almost every policy of the conservative government that appears to promote social justice has its dark side, which presents it not so much as an expression of authentic desire to support those who may fall through in the transition process, but much more as an unavoidable compromise in the realisation of the government's conservative goals, in a strategic sense.

The second clearly distinguishable political group on the Czech ideological scene are the former communists. Their ideology is familiar, and their chances for any important political success were not very likely until the beginning of 1995, when these groups attempted to forge a political alliance with the Social Democrats. The communists are very vocal in supporting the heavy-handed policies of social control, and especially the reintroduction of the death penalty, which was debated particularly intensely during 1994.

The third distinct political and ideological group today are the Social Democrats. The Social Democratic Party (Československa socialdemokracie), led by Miloš Zeman, has considerably increased its political influence and public support. Their programme is based on moderate political and economic principles, and especially the need to reconcile the needs and legitimate interests of marginalised social groups, such as the elderly and the unemployed or insufficiently employed, with those of businesses and the new market economy. Social Democrats play a very important role in Czech society, because they may be able to tap the dissatisfaction of marginalised groups that are otherwise a natural electoral base for reactionary forces. The most worrying political force in the Czech Republic today is the Alliance for the Republic — the Czechoslovak Republican Party (Sdruženi pro republiku — Republikánska strana Československa) led by the controversial Miroslav Sládek, and the former communists grouped under a string of political flags, most openly so in the Communist party of Bohemia and Moravia (Komunisticka strana Čech a Moravy).[21]

Consequences and implications of ideology for crime-control policy

The consequences of political ideologies for crime-control policy in Czech society today are not merely a reflection of 'pure' political principles adopted by the ruling conservative-liberal group. It is certainly true that the Civic Democratic Party (Občanská demokráticka strána - ODS) and the government it dominates have tried to make the criminal legislation less harsh after the 'Revolution'. Yet the criminal justice system has shown serious signs of being affected by widespread corruption and abuse of authority. A whole sequence of cases have occurred since 1989, and one of the politically most symptomatic and dramatic ones was the incident described below that shook the nation and led to the sacking of the director of the Czech Prison System in April 1994. On this occasion a prisoner accused of abduction and murder of a son of one of the Prison System's officers was murdered, allegedly by the colleagues of the murdered boy's father. This case could be the source of insights into the beginning of reforms geared at increasing the amount of responsibility of prison officials.

On April 8, 1994, soon after he had confessed to the sexually motivated abduction and murder of the ten-year-old Tomaš Belica, František Kahánek, aged fifty-one, died in the Horńi Slavkov Prison, in western Moravia. Kahánek's autopsy confirmed that the death had occurred because of a fatal head injury, but that other injuries typical of physical maltreatment were also evident, including broken ribs and chest bone. Prosecution began against four prison guards who were suspected of being connected with Tomaš Belica's father, who was an officer in another Czech prison. After visiting the Horñi Slavkov Prison, Czech Minister of Justice Jiři Novák sacked the Director General of the Czech Prison System, Zděnek Karábec, on April 24, 1994. The Governor of the Horñi Slavkov Prison, Alexandr Kozelka, and his deputy, Jaroslav Petrzelká, were also sacked. After all these events, the Public Prosecutor for Western Bohemia, Augustin Hrbotícky, issued a public statement through the Czech news agency ČTK, announcing that the commencement of criminal prosecution against the four guards should not be understood as in any way excluding the possibility that other police officials and prisoners might have also been involved in the murder. Hrbotícky announced that a comprehensive investigation of all possibilities was pending. The four accused guards faced prison penalties up to twelve years, if convicted.

According to the information available, immediately after arriving at Horñi Slavkov, Kahánek was placed in a shared cell with *ten* other prisoners, which in itself was an unusual procedure. After a short time, Kahánek allegedly 'fell' against the iron bars of the cell and was subsequently placed in solitary confinement, where he died from massive head and chest injuries. For some reason, Kahánek also apparently signed a declaration declining the right to medical help, while he was in a solitary cell with several prison guards. In the same cell, and, it appears, in the same circumstances, Kahánek also signed a confession of murder.

As was mentioned earlier in the discussion of the Yugoslav crime control system, brutal treatment of prisoners is not a rarity in the region. The Kahánek case and other examples that have been detected have led to at least 'cosmetic' attempts to change the dubious standards of conduct and supervision in repressive institutions. The Kahánek case also revealed an interesting phenomenon for criminal justice systems in transitional circumstances. Although corruption is usually based on bribery, kick-backs, and other illegitimate means of career advancement, in the contemporary Czech Republic corruption in the criminal justice system is often motivated by entirely private and personal reasons, such as private revenge. This by no means suggests that in other societies abuses of official positions for entirely personal and emotional reasons, including revenge, do not occur, on the contrary. However, what is rare is that such a personal campaign stretches throughout the system, in cases where the relevant individual is neither at, or near, the top of the official organisation's hierarchy. In such a situation, one must depend on a large number of others who are willing to risk their own careers. In Kahánek's case, the whole system was allegedly put in motion in the service of private revenge of an individual who did not occupy a high position in the official hierarchy of the system.

Many such abuses arise from the impression that, if the most serious cases were left to the criminal justice system, 'justice' would not be fulfilled. In other words, distrust of the efficiency and fairness of the system itself is a possible reason for further abuses of the system.[22]

In the Kahánek case, the police establishment showed a willingness and readiness to implement a comprehensive investigation and penalise the perpetrators, partly because the case detonated deafeningly abroad.

International human rights groups are still carefully monitoring what is happening in the Czech Republic. This country also has many unresolved problems in the area of international relations with particular member-countries of the European Union, which could use problems arising from human rights issues, such as those in the Kahánek case, to block the Czech Republic's entry into the Union's common institutions.[23] What is particularly worrying, however, is that, although the political circles have shown readiness to resolve the Kahánek case, Czech public opinion did not react strongly to this event. Because of the publicity and the political importance that this case was given, several public opinion polls were conducted, many by daily newspapers, and the general impression from the results was that most of the population considered that in a fair trial Kahánek probably would not have been sentenced to an appropriate penalty. In other words, the legality and legitimacy of a penalty did not seem sufficiently important to the public to prevent, or at least to unequivocally condemn, 'customary justice'.

The perception among the Czech population that the criminal justice system is unlikely to apply sufficiently severe penalties for major crimes is largely incorrect. Although Czech criminal legislation does not contain the death penalty, this certainly does not mean that it can automatically be understood as a particularly mild and forgiving criminal legislation. The Czech criminal justice system contains very severe prison sentences, including life imprisonment within the exceptional or special penal measures, briefly discussed earlier. The Kahánek case, if it had ever reached the court, would probably have been treated as an exceptional crime for which, if Kahánek had been convicted, an exceptional penalty might have been applied. This penalty would have probably been life imprisonment.

The argument that private justice is justified on the basis of the unjustified mildness of the Czech criminal justice system is therefore unfounded. The main reason for public distrust of the system is the inefficiency and perceived lack of integrity of the police and other control organisations. It is this unreliability of the social control service in the Czech Republic that made the tragedy of František Kahánek possible.

Benevolence, parole, and possible directions for the future development of control policy

Generally speaking, since the end of communist rule in 1989, the Czech criminal justice system has faced two mutually contradictory streams of change. In the first period, immediately after the 1989 'Revolution', efforts were made to make the system more forgiving and lenient, and on a general level less restrictive. However, this initial trend soon led to a perception that criminal deviance had risen exactly *because of* the initial changes to the control system. This, in turn, led to a backlash in conservative circles, starting in 1993. It has led to the introduction of more severe penal regulation, more flexible procedural restrictions on police work and the work of other control agencies. The discretion of the police, prosecutors, and the courts was thus increased. One of the more obvious parts of the criminal legislation where these types of changes are evident is the application of parole as opposed to effective imprisonment.

Article 61 of the Czech criminal law determines that the court may decide to release a prisoner on parole after he has served one-half of the entire sentence, if a significant *improvement* in the convict's behaviour has occurred. Parole also depends on whether or not the court is satisfied that the *reformatory* aims of the penalty have been achieved. In Czech criminal legislation, there are also provisions for the passing of suspended sentences, including non-custodial sanctions such as prohibition to engage in an occupation or a profession, banishment from a particular part of the country, or expulsion from the country. At first sight, these provisions seem liberal. However, their application is subject to large restrictions. Parole and suspended sentences are applicable under particularly restrictive conditions for certain specific categories of crimes, including:

(1) grand treason,
(2) subversion of the state,
(3) terrorism,
(4) intentional causing of damage to the public,
(5) sabotage,
(6) espionage,
(7) treason in war time,
(8) violation of the state border in particular circumstances,
(9) causing of public danger in particular circumstances,
(10) unauthorised acquisition of psychotropic and intoxicating substances,

and a sequence of other crimes.[24] Offenders convicted of these crimes can be released on parole only after they have served two-thirds of their sentences. Similarly, offenders sentenced to life imprisonment can be released on parole only in exceptional circumstances, after they have shown an 'unexpected improvement', and *only after* they have served at least twenty years of imprisonment. The 'unexpected improvement' is a term that is required for strictly logical reasons here, because it is assumed that the passing of a life sentence is a result of the court's conviction that the chances of the offender's 'improvement' are negligible.

As can be seen from the partial list above, for some of the specially parole-restricted crimes, many other countries prescribe the death penalty (war-time treason, grand treason, terrorism, etc.). However, this list also includes crimes that are not typically on the list of most serious crimes, such as 'causing damage to the public' or, even more obviously, possession of prohibited psychotropic substances.

The length of probationary periods for parole and suspended sentences is determined in a relatively flexible way, and ranges from one to seven years.[25] For parole or suspended sentences for the penalties of expulsion from the country or prohibition to engage in an occupation or profession, probationary periods cannot be longer than five years.[26] During the probationary periods, the court may abolish the probation and decide that the offender be sent back to serve the initial sentence. At the same time, when passing a parole or suspended sentence, the courts have the right to apply *any* restriction they may deem necessary.[27] This means that the courts have practically unlimited powers to shape conditions for the application of 'lenience measures'. It also means that parole and suspended sentences are not so much authentic signs of lenience and 'mildness' of the system, as they are alternatives often used because of the organisational needs and limitations of the control system itself.

Czech criminal legislation reveals a certain degree of overregulation *and* underregulation. The overregulation includes the excessively restrictive conditions for the application of 'lenience measures'. The underregulation arises from the extremely high degree of discretion in the initiation and application of these measures. These phenomena should probably be ascribed to the relatively early stage of development of Czech legislation after the 1989 changes, with a relatively undeveloped systematisation of crimes and relatively old-fashioned, still insufficiently reformed, aspects of the penal code. In the context of the values declaratively adopted by the Czech political system in its liberal robes, criminal legislation needs to be additionally reformed, to become less restrictive towards offenders and to facilitate more releases on parole and suspended sentences, more grounds for ascription of mitigating circumstances, etc. These are all authentic determinations of a liberal, humanist, democratic legislation which, for now, are still not entirely clearly visible in the Czech system of social control.

One of the main reasons for doubt in the 'benevolent' and 'liberal' character of the provisions regulating releases on parole and suspended sentences in Czech criminal legislation is that 'lenience' simply cannot be left to the mercy and will of the judges, prison administrators, and other agents of the criminal justice system. That amounts to a reliance on a *personally* determined 'benevolence' of those individuals who hold positions of power. If parole and suspended sentences are to be an authentic sign of 'lenience' of the *system*, then there must be more independent, legal provisions, which would *guarantee* parole and suspended sentences in particular types of cases. This would then mean that parole and suspended sentences *must* be available in certain cases, not that they *may* be available, depending on the judge. Should such measures not be applied, an appropriate explanation would be required from the courts.[28] Only in this way could the system increase its respect for the personality and inherent interests of the 'bad' members of society. It was mentioned earlier that this is fundamentally important in order to *avoid* the division of society into two mutually structurally confronted 'classes', marked by antagonism.

Any further changes to the procedural aspects of policing, judicial work, and penal administration, can be introduced by legal acts such as those that are being enacted extremely frequently and in extremely large numbers in the Czech Republic today. For example, only by one act (Act no. 82/1995), introduced in the Parliament on April 18, 1995, the previous act of the Czech National Council about infractions was changed (Act no. 200/1990), along with Act no. 283/1991 about the Czech Republic's Police Force, and Act no. 553/1991 about regional police.[29] Some of these changes were made several times in the same year. For example, on June 28, 1995, the above-mentioned act about regional police was changed again, by Act no. 153/1995, section no. 48. It is clear that changes to the procedural and operational aspects of the criminal justice system are being made even in relation to the legislation introduced *after* the political changes of 1989. The above-mentioned changes relate to the acts from the early 1990s. The redefinition of those aspects of the regulations that are still controversial, such as those that allow an excessive amount of discretion, would therefore not disturb the ongoing dynamics of legislative activity.

Notes

1. See Jiři Pehe (1994), 'Czech Republic's crime rate slows down', in *Radio Free Europe/Radio Liberty Research Report*, vol. 3, no. 8, February 25, pp. 43–8.

2. ibid.

3. ibid.

4. During 1993, 1994, and 1995, several international and local conferences and seminars were held in Prague on the theme of business ethics, where this problem was singled out as the most significant obstacle to conducting business in the Czech Republic.

5. Law on the acquisition and loss of Czech citizenship, article 7.

6. Article 12 of Czech criminal law — see Jiři Jelínek & Zdeněk Sovák (1994), *Trestní zákon a trestní řad*, edited text as of September 1, Linde Praha a. s. — Právnické a ekonomické nakladatelství a knihkupectví Bohumily Hořínkové a Jana Tuláčka, Prague. The original text of the article reads: 'The offender who, because of a mental disorder at the time of committing the offence, could not understand the danger caused by the offence to society, or could not control one's actions, is not criminally responsible for that offence'. ('Kdo pro duševni poruchu v době spáhání činu nemohl rozpoznat jeho nebezpečnost pro společnost nego ovládat své jednání, není za tento čin trestně odpovědný.')

7. 'Čin jinak trestný, kterým někdo odvrací přimo hrozící nebo trvající útok na zájem chráněný tímto zákonem, není trestným činem. Nejde o nutnou odbranu, byla-li obrana zcela cjevně nepřiměrená spusobu útoku.'

8. Article 4 of Yugoslav federal criminal law and article 16 of Czech criminal law.

9. Throughout the eastern European region, there were 'committees for the investigation of origin of property', which often targeted people who were perceived as unusually wealthy. In the former system, this policy curiously co-existed with widespread corruption and abuse of official positions by members of the ideological élite themselves, but that is not

directly relevant to the meaning of ideological presuppositions of the system that are discussed here.

10. 'Peněžity trest ve výmere of 2 000 Kč do 5 000 000 Kč může soud uložit, jestliže pachatel úmzslnou trestnou činností získal nebo se slažil získat majetkový prospěch.'

11. Article 51.

12. Article 57.

13. Article 57a.

14. In the Czech lands all residents, both citizens and foreigners, must have a special residency permit, which can be temporary or permanent, and which is issued by the police. Many documents, necessary for attendance to daily business, can be obtained only from the authorities of the municipality where one holds permanent residency. It is therefore understandable that banishment cannot apply to that place or region where the offender permanently lives. However, this measure can be applied to a place where the offender temporarily resides, or visits frequently. In other words, this measure often means a ban on travel to particular parts of the country, and in that sense it is somewhat different from 'banishment' in the traditional sense, which implies banishment from the place where the individual permanently lives. In this, as in many other parts of the criminal legislation, courts are allowed a great deal of discretion when deciding on what represents a 'threat to public interest' in particular cases.

15. Article 39, paragraph 1.

16. Article 219, paragraph 2.

17. As per article 91, with aggravating circumstances and consequences determined by article 29, paragraph 3.

18. In accord with articles 93 and 93a, paragraph 3, also with aggravating circumstances determined by article 29, paragraph 3.

19. As per article 179, paragraph 3, also with aggravating circumstances.

20. As per article 259, with aggravating circumstances.

21. Sládek's 'policies', as an illustration, include calls for military annexation of the Silesian areas within Poland to the Czech Republic, expulsion of the Romany minority, a reintroduction of the death penalty, and sharp legislative and other regulatory distinctions in civil rights between ethnic Czechs and other citizens, as well as between the

citizens of the Czech Republic and foreigners who live and work in the Czech Republic.

22. Distrust of the integrity and efficiency of social control institutions is extremely widespread in the region — see for example the report of the United Nations Criminal Justice Information Network entitled *Crime and justice letter*, vol. 1, no. 1/2, section entitled 'Citizens' experience and satisfaction with police', electronic version.

23. This, for example, has related ever since the end of the Second World War to Czech-German relations, which have been soured over the question of restitution of property and citizenship to the descendants of the Sudeten Germans, who were expelled from Czechoslovakia after the Second World War under the accusation of collaboration with the Nazis. Czech government and public opinion are strongly against the German demand for restitution of property and citizenship to these groups, which has been one of the major problems of Czech foreign policy for a long time. Early in 1997, the Czech and German governments signed an agreement designed to put an end to the ongoing problem in mutual relations. This includes German apologies to the Czech people for war-time aggression and criminal atrocities, and a Czech apology to the Sudeten Germans for expelling them, but this does not include any compensation, restitution, or return of citizenship to the Sudeten Germans. In January 1997, both the German Bundestag and the Czech Parliament promptly ratified the agreement, hoping to put an end to a long-lasting and embarrassing problem. There is very strong opposition among Czech people to the agreement, however, and the Czech government might suffer political consequences at the next election because of signing the agreement.

24. Article 62 of Czech criminal law.

25. Article 63, paragraph 1.

26. Article 63, paragraph 2.

27. Article 63, paragraph 3.

28. According to the Czech Republic's Constitution, adopted in December 1992, the Czech judicial system consists of the Supreme Court, the Supreme Administrative Court, high, regional, and municipal courts. Until December 31, 1993, the judicial system also included the military courts. In addition, the Czech Republic has a Constitutional Court with fifteen member judges.

29. The same act also changed Act no. 528/1990, which concerned not crime control, but currency exchange.

4 The Hungarian criminal justice system: An advanced reform

Policy- and law-makers in all central-eastern European countries are aware of the need to reform and reintegrate their criminal justice systems. In most countries of the region, steps have been taken towards such reform. In Hungary the reform has progressed the furthest, not only in the implementation of particular new policies and practices, but also, and perhaps more importantly, in the sense that the government systematically encourages and sponsors criminal justice research. This research and its results are being used in the construction of an entirely new crime-control system.

The advanced research is largely the reason why more comprehensive information is available about Hungary's criminal justice system than about any other central-eastern European country's criminal justice system. The reform and research of criminal justice in Hungary have included a number of aspects, ranging from the study and analysis of the crime rate and its structure to policing and reform of criminal law and penal policy. The analysis of the Hungarian criminal justice system in the so-called transition period is therefore likely to provide insights into those aspects and problems of criminality that are equally present and relevant in other countries of the region, but may not be so elaborately conceptualised because of the early phase of the reforms in these countries. In other words, perhaps the study of Hungary can highlight any important common needs and directions for further development that Hungary essentially shares with the rest of the region.

Criminality and socio-political changes after 1989

It was mentioned before (in the context of both Yugoslavia and the Czech Republic) that the collapse of the strong communist control-based state had brought a certain general perception of a crisis of security, including a fairly dramatic increase in crime rates. This perception is often at odds with the official statistics, which sometimes suggest a far less dramatic deterioration of the security situation. This has sometimes been explained by reference to the inefficiency of the detection system and the so-called 'dark figure' of crime (all those crimes that might have gone unreported, undetected, etc.). It has been suggested that the dark figure accounts for the sometimes very considerable discrepancy between the official statistics and the public perceptions of a security crisis.

Another popular line of argument goes one step further and argues that, although the internal security situation has evidently deteriorated after the liberalisation, this deterioration is not in any direct way a result of the new liberal ideology and the new economic and political systems adopted in many post-communist countries. Rather, it is argued that the deterioration of the security situation was caused by the disappearance of the 'artificial', oppressive control machinery of communist times. It is further argued that the very low crime rates and the corresponding very high degree of security under communist régimes were somehow artificial and unsustainable, and the increase in crime rates along with societal liberalisation was therefore natural. This suggests that such an increase has little to do with any political or social causes of criminality, but rather with the smaller quantity of institutional repression.

On the one hand, this explanation seems fairly appealing and simple. On the other hand, this rhetoric is reminiscent of the communist rhetoric, according to which capitalism was destined to collapse and rotten from the inside, so that the question of realisation of an international proletarian state was understood as only a matter of time. Neither explanation really has any equivalent in the social realities of either the post-communist or the more western part of the world. Some authors have pointed out that any correlation between liberalising political changes and a crisis of security is highly uncertain, and that the evidence that is quoted to support it is highly doubtful.[1]

There are differences between central-eastern European countries in this respect which could make the discussion of this issue more complex than it seems at first. It may simply not be true that the developments in crime rates are the same in all countries of the region, and their correlation with the socio-political changes may differ from one country to another. This particularly applies to differences between Yugoslavia and the other countries of the region. The increase in crime rates in Yugoslavia was undoubtedly very dramatic, but it might have been more a result of the outbreak of civil wars and a number of political circumstances arising from international isolation and introduction of trade sanctions than of any collapse of the communist state, which was based on the ideology of control. On the one hand, any change in political régime is closely linked with changes in the structure of state organisation, especially if the disintegration of the state is caused by a civil war. On the other hand, the internal security consequences of institutional collapse have a material and strategic dimension which is primarily the result of military conflicts and social disintegration, but which is not necessarily conceptually, and even practically, connected with the underlying ideological change itself. This distinction should be kept in mind, because many states have passed through changes in political systems, even institutional disintegration, without a civil war and those aspects of a security crisis that are connected with the social consequences of civil war.

In the Czech Republic, at the same time, much of the increase in crime might have been caused by increased business and other financial opportunities, increase in the social and occupational mobility of people, ownership of resources that no longer have to be accounted for to the same extent as under the previous régime, and a number of other factors that have changed, and once made crime more difficult under communist rule. Undoubtedly greater liberty provides greater opportunities to commit crime, and in this sense there certainly has been an increase in opportunities to engage in crime in the Czech Republic. In itself, however, this may not necessarily be the key factor that contributed to actual increases in crime rates, but that is a different matter. It was mentioned before that there may be certain motivational factors for actually engaging in crime which, in accordance with the theory of relative deprivation, may be more directly politically responsible for the worsening of the transitional security situations in eastern Europe than the mere increase in criminal opportunities arising from societal liberalisation. This illustrates the relevant difference between Yugoslavia and other countries of the region: the causes of criminality in Yugoslavia are less directly a result of the ideological change itself than they are in other countries, including Hungary.

Although the rise in the official criminal statistics is relatively moderate in Yugoslavia and the Czech Republic, and the discussion of a security crisis is therefore largely centred on speculations about the dark figure, in Hungary the statistics reflect a true crisis of security. However, some commentators have expressed the view that in Hungary the dark figure was high during communism, and has subsequently merely translated into official statistics, because of the more efficient criminal justice system. It was thus argued that the statistics for some types of crime, especially white-collar crime, were inaccurate under the previous régime, and the perceived increase in these crimes is merely the result of more accurate statistics.[2]

This is an interesting argument, because it implies that the security situation under communist rule was in fact no better than it is today, and the crisis of security was merely hidden in the official information. It is an argument that cannot be found in other countries of the region, where there is a fairly widespread consensus that societal liberalisation is followed by an increase in the number of crimes. The argument itself is, of course, not uncontroversial, because it does not explain how it was possible for the security situation under communism to be as bad as it is today, while at the same time there was no widespread public perception of such a crisis. It could be argued that, if crime was so prevalent during communism, there would have been an independent perception of it among the populations in the region, and there would be a corresponding distrust of the statistics, which painted a rosy picture of internal security. Conversely, today there is a perception of a security crisis *despite* the statistics which, in many parts of the region, show a satisfactory degree of internal security. Crimes can be hidden in statistics, but the crisis they cause cannot be hidden as easily, nor can the people's reactions and awareness of the real status of criminality in society be entirely ignored in the long term. This may be somewhat of a reason to take the above argument with a certain degree of caution.

As far as the figures contained in the statistics are concerned, increases in crime rates in Hungary have been phenomenal since 1989. The total reported number of crimes, which was on a slight rise in the second half of the 1980s — from 165 816 in 1985 to 185 344 in 1988 — jumps to 225 393 in 1989, and 341 061 in 1990. A more complete picture of the developments in crime rates is given in Figure 1.1.

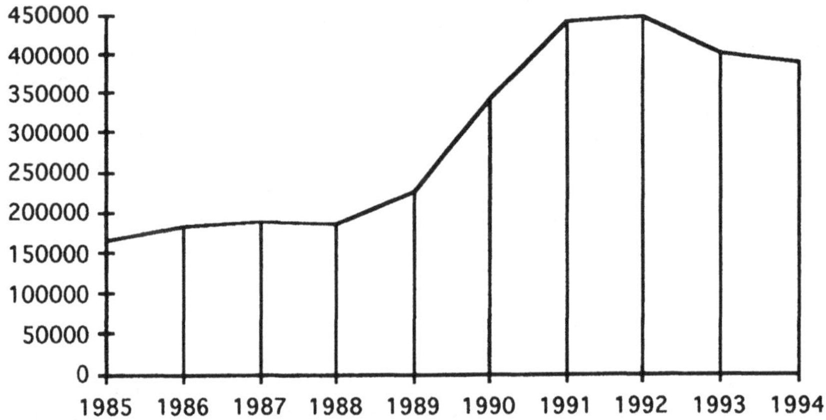

Figure 1.1: Total number of reported crimes per year, 1985–94

As the figure above shows, the most dramatic increase in reported crime occurred in 1990 and 1991, the two years following the political changes. Crime has jumped from 341 061 in 1991 to 447 215 in 1992, with the rate becoming relatively stabilised around the figure of 400 000 in 1993 and 1994. When this stable rate is compared with the average of slightly above 180 000 in the years 1986, 1987, and 1988, the crisis of security, at least in numbers, becomes obvious: the post-communist crime rate is more than twice the communist one.

This discrepancy may be partly explained by the assumption that many types of crime, particularly corporate and large-scale economic crime and fraud committed by party apparatchiks, were not reported, investigated, or recorded in statistics during communist rule. In cases such as corruption or bribery, there is little reason for the assumption that there is significantly greater accuracy in reporting this type of crime today than there was during the communist régime.

There is probably a case for arguing that economic changes have provided many white-collar criminals, both those who were criminals under communism and those who engaged in this type of crime for the first time, with ample opportunity to commit fraud and large-scale theft. The change in régimes meant a degree of disintegration of the institutions and a loosening of the control mechanisms, especially during the transitional period. It therefore might not be accurate to say that the former communist régime concealed economic crimes any more than they are concealed today. However, even if this is granted, communist institutions and the party might have concealed offences such as mass fraud and embezzlement of state resources, and in all of the white-collar crime rate these crimes are very few, although the damage they cause is far greater than that caused by petty crimes. Statistics quoted here are concerned with the number of crimes, which means that their emphasis is on the social dimension of deviance, rather than on the economic aspect of evaluating material damage caused by particular types of crimes. The perception that is contested by some analysts is that the post-communist change has brought with it a dramatic increase in deviance, which is reflected in the number of crimes committed. The greatest proportion of all crimes in most societies, and thus also in Hungary, are petty offences against property — in other words, petty theft, pickpocketing, shop-lifting, and similar offences. These offences were not concealed by the communist régime, simply because there was no ideological or any other convincing reason to conceal them. The number of large-scale economic crimes is small in the overall structure of the crime rate in any society, and any concealment of these crimes would therefore have had little impact on the statistical picture of crime during communism. In other words, if one wants to argue that crime under communism was as prevalent as it is today, one needs a better argument.

For this reason, it is hard to believe that the truly dramatic rise in the official crime rates in Hungary after the socio-political changes of 1989 has been entirely fictitious. This becomes clear when the structure of the Hungarian crime rate is examined more closely. Offences against property comprised 73.7% of all reported crimes in 1994. They are, therefore, the most significant type of crime in the analysis of the overall increase in the crime rate after the 'Revolution'. Violent crime is the smallest part of the crime rate, being at just 4.14% of the overall crime rate in 1994. Offences against public order make up 11.3%, traffic offences 6.81%, and all other offences 4.05% of the total 1994 crime rate.

The rapid increase in the number of offences against property really consists of a sharp rise in petty thefts and other small property-related offences. They are probably connected with economic hardships that have been inflicted on a large proportion of the population by the transition to market economy and the lifting of safeguards of continuing employment. Unlike the past, a large number of employees are no longer able to count on permanent employment. Short-term contracts have become considerably more prevalent in the past few years, sometimes with attached probationary periods that stretch through most of the duration of the contracts.

These industrial and economic changes have in a certain sense had more devastating consequences for Hungarian society than those of crime, and they will be analysed in more detail in the next chapter, where social policy issues and social crisis are discussed. There is little doubt, however, that the impoverishment of large masses of people, which was a direct result of rationalisation of industry, massive layoffs of the workforce as a result of privatisation, and the introduction of market competition, and the concomitant creation of the first phenomenon of 'structural unemployment', have played a major part in the creation of the high rates of property-related crimes.

The increases in crime rates after 1989, particularly the dominant role that property-related crime has in the overall crime rate, can be related to the increase in the amount of societal insecurity, unemployment, and the normative cultural disintegration that often follows social crises. The social transformation of Hungarian society, which started in 1989, and which is ongoing, has largely caused problems of social control. There are more crimes and greater incentives to engage in crime (especially property-related), and thus more resources and more effort are needed to maintain effective crime control.

These observations by no means imply that there is any real crisis of security in Hungarian society today, at least not in any significant sense, despite the widespread perception of a crisis because of the emergence of crimes that were once unfamiliar and an increase in the overall crime rate. The security situation has worsened, but compared with the wider European situation this does not amount to a security crisis. This especially needs to be taken into account in the context of the reform of the criminal justice system, and in particular in the discussion of penal provisions envisaged by the criminal law. Petty crimes cannot be fought with harsh penalties — perhaps the only way to prevent these crimes is by more effective policing. Their heavy penalisation causes very serious moral and cultural dilemmas, because of the very small danger they present.

The transformation of criminal justice in Hungary, as elsewhere, inevitably involves the issue of penalties. Concerns arising from fear of crime and political pressures for harsh penalties are often based on the assumption that higher crime rates imply substantially more violent, dangerous crime, which is traditionally confronted by stiffer penal legislation. Yet the analysis above clearly shows that violent crime in Hungary remains only a very small part of the overall crime rate, and it has not dramatically increased since the shift to social and political reforms in 1989. There is therefore no security crisis in this sense, and no need for Draconian penalties. The emphasis of the reform ought to be on policing minor deviance, which is related to the new economic circumstances, and which is therefore probably there to stay. The Hungarian law-makers have largely well understood this aspect of post-communist developments, and later in the text some of their most important strategies are examined.

It was mentioned that white-collar crime constitutes a comparatively small proportion of all crimes, but the relative damage it causes is often far greater than that of the more numerous, small property-related offences. In the economic sense, white-collar crime, or economic crime as it will be referred to here, is a very important problem for Hungarian transitional society.

Economic crime

The most prevalent types of economic crime in Hungary today are credit fraud, embezzlement, insurance fraud, offences related to currency exchange and customs regulations, fraudulent tax and VAT claims and declarations, fraudulent accounting, abuse of state subsidies, and breaches of environmental regulations.[3]

Some of the more numerous white-collar crimes involve various types of oil fraud, such as using heating oil (which is heavily subsidised) in cars instead of diesel, with the help of discolouring chemicals. The difference in VAT rates for diesel fuel and for oil for heating is 19% (25% as opposed to 6%), which makes it easy to see what amount of tax would have been evaded by this type of fraud. The level of credit fraud has also increased in the past few years. This development is indicated by Figure 1.2.

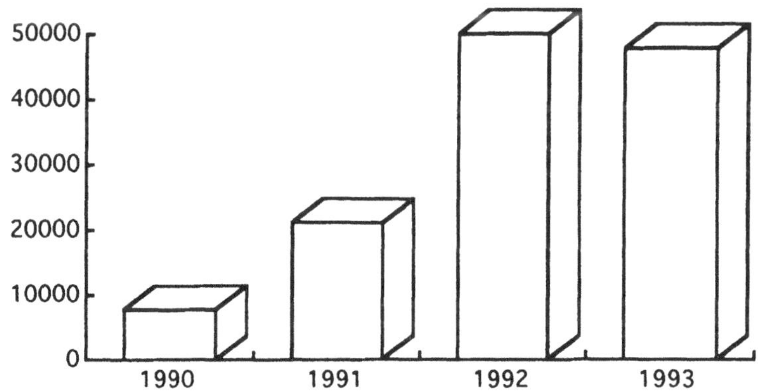

Figure 1.2: Recent developments in the credit fraud rate in Hungary

Credit fraud is usually based on the failure of banks to verify the financial background of a loan seeker, or on the failure of business associates to check the background of their business partners. The latter sometimes meant that fraudulent businesspeople registered their companies to homeless people, whom they payed to act as decoys. Once a substantial amount of goods became available to them, they simply took the goods and disappeared, leaving it to the police to trace the company to the homeless person whose whereabouts may be difficult to ascertain, and who knows nothing about the scheme.

In cases of insurance fraud, one of the major problems encountered by insurance companies and law-enforcement agencies has been the cooperation between employees of large insurers with perpetrators of insurance fraud. Corrupt employees would often accept insurance claims which were invalid, for a percentage of the fraudulently obtained money. The most notorious instances of insurance fraud occurred in connection with the famous 'new value insurance', which was initially designed to encourage more owners of new cars to buy insurance. The scheme essentially provides full reimbursement for the value of a new car during the first five years after its purchase, which made it very easy to dispose of several-year-old cars either by damaging them on purpose, or by arranging for them to be 'stolen', with the intention of obtaining the value of a new car instead. This problem was aggravated by the very high rate of motor vehicle thefts, which meant that it was very easy to arrange car thefts. The scheme was stopped, and today no insurance companies in Hungary offer 'new value insurance'.

Other problems are similar to those in the Czech Republic and all other countries of the region, and concern the presence of capital of unknown origin in the flow of investment. The origin of suspicious money is very difficult to ascertain, and money-laundering is widely suspected to be happening on a very large scale, not only in Hungary, but also elsewhere in central-eastern Europe. Policing white-collar crime has become a major issue in Hungary, related both to the social problems arising from the increase in deviance and to the economic problems, because of the extremely large damage that it causes.

Policing in a post-communist society

To facilitate the enforcement of policies against white-collar crime, the Hungarian Penal Code was modified three times, once in 1993, and twice in 1994. The changes introduced penalties for a number of white-collar crimes that had not been sanctioned under the previous communist régime, including forgery of bank bills, false labelling of merchandise, misuse of revenue, money-laundering. Many of these crimes were virtually non-existent during the fifty years preceding the political changes in the region. The need of central-eastern European countries for the influx of fresh capital has meant that large investors were not asked many questions about the legality of the origin of their resources. In this situation, companies established by investments of illegally obtained resources can automatically become perfectly legal, especially if unquestioned during the initial years of operation. If the company itself is not involved in criminal activities, if its operations are legal, the financial institutions will not question the origin of the initial investment. In central-eastern European countries, in need of economic growth against a background of global recession, there is an understandable reluctance to cause investors difficulty by imposing more stringent procedures for the verification of the origin of their capital. Once dirty capital is brought in and invested, the longer the companies established by it operate, the less feasible it becomes to trace the origin of their resources successfully.

Policing in Hungary has been the subject of much debate since 1989 and 1990, and this was partly because of two major scandals which shook the law-enforcement structure and led to radical reforms of the policing policies and chains of command.

The first scandal was connected with the involvement of the secret service agencies in the illegal surveillance of opposition parties and their leaders before the first multi-party elections in the spring of 1990. This affair, labelled 'Danube-Gate', led to an institutional separation of intelligence agencies from the police structures, and to a stricter regulation banning government ministers from interfering in law-enforcement operational matters. One of the most important restrictions that resulted from Danube-Gate was the abolition of the power of the Minister of the Interior to issue direct orders to the police. These changes occurred shortly before the 1990 election, and the newly elected government subsequently largely took it for granted that all major problems in policing had been solved by these measures.

After the elections, efforts were made to reduce the centralised organisation of the police, to make the police force more democratic, more sensitive to community concerns, and more accepted by the community. In short, community policing became the desired direction for the development of the Hungarian police, which has been traditionally organised for military policing.[4] In this context, appointments of police commanders were made more competitive, and open to applicants from outside the police organisation. The Ministry of the Interior started work on a draft *Code on the Police*, which was intended to conceptualise and sanction the reform of these policy objectives.

However, these changes were brought to an abrupt halt in October 1990, after the government had announced sharp increases in the prices of petrol, which led to major street demonstrations and the blockade of all important border crossings, roads, and intersections, thus paralysing the traffic. The police were reluctant to apply force, and calls from within government ranks for a crack-down against the demonstrators were ignored by the police establishment. The demonstrations were eventually concluded by peaceful negotiations. This was a positive result of the strategy adopted by the police, but it nevertheless led to a perception among the public that the police were unable to maintain law and order. The government subsequently halted the reform towards community policing. More right-wing views on policing eventually prevailed, and the draft *Code on the Police* was temporarily withdrawn from consideration to be revised. Finally, in 1994, the Parliament passed a new *Act on the Police*, which was substantially different from the spirit of the reforms envisaged by the draft *Code on the Police*.

The *Act on the Police* was based on the principle that 'civil liberty', guaranteed by the law, extended only to those who obey the law.[5] The concept of liberty here was unclear in scope. One possibility was that it stood for the specific 'civil' or political liberties, such as the right to hold public office, to vote, and to exercise other civil and political rights. Alternatively, it could stand for basic human rights, which appeared more likely given the context in which the concept of legal guarantees of liberties was depicted. If the latter possibility had been intended by this term, then this formulation of legal guarantees of liberty would have been in conflict with the basic constitutional guarantees of respect for human rights and liberties on a universal basis. These guarantees extend to every person, and normally imply that no one's human rights may be infringed, whether that person has committed a crime or not. The *Act on the Police* referred to citizens' rights in relation to the police, which suggested that what was really intended were human rights. Constitutional guarantees imply that human rights are guaranteed to everyone, both to law-abiding citizens and to those who are accused of crimes. According to the Constitution, even if someone is convicted of a most serious crime, that person must not be mistreated, coerced to engage or refrain from engaging in certain actions beyond the domain guaranteed by the law, nor may one's other human rights, including the right to the respect of personal and individual dignity, be infringed. The *Act on the Police*, on the other hand, did stipulate that constitutional safeguards were to be observed, but the very principle of respect of the civil rights of only those citizens who abide by the law suggested a certain right turn, towards greater police powers, and might suggest, depending on the interpretation of the scope of the civil rights referred to in the act, that the *human* rights of those who were accused or convicted of crimes did not 'apply' to the same extent as the human rights of other citizens. From a principled point of view, this would have been a problematic assumption, because in a democratic society one cannot leave it to the police to decide who has broken the law and who has not, given that such decision-making is normally in the exclusive jurisdiction of the courts, and that every citizen has the right to be presumed innocent until proven guilty. The problem consisted in the fact that the *Act on the Police* clearly and directly suggested that the suspicion that someone might have committed a crime, during police investigation, and before guilt could be established in the court, might guarantee the police the right to infringe on the suspect's civil (or possibly human) rights. This principle would not be considered acceptable in any consistent democratic system.

The *Act on the Police* did not stop at this point. Some of the rights it gave to the police extended into the domain of penal measures, although under the Hungarian Constitution the passing of penalties and other criminal sanctions was in the exclusive jurisdiction of the courts. A potential conflict between the act and the Constitution was hidden here, although certain conceptual distinctions on a technical level might serve as a justification for the use of penal measures by the police, without a court's consent.

Hungarian law also distinguished between crimes and administrative infractions, which in the conceptual sense were not the same as infractions in Yugoslav or Czech criminal legislation. Unlike Yugoslav legislation, where infractions are the subject of a separate *Law on infractions*, in Hungarian legislation the *Criminal law*, up until 1978, allowed the discretionary qualification of certain minor offences by the police as either infractions or crimes. The category of administrative infractions was a borderline category, which usually included the so-called petty crimes such as shop-lifting or pickpocketing. In these borderline cases the police formally had the right to impose penalties without beginning criminal prosecution, meaning without a conviction in court. This clearly directly threatened the right of the accused to a presumption of innocence, which is a right guaranteed by the Constitution.

Contrary to the hopes that had been initially connected with the draft *Code on the Police*, the final *Act on the Police* did not in the least water down the centralised structure of the police organisation. This organisation is still structured along military lines today. All command activities are centralised in the National Police Headquarters in Budapest, in the hands of the National Police Commissioner, who is appointed by the Prime Minister. The Commissioner delegates some of his competences to the two Directors General, one of whom is responsible for criminal investigation, and the other for public order and security policing. There are about 30 000 police officers in Hungary today, along with an additional 10 000 civilian employees working in the police organisation. The force is facing serious personnel problems, because of low salaries, so that about 300 police officers leave the force every month. The government's attempt to fill 3000 vacancies on the force in the early 1990s was not entirely successful.[6] Decision-making about law-enforcement policies is marked by a high degree of discretion and most operational and strategic decisions are made entirely within the police structures, with no or very little consultation with the public, or even with the government.

Although these most recent trends have meant that initiatives for community policing were largely abandoned, some operational advantages of the centralised approach have been reflected in the performance statistics of the police force. A survey of clearance rates for crimes shows that the attempts to diversify the police structure, combined with the socio-political changes, initially led to the lowest clearance rates in the past decade in 1990 and 1991. From 1992 onwards clearance rates have improved, and in the mid-1990s they reached roughly the same level as in the late 1980s, before the post-communist revolution. Public responses to law-enforcement strategies have shifted accordingly, from a sharp drop in public confidence in the police in 1990 (29% confidence rate), to some improvement in 1992 (39% confidence rate).[7]

Informal crime control

Social mechanisms for crime control which go beyond government agencies and police structures have been known for decades in Hungary. During communist rule, the so-called 'Volunteer Police Units', drawn from the community at large, supplemented the activity of the police. They were equivalent to what is known in western countries as 'citizen guards' and similar organisations. After the 1989 'Revolution', Volunteer Police Units were disbanded because they had become severely politically compromised, and had been acting in the service of the régime against its opponents. The gap created by their disbanding was filled by another volunteer citizens' organisation — the 'Civil Guards'. Today this organisation has a cooperative and positive relationship with the police, and is generally considered to be contributing substantially to public security in Hungary. Some accusations have, however, been brought against Civil Guards for vigilantism and violence against national minorities, excessive use of force, etc.[8]

The issue of crime prevention in addition to policing became a prominent part of the public agenda after the enactment of the Criminal Code, Parliament Act no. 4, 1978. The code sparked initiatives that eventually led to the establishment of an informal crime-prevention network, which consisted of the 'Crime prevention Councils' in Budapest and in several country districts or counties. These councils were responsible for the local coordination of the government's crime-control policies, mainly emanating from the Ministry of the Interior and the police. Yet the fate of the Crime prevention Councils was no better than that of Volunteer Police Units or Civil Guards: the councils were acting in the service of the communist élite, they were extremely formal in their organisation, and they did not mobilise wide public support. The councils thus never went beyond the state of being a mere experiment in social control.

After the changes that occurred in 1989 and the early 1990s, enthusiasm for informal crime-control mechanisms largely disappeared, and crime prevention was entrusted solely to the police, in accordance with the spirit of highly formalised and militarised law enforcement in Hungary. The need for a specific crime-prevention service, to some extent separate from law enforcement in the strict sense, was there, however, as fear of crime grew in the population, especially in larger cities, where increases in crime rates were most rapid. The legal regulation dealing with the incorporation of crime-prevention services into the police organisation was developed in 1994, in the *Act on the Police*, although the formation of specialised crime prevention units had already started in 1989 and 1990.[9]

In light of the already mentioned high crime rates in Hungary, crime-prevention strategies have not proven to be very effective. As a result of the perception of a security crisis and the apparent failure of the formal organisations to halt the rise in crime, numerous organisations for citizens' self-protection have sprung up. Today there are around 600 such organisations, with around 40 000 members, and only about 200 are legally registered and operate legally. Initiatives originating from individual, informal crime-prevention organisations are considered within the 'National Civic Guard Association', which has a cooperative agreement with the Crime-Prevention Department within the National Police Headquarters. There is a designated police officer at the National Headquarters whose primary task is liaison with the informal crime-prevention organisations. The police also provide support and assistance to the neighbourhood watch program, which in Hungary is called 'Neighbours for Each Other Movement'.[10] This program, as well as other informal crime-prevention initiatives, can be understood in much the same way as the equivalent measures and organisations in western countries. Unfortunately, their success is no greater than the success of equivalent organisations in the West. The economic hardships inflicted by the introduction of a free-market economy, as well as the political liberalisation and the so-called transition, have been accompanied by higher levels of criminality. It seems that these crime rates cannot be substantially reduced by measures that have been applied within the social and institutional arrangements of other societies which are also affected by high crime rates. Crime control obviously remains an open issue for Hungary, and for the other countries of the region. What it reveals is that, if the dramatic worsening of the security situation that has occurred since 1989 is to be connected with the socio-political changes that began at the same time and are still going on, then there may not be much reason for optimism, and any expectation of a return to the pre-'Revolution' low crime rates may be unrealistic.

Questions of legal reform: Constitutionality and the judiciary

Constitutional determinations

The first and most important step towards a fairly comprehensive legal reform in Hungary was taken immediately after the post-communist changes, in 1989, with amendments to the country's Constitution. A number of the provisions relating to civil rights and liberties were introduced, and the ones characteristic of the former system, allowing for intrusive controls and those defining the former socialist system of governance, were eliminated.

Generally speaking, the provisions of the Constitution were adjusted to facilitate legal reform along fairly liberal guidelines, which at the end of the 1980s in Hungary also implied a fairly strong anti-communist tone. This change to the Constitution was guided by the need to liberalise the markets and increase the role of private incentives and private capital.

Of particular interest for this book are the provisions that reflect the structure of the Hungarian criminal justice system. This system is partially defined by the Constitution, and in far greater detail by the Hungarian criminal law (or Penal Code), which will be discussed shortly, and which has also passed through important changes. The constitutional provisions deal mainly with the judiciary and prosecution, thus they outline the structure of this part of the criminal justice system.

The highest court in Hungary is the Supreme Court. Apart from the Supreme Court, the Hungarian judicial system comprises the Court of the Capital City, county courts, and local courts. The Constitution also allows for the establishment of special courts for certain (but unspecified) groups of cases. These special courts are established by special laws. The main legal principle is that judicial decisions can be taken only by professional judges 'and lay assessors' (this probably refers to jurors). However, the Constitution also allows that special laws may be used to provide for exceptions to this rule.

The Supreme Court sets principles and directions for the work of all courts in Hungary; its decisions and recommendations have binding power over all other courts in Hungary.

The President of the Supreme Court is nominated by the country's President, and the appointment is approved by Parliament with at least two-thirds of the votes. The President of the Supreme Court nominates the Vice Presidents, who are formally appointed by the country's President. The President of Hungary is also responsible for the appointment of professional judges. The adoption of any law on the judiciary in Parliament requires two-thirds of the MPs' votes. These requirements were designed to ensure the stability of the structure of the judiciary and its independence of the government in times of political change, which can be accompanied by social instability.

The Constitution also defines a very broad and powerful role for the state prosecution. The prosecution is entrusted with the supervision of police investigations, especially with overseeing the operations performed by plain clothes police officers. It also performs the usual functions of prosecution in the court. What is particularly important, and dangerous, in the competences of the prosecution is that it has the right and duty to 'exercise supervision over the observance of legality in the administration of penalties'.[11] This, in effect, means that the prosecution has the right to oversee the operation of prisons, and to implement changes in penal policies and procedures. Such checks on the operation of the penal system are traditionally seen as being exclusively in the jurisdiction of courts and the Ministries of Justice in most countries. The problem here is that the strategic position of the prosecution is directly opposed to the position of the accused offenders, and thus does not have the necessary degree of impartiality and neutrality for it to be entrusted with the ultimate authority over the implementation of penal measures. This problem is probably less pronounced where the administration of penalties is within the competences of the Ministry of Justice. If the prosecution accuses the offenders, pursues their cases in court, and ultimately penalises them, then there is not enough separation of powers within the criminal justice processes to ensure the fair treatment of convicted offenders within the penal system.

The Chief Prosecutor and Deputy Chief Prosecutors are appointed in the same way as the President and Deputy Presidents of the Supreme Court — the President of the Republic nominates the Chief Prosecutor, who is then appointed by Parliament. The Chief Prosecutor then nominates the Deputy Chief Prosecutors, who are formally appointed by the President of Hungary. The Chief Prosecutor appoints all other prosecutors, and is directly responsible and obliged to report to Parliament. Professional judges or prosecutors are not allowed by law to hold any political affiliations, because of the need to protect the integrity and political neutrality of the judiciary and the criminal justice system.

Most of the constitutional provisions relating to the judiciary and the prosecution are intended to maximise the accountability of these extremely sensitive parts of the criminal justice system, to minimise the possibility of abuse of office or negligent performance of duty. However, there are also several worrying provisions in this area.

Apart from excessive authorisations being granted to the prosecution, including the authority to oversee the administration of penalties and prisons, some concern also arises relating to the provision which facilitates the setting up of 'special courts' for 'special' groups of cases. It is questionable under what circumstances it is possible to exercise full control over the application of such exceptional legislative measures. In unstable socio-political circumstances, it is entirely conceivable that these constitutional provisions could be used for oppression against citizens' rights and liberties, in the service of a particular political ideology, greater institutional repression, and for the relativisation of standards of legitimate judicial procedure and respect for the law.

This last possibility is aggravated by the constitutional provision allowing that under 'certain', and yet unspecified, conditions, lay persons may make judicial decisions. This can to some extent be explained by the need for a democratic conduct of judicial decision-making with a jury whose members do not have to be lawyers. However, the Hungarian Constitution goes further than that, and allows for the introduction of 'special' legislation, leading to the establishment of courts with lay *judges*. This is a controversial point in the Constitution which could lead to abuses of the legal system in times of political and social trouble. The relevant constitutional provisions relating to the judiciary would need to be further revised if they are to present a stable and solid basis for further comprehensive legal reform.

The communist 1978 Criminal Code, before revisions

The enactment of the 1978 Hungarian 'Criminal Code' (to be referred to as 'criminal law' henceforth) which is still in force, with subsequent amendments, was met with a great deal of enthusiasm. This criminal law came one century after the country's first criminal law, and it contained some extremely important legal improvements concerning the definition of a crime and criminal responsibility, as well as provisions regulating the operation and governance of the criminal justice system.

The 1978 law included a new definition of the criminal act, which incorporated the principle of *nullum crimen-nulla poena* (there can be no penalty for actions that are not qualifiable as criminal). This definition is today standard in most modern criminal laws world-wide, but it was introduced into the Hungarian legislation only in 1978. Its exact formulation is: 'A criminal act is an action committed intentionally, or by negligence, if the law also criminalises negligent perpetration, which is dangerous for the public, and for which a penalty is prescribed by law'.[12] However trivial this definition might sound today, it envisages an important direction for the development of the conceptualisation of social control through the criminal justice system. This conceptualisation relies on the principle that no act can be qualified as criminal within the criminal justice system, by institutions of that system alone, unless it is independently and in advance qualified as criminal by the criminal law. It was mentioned before that for a long time the Hungarian criminal justice system contained provisions about the so-called 'administrative infractions' or minor faults, where the police had substantial powers of discretion in deciding how to treat the perpetrators. Many offences were in the overlapping area, potentially qualifiable both as crimes and as administrative infractions, such as petty theft. The police therefore had the authority to decide whether or not such actions will be prosecuted in court, or sanctioned by administrative sanctions. Administrative infractions still exist today, but they are defined more narrowly, and it is clearer which acts must be prosecuted as crimes, and which ones are minor faults. The 1978 law made it clear that crimes can be specified only by the criminal law, and that discrimination between those offences that are crimes and those that are not cannot be within the obviously discretionary authorisations of the police. This was obviously a progressive step, which made arbitrary prosecution and penalisation both less likely and more clearly definable.

However, as Jószef Földvári pointed out in his commentary on the 1978 Code, for the principle of *nullum crimen - nulla poena* to be truly upheld, it may not be sufficient to curb the discretionary rights of the police in deciding the nature of particular acts and the need for prosecution.[13] What is needed here is to approach the discretionary powers of the Supreme Court with a great deal of caution as well. As mentioned before, the new Hungarian 1989 Constitution (like the previous communist one) determines that the Supreme Court has a policy-making authority over the entire Hungarian judiciary, and that its decisions on matters of principle are binding for all other courts. The justification of this measure clearly lies in the need to provide a uniform and fair interpretation of the law in the entire territory of Hungary. However, the danger here is that the Supreme Court may rule on the interpretation of legal definitions of crimes and faults in problematic or controversial ways. In other words, from a procedural point of view, the same dangers that are inherent in police discretion in discriminating between crimes and infractions may also be present in the policy-making and discretionary powers of the Supreme Court. On the one hand, the law makes it clear that even the Supreme Court is not empowered to establish new qualifications of what a crime is. On the other hand, in practice, this principle may be compromised because the Supreme Court rules on a wide range of judicial policies and interpretations of the law, and these interpretations, if controversial, can set precedents resulting in controversial judicial policies on many issues, including the treatment of particular actions as prosecutable or non-prosecutable.

To be fair, one must note here that this problem is largely academic and strictly procedural. The Supreme Court, as any other court, operates on the assumption of integrity. Its judges are accountable to Parliament. The point of Földvári's remark here is not to criticise any part of the criminal justice system, but simply to emphasise the ramifications of giving substantial discretionary powers to any part of that system, and the need to be very precise and exhaustive in the formulation and application of legal definitions.

Another relevant feature of the above definition of a criminal act, apart from the principle of *nullum crimen - nulla poena*, is that, for an act to be considered criminal, it must be dangerous to society. The 1978 law determines that only those actions which represent a substantial threat to society are prosecutable, which reveals the theoretical and principled assumption of the legislation that criminal prosecution is understood only as the *ultima ratio* strategy of social control.[14]

Assessments of the threats to society that are present in particular actions are envisaged in solely objective terms in the law, that is in terms of the description of crimes and their inherent danger to society. This type of solely objective characterisation leaves out the entire realm of subjective danger, which is posed by the person (or personality) of the perpetrator. The subjective dimension traditionally captures the relevant concept of guilt in the narrowest sense, which is strangely absent from the entirely objective characterisation of 'danger to society'. According to Földvári, the rationale for leaving subjective considerations aside in characterising the criminal offence as a legal concept is that the assumption that the subjective danger to society will be taken into account in the sentencing process, where the decision on the penalty always partly depends on the personality of the perpetrator and the danger one subjectively poses to society; even the letter of the law does not provide for this explicitly.[15]

Most of the important penal provisions and criminal characterisations in the Hungarian 1978 criminal law are the same as, or very similar to, those of the Czech Republic and Yugoslavia. It is therefore unnecessary to devote special attention and interpretation to them again here. The forthcoming discussion will thus focus on some of the most characteristic and ideologically important aspects of the 1978 Hungarian criminal law, the relevant differences between it and the legislation of Yugoslavia and the Czech Republic, as well as the changes to the 1978 Hungarian law which were introduced by parliamentary acts after 1989, in the period which is of particular ideological significance, and which is the primary theme of this book.

The first striking element is the first section of the 1978 criminal law, describing the purpose and meaning of the law. According to this provision, the purpose of the law is 'to provide protection against actions dangerous to society, to educate people to abide by the rules of socialist coexistence and to respect the law'. The preventionist, strictly utilitarian purpose of the criminal legislation is more apparent here than in either the Czech or Yugoslav criminal laws. Interestingly, the notion of fulfilment of justice is not even mentioned as one of the aims of the legislation, nor does the notion of individual responsibility play any significant role in this formulation and in the conceptual context it generates. Contrary to these traditionally 'deontic', moralising categories, the Hungarian legislation presents criminal culpability not as made up of any ontological or moral guilt and transgression of a moral principle, but primarily as consisting of the very danger which arises from the commission of the criminal action. This is the case to such an extent that even the conditions for granting excuses from culpability are described in terms of the perpetrator's awareness or lack of awareness of the action's danger to society. Thus section 27, paragraph 2 determines that 'A perpetrator who commits a criminal act due to the erroneous assumption that it is not dangerous to society, if one has had weighty reasons to believe it not to be dangerous, is not liable to a criminal penalty'. This implies a full excuse from culpability for an action committed under the assumption that it is not dangerous, if that assumption was reasonable. A clear utilitarian tone is discernible here, much more open than that in the relevant formulations of the Yugoslav or Czech criminal legislation.

Other provisions of culpability in the Hungarian legislation are largely the same as those in the Czech law, and to some extent in the Yugoslav laws. For example, the retrospective application of a law that has been enacted after the commission of the offence is limited to cases where the later law is more lenient to the offender than the law which was effective at the time of the commission of the offence. The same is the case in both the Czech law and the Yugoslav laws. The minimum age for criminal prosecution in Hungary is fifteen years, which is the same as in the Czech Republic, but stricter than in Yugoslavia, where the minimum age is sixteen. The death penalty does not exist in Hungarian criminal legislation today, but it did exist in the first version of the 1978 criminal law. According to that law, the death penalty could be implemented only against a person who was at least eighteen years of age (or who has 'completed one's 18th year of age'), which is the same as it is in Montenegro today (beginning of 1997), and stricter than in Serbian criminal law, according to which the minimum age for the death penalty is twenty-one years. [16]

The Hungarian 1978 law distinguishes between penalties and measures, as well as between principal and supplementary penalties. Until the last changes to the law, since 1989, the principal penalties included:

1. the death penalty,
2. imprisonment (or 'deprivation of liberty'),
3. forced 'reformatory and educative labour' and
4. monetary fines.

The supplementary penalties were:

1. interdiction from public affairs,
2. interdiction from practising a profession or engaging in an occupation,
3. interdiction from driving a motor vehicle,
4. local banishment within the country (this penalty also exists in the Czech criminal law),
5. expulsion from the country,

6. confiscation of property, and
7. fine as a supplementary penalty.[17]

The 1978 law allowed both the death penalty as the principal penalty and confiscation of property as a supplementary penalty. This was to some extent characteristic of communist social control systems, where penalisation of political opponents was often pursued to the very maximum, and sometimes included deprivation of both life and property.

Similar to Czech criminal law even today, the duration of imprisonment according to the Hungarian 1978 law was 'generally' limited in a fairly liberal way to fifteen years, but the law also allowed life imprisonment in some cases. The provisions relating to the implementation of prison penalties were elaborated far more extensively in the 1978 Hungarian criminal law than they are even today in Czech criminal legislation. The 1978 law made a distinction between three different levels or grades of remand institutions, and thus also of prison penalties served in these institutions. The strictest prisons in Hungary are called 'convict prisons', or 'penitentiaries'. All life sentences, prison sentences passed instead of the death penalty, as a result of presidential pardons, and any prison sentences of three years and more passed for crimes against the state or against humanity, terrorism, hijacking of aircraft, homicide, rape, indecent assault, causing danger to the public, and 'robbery of major gravity' (this usually implies armed robberies with violence), are served in convict prisons. The same applies to military crimes that can be alternatively penalised by the death penalty, and for all prison penalties of two years and more where the perpetrator is a 'habitual offender'.

The prison sentences for all crimes not included in the above categories are served in the 'common prisons'. These are medium grade prisons. Sentences for misdemeanours are also served in common prisons if the offender is a recidivist.

The third, and lowest grade in severity of custodial institutions are the 'houses of detention', where first-time offenders convicted of misdemeanours serve their sentences.[18] The word 'detention' here signifies the actual serving of a prison sentence, and not just remand in the expectation of a trial or sentencing, which is perhaps the more standard meaning of this term.

It was mentioned before that according to the 1978 law the notion of objective danger to society is the sole ground for deciding whether or not an act is to be considered a crime and how it will be prosecuted, that is whether or not criminal prosecution or prosecution for a misdemeanour will proceed. It was also mentioned that the subjective danger, that is the danger to society arising from the personality of the offender, is taken into account in the judicial process, in the sentencing component. It is relevant to note that the subjective danger is also explicitly taken into account when deciding on *what category of prison* to commit the offender to. In other words, depending on considerations of the offender's character and motive for committing the offence, the offender may be committed to a lower, or higher, grade of prison. Similar considerations apply to the offender's behaviour while serving the sentence: good behaviour may be accepted by the court as grounds for the offender's transfer to a lower grade facility, and *vice versa*, bad behaviour might lead to transfer to a higher grade prison.

The 1978 law was particularly strict in the part where it regulated conditions for parole. In deciding on parole, the courts took into account the grade of prison to which the offender was committed.

Parole for sentences that were served in convict prisons could be granted only after at least *80%* of the sentence had been served; for sentences served in common prisons, after at least *75%* of the sentence had been served; and for sentences served in houses of detention, after *two-thirds* of the sentence had been served. For reasons of comparison, current Czech criminal law determines that prisoners are eligible for parole after serving two-thirds of their prison sentences in all cases where eligibility for parole applies at all. The Yugoslav legislation (before the expected enactment of the new federal criminal law) provides that parole can become available after serving two-thirds of the sentence, and in exceptional circumstances after serving one-half of the sentence. In addition, the 1978 Code did not allow parole for habitual offenders and those offenders who had not served at least three months of imprisonment, regardless of the above criteria of proportionality. Some other classes of prisoners are also excluded from the possibility of being granted parole. (Prisoners serving life sentences in Hungary today can be placed on parole only after they have served at least twenty years, which is the same provision as in the Czech criminal law. It does not have an equivalent in the Yugoslav criminal legislation, because that legislation, at least before the expected introduction of the new federal criminal law, does not as yet contain the possibility of a life sentence being passed, given the availability of the death penalty under the republican criminal laws of both Serbia and Montenegro.)

In the Hungarian 1978 criminal law, the penalty of forced labour, or 'reformatory and educative labour' was described in a particularly interesting way. This penalty involved committing a person to performing certain tasks, sometimes under close supervision, in a particular workplace, *for a wage*. The punitive component of this penalty was represented by two elements: first, the obligatory nature of the work, which is determined by the court (not free employment), and second, the fact that the state retained 5% to 10% of the wage. This penalty probably had the same intent as the relatively popular community service order in some other countries, the difference being that community service normally does not include a wage, whereas the 1978 Hungarian law provides a wage for this type of 'forced labour'.

Other penalties provided for in the 1978 law that are strikingly similar to those in the current Czech criminal legislation are local banishment and confiscation of property — neither of which exists in Yugoslav criminal legislation.[19]

Apart from penalties, the 1978 law also provides for 'measures', which include:

1. court admonition,
2. respite,
3. compulsory medical treatment,
4. compulsory detoxification of alcohol addicts,
5. confiscation (also used as a penalty),
6. 'custody of varying severity', and
7. supervision while on parole or probation.

Most of these measures are self-explanatory and familiar from the preceding discussions of Yugoslav and Czech criminal legislation. According to the 1978 law, they can be applied independently, as self-sufficient measures, in which case they served as sanctions for misdemeanours, or combined with penalties, in which case they served as sanctions for crimes and repeated misdemeanours.

A 'Special part' of the 1978 law dealt with 'offences against the state', including 'conspiracy', 'sedition' (participation in, or support of, an anti-state riot), 'sabotage', 'destruction of property', 'murderous attempt', 'treason', 'treachery', 'supporting the enemy', 'espionage', 'subversive activity', and 'misprision' (failing to reveal information about the preparation of any of the preceding crimes against the state).[20] Some of these criminal characterisations are peculiar to communist states, others are present in the criminal laws of many countries. Particularly noteworthy was the provision in the 1978 law according to which any of the above-mentioned offences, if committed against another socialist state, was equally culpable in Hungary as if it had been committed against the Hungarian state. This element was not always present, even in the criminal laws of other communist countries.

The 1978 Code also criminalised abortion, and threatened imprisonment for up to three years for it. This sentence would normally be served in a convict prison, or penitentiary, which suggested that abortion was considered a serious crime.

In many aspects the 1978 criminal law presented a strong case for the view that ideological determinations were of crucial importance in any system of social control. The importance of ideology for social control becomes particularly obvious when Hungarian communism, which was very internationalist and faithful to the letter of the Stalinist version of Marxism, is seen as the ideological background of the 1978 law. The strong, intrusive state, the notion of a community of socialist countries battling their way through the corruption and decay of the capitalist world, and many other communist theoretical and strategic assumptions, are clearly discernible in the particular provisions of the 1978 law. However, since 1978 numerous changes to the criminal law have been implemented, and, although there has been no new law (the 1978 law is still formally in force), the present shape and spirit of the Hungarian criminal legislation are considerably different from what they were in 1978. This does not mean that further changes and, preferably, a new criminal law, would not be desirable from the point of view of the need for a further liberalisation of the criminal justice system.

The post-1989 parliamentary amendments to the 1978 criminal law

Most of the amendments to the 1978 criminal law have led to more lenient and benevolent provisions for offenders, and since 1989 most of the changes have directly targeted the most obvious ideological assumptions of the original communist version of the 1978 criminal law. Several of those are directly relevant to this discussion.

In 1992, by Parliament Act no. 11, a number of sentences passed for crimes committed between 1963 and 1989 were pronounced void. Not surprisingly, these were mostly crimes committed against the state and the political régime.

They included: 'conspiracy', 'incitation', 'revolt', 'crimes against another socialist state', 'insult of authority or official personage', 'insult to the community', 'incitation against the law or an authority's order', 'misuse of the freedom of association', 'unauthorised crossing of the frontier', 'refusal to return [to the country]', 'crimes against the freedom of the peoples', 'misdemeanour against the press law', 'propagation of disquieting rumours', 'failure to denounce, if the obligation to denounce relates to the offences against the state', and 'abetment'. *All* sentences for these offences which had been passed between April 5, 1963 and October 15, 1989 were pronounced void on the grounds that they had been contrary to the Hungarian Constitution at the time when the judgments had been made, that they had breached human rights and citizens' liberties, and that, although the law could not fully rectify these wrongs, 'victims of the communist régime' had to be given some satisfaction for their suffering.

The mentioned pardon also included any other crimes that had been committed alongside the above-mentioned 'crimes against the state', for which (i) cumulative sentences had been passed both for those crimes and for the connected crimes against the state, *or* (ii) these related crimes had been committed in close connection with crimes against the state for which penalties had been passed, *and* (iii) the penalties prescribed by the law for these related crimes did not exceed in severity the penalties for the connected, relevant crimes against the state to which the pardon refers directly. In other words, the pardon of crimes related to, or committed alongside, the crimes against the state excluded those crimes which were so grave that they normally led to a more severe penalty than the relevant crime (or crimes) against the state. It could be assumed, however, that the number of such extremely serious related crimes would have been very small, if not negligible, for the simple reason that, given the nature of the previous régime, crimes against the state generally carried the most severe penalties.

In all cases where aggregate penalties had been passed for a combination of crimes against the state and other crimes, and the relevant other crimes did not qualify for the voiding of penalties under the conditions described above, the aggregate penalty was to be reduced by the amount of penalty which, according to the court's analysis, had been passed for the crimes against the state which had been part of the relevant charges at the time of sentencing. All cases that had been tried under charges for the crimes described above, but where the serving of penalties had not begun, were to be re-tried by normal courts.[21]

The Hungarian Parliament gradually adopted a more aggressive approach to dealing with the communist past in it legislative activity. In 1993, it passed an act banning the propagation, public use, and presentation to the public of the so-called 'symbols of despotism'. These included the following: the swastika, SS symbols, the arrow-cross, the *sickle and hammer*, the red pentagram, and any related symbols. These provisions, and especially the one relating to the symbol of the sickle and hammer, which was the symbol of the international labour movement, were very close to the criminalisation of political beliefs represented by the symbols, especially the communist ones. Penalties for these offences were fines, but the criminalisation of the symbols had an extremely clear political meaning. The only two contexts where public use of the above symbols was not to be considered a crime were when the symbols would be presented for educational, teaching, artistic, or information purposes, and when they might be the official symbols of other states.

In the 1990s there was great deal of activity in the Hungarian Parliament, which passed numerous amendments to various legal provisions relating to the criminal law and other relevant documents. These changes cannot all be explored here, because they are largely legal technicalities whose relevance and spirit are reflected in the major changes to the 1978 criminal law which are discussed here.[22]

The removal of sentences for crimes against the state which had been passed between 1963 and 1989 and the criminalisation of propagation and public use of communist (and other mentioned) symbols, reflected the determination of the Hungarian parliamentarians and government to shed any communist connotation and remaining communist content from the criminal law. However, by far the most important and substantial amendments to the criminal law were introduced in *1993* by *Act no. 17 'on the amendment of the rules of the criminal law'* — a 79-page document detailing unprecedented changes to the criminal law. This document epitomises most of the changes to political ideology in Hungary after 1989, and their bearings on the criminal justice system and the judiciary.

The 1993 Parliament Act no. 17 introduced major changes to particular sections and articles of the 1978 law, which directly reflected the new post-communist values. The changes included a full replacement of section 33 of the law, specifying legal limitations to penalties. One of the main, great post-communist changes of the 1978 law was that *the death penalty was abolished*, and therefore in 1993 section 33, which formerly determined that imprisonment was limited to twenty years in cases where alternatively the death penalty could be passed, was replaced by the provision that imprisonment was limited to twenty years in cases where alternatively a *life sentence* could be passed. Life imprisonment was introduced *to replace the death penalty*.

This was of course a technical change, which resulted from the relevant changes to section 38 of the criminal law. Section 38 specified the types of penalties legally available to courts in Hungary.

Initially, section 38 enumerated the principal penalties in the following way:
1. the death penalty,
2. 'deprivation of liberty',
3. 'reformatory and educative forced labour', and
4. fines.

Section 2 of the 1993 Act no. 17 changed the above specification to:
1. imprisonment,
2. work for public benefit, and
3. fines.

It is important to note here that, apart from abolishing the death penalty, Act no. 17, 1993 also changed the formulation of the other two principal penalties. The rhetorical masquerade of imprisonment in the expression 'deprivation of liberty' has been eliminated, and forced labour is no longer described as 'reformatory', 'rehabilitative', or 'educational'. Given the widespread opinion that forced labour does not have any of these reformatory characteristics, it is now described in the law to simply emphasise its benefit to society (work for public benefit).

Before the changes implemented in 1993, section 40 of the 1978 criminal law provided that the shortest period of imprisonment was for three months. This provision was changed in 1993 so that the shortest period of imprisonment can be only one day. The maximum periods of imprisonment remain the same — fifteen years in 'normal' cases, and twenty years in aggregate penalties (for several crimes cumulatively). However, in all central European criminal laws the provisions relating to the maximum length of imprisonment are extremely vague, because 'special' circumstances often allow the passing of life sentences, or generally longer periods of imprisonment than those allowed under normal circumstances. Thus, section 40 of the Hungarian criminal law provides that the maximum length of imprisonment, even under special circumstances, and even for aggregate sentences, is twenty years, while at the same time section 38 of the same law allows the passing of a life sentence. Such points of lack of conformity, at least on a terminological and structural level of the legislation, are an impediment to the practical implementation of the relevant provisions by courts, and they thus at least potentially undermine the guarantees of equal and fair treatment of all offenders.

The changes introduced to the criminal law by the 1993 Act no. 17 have not all been emancipating. This reflected the dramatic worsening of the criminality situation in Hungary after 1989, especially when the number of property-related crimes is considered. For example, fines and the rules for the conversion of unpaid fines and unserved forced labour into prison penalties have generally been by the 1993 Act no 17. As an example, two days of forced labour used to be convertible to a one-day imprisonment before the Act. After the Act was introduced, unserved 'work for public benefit' is now convertible to imprisonment on a 1:1 basis. This regulation is still in force in Hungary.

At the same time, some provisions, such as those that regulate the application of parole and probation, have been made less severe. According to the criminal law before the 1993 changes, life sentences could be converted to parole only after at least twenty years of the prison sentence have been served. Today this is possible after fifteen years, up to twenty-five years, where courts have a large measure of discretion in deciding on this matter. Similarly, before the 1993 changes, principal penalties passed for crimes, as opposed to misdemeanours, could be replaced by supplementary penalties (e.g. fines) only for crimes for which the following was true:

(i) there was a low likelihood of repeat, and

(ii) by law, only penalties up to two years of imprisonment could be passed for those crimes.

After the 1993 changes, principal penalties could be converted into supplementary ones where the following applied:

(i) the crime could be penalised only by up to three years of imprisonment, and

(ii) there were convincing reasons to believe that 'the aims of penalty could be achieved without imprisonment'.

These changes reflected trends in the post-communist social and value milieu of Hungary. On the one hand, many provisions of the criminal law that were seen as more down-to-earth in their ideological dimension, and thus many penal provisions which had been relatively mild under the former régime, had been made more severe, and are continuing to be made even more severe, alongside the perception of an increasing need to sanction and control certain particularly threatening types of criminality more strictly. These crimes mainly include those which are occurring more frequently, and which are thus increasingly becoming a real concern for the population and social relationships, and thereby also for policy- and law-makers.

The conditions for the abolition of penalties at the courts' discretion were also liberalised by the changes introduced in 1993. The initial version of the criminal law contained complicated provisions in this regard, based on the types of crimes and sentences passed for them, and on the number of years of imprisonment that had already been served. The 1993 Act empowered courts to grant abolition of penalties to offenders who were considered 'worthy of clemency', and who have, as a general rule, served at least one-half of their prison sentences. These provisions are similar to the relevant provisions in Yugoslav criminal legislation, although the Yugoslav legislation is even more liberal, because it empowers the courts to grant an abolition of penalty after one-third of the sentence has been served, in certain circumstances.

The 1993 Act also introduced more specific provisions regulating matters that had either not been regulated at all in the 1978 criminal law, or had been insufficiently regulated. These provisions concern the rules and sanctions pertaining to the treatment of crimes including the protection of information, especially of electronically stored information, business relations (especially in the context of privatisation and private enterprises), tax evasion, fraud in social security allotment claims. Crimes arising from these matters are to a large extent in the domain of white-collar crime, which was not high on the list of priorities of legal institutions during communism, but which has gained a certain prominence after the changes in the late 1980s.

For all these reasons, it can be concluded that the changes to the 1978 criminal law have been indicative of the progressive, qualitative moves ahead which have taken place in Hungarian society since the beginning of the post-communist changes. The general direction of these changes has been towards decentralisation, democratisation, and a greater emphasis on diversity and the principle of subsidiarity, which is a principle whereby social policy problems are addressed at the lowest appropriate hierarchical and organisational level in society, and not exclusively by central authorities. However, it must be noted that many aspects of the criminal justice system have remained extremely centralised. This fact has already been mentioned in the discussion of the organisation of the Hungarian police. There are also other areas of social control where a certain natural and unavoidable isolation of criminal justice institutions from the 'mainstream' of the societal political discourse can cause dangers for human rights and moral standards in the treatment of individuals by institutions. One such sensitive area, which certainly deserves a separate discussion, is the prison system.

The Hungarian prison system

The Hungarian prison system structure is fairly elaborate. The 'Prison Administration' (which is another, official name for the prison system) consists of two types of institutions. The 'directing institutions' comprise the National Prison Administration, which acts within the legal and institutional guidelines set by the Ministry of the Interior. The chief officer of the National Prison Administration is the Director General, who is assisted by two Deputy Directors. The Director General is directly responsible for the Department of Internal Supervision, Department of Human Resources, the Secretariat, and the Department of Research and International Relations. One Deputy Director General is responsible for the Legal Department, Department of Corrections, Department of Prison Security, and Medical Department. The other Deputy Director is in charge of the Department of Prison Enterprises, Department of Finance, and Department of Computer Informatics.

After the changes in the late 1980s, a great deal of emphasis has been placed on openness and cooperation with the public and other governmental and non-governmental organisations. This is witnessed today by the fact that one department in the National Prison Administration is solely concerned with research and international relations, which would have been considered very extraordinary under communist rule, where the activity of criminal justice institutions was usually treated as confidential and as a matter of the country's sovereignty, meaning also that any such information would probably not be allowed international circulation. At least procedurally and formally, the willingness of the prison system to engage in the exchange of ideas with the outside world and the existence of an international relations section within it provide a chance that custodial penalties might in the future be applied with still greater social purpose, and that more information may be provided to the public about this generally hidden, but by its very nature extremely controversial and liable to questions of legitimacy, part of the overall system of criminal justice.

Apart from the directing institutions, the prison system contains the 'executive institutions', including county gaols, prisons, and 'prison enterprises', and other custodial, medical, training, education, and social welfare institutions, as well as the Central Institution for Maintenance and Supply. The executive part of the system consists of the following departments: Central Executive Staff, Department of Human Resources and Social Welfare, Department of Sentence Implementation, Department of Prison Security, Department of Finance, and Medical Department.[23]

Similar to the practice in other countries, county gaols are used mainly to house pre-trial detainees, rather than convicted prisoners, as well as a limited number of convicted offenders who are serving short sentences for misdemeanours, rather than crimes. At present there are seventeen county gaols in Hungary.

Prisons (or prisons proper) house convicted prisoners who have committed crimes. They are designed for the execution of penalties, their régime is harsher, and they are more intrusive and restrictive than gaols. There are minimum, medium, and maximum security prisons in Hungary, the same as in many other countries. This classification is based not only on security considerations in the sense of the institutional security arrangements at particular institutions, but also on the profiles of prisoners who serve sentences in those institutions. The classification is reflected in the geographical setting of the prisons (maximum security prisons are more isolated from human settlements, and presumably more difficult to escape from). The security classification is also reflected in the nature of compulsory work for prisoners, as well as in a number of other features.[24] Prisoners serving their sentences in maximum security prisons, for example, do not do work requiring the use of tools that could be used as weapons, for escape, attack on other prisoners or guards, starting a fire, producing an explosion, etc. In such prisons, rules are more restrictive, such as those regulating the assembly of prisoners in groups, their mutual communication, the equipment and security of cells, corridors and other rooms, guards' training and arms, etc.

Apart from the above-mentioned division, prisons are also divided into open and closed ones. This division is primarily reflected in the nature of work assigned to prisoners. There are nine closed prisons in Hungary at present. In such prisons, prisoners mainly do industrial work in enclosed environments. There are also four open prisons, where the main type of work is agricultural, and it therefore takes place outdoors, often outside the prison walls. The Hungarian prison system also contains 'transitory prisons'. These institutions are designed as half-way houses, where prisoners who are soon to be released are housed. The restrictive régime in transitory prisons is reduced, to facilitate the reintegration and adaptation of prisoners to life in the society at large after their release.

The two medical institutions within the prison system are the Central Hospital for Prison Administration, and the Institution for Forensic Observation and Mental Hospital for Prison Administration. These two institutions provide all medical services for prisoners. The Institution for Forensic Observation and Mental Hospital for Prison Administration also conducts all types of psychiatric and psychological assessments and treatment, including the assessment and treatment of psychoses, other mental disorders, and personality disorders, or psychopathies.

The average annual prison population ranged between around 24 000 (in 1986 it was 23 903) at the upper end and 13 000 (13 307 in 1990) at the lower end between 1983 and 1992. These numbers suggest that rates of imprisonment had been high during communist rule, and that they dropped substantially immediately after the beginning of the political and social changes in the late 1980s — hence the low figure in 1990. However, after 1992, increased crime rates and increased rates of imprisonment have been recorded. This has been perceived as a security crisis.

Of all Hungarian citizens who are in custody on an average day, approximately 27% are pre-trial detainees, that is, those charged and awaiting trial, while the rest are convicted offenders. The ratio of male to female offenders is similar to that in most other countries. Nearly all prisoners (approximately 94%) are male, with only about 6% female. The figures reflecting the duration of pre-trial detention, at least those derived from the available data until 1993, are worrying. For example, in 1993, of 3557 individuals detained for trial, 674 had been detained for more than twelve months without a trial and 161 had been detained for more than *twenty-five months*; 1668 detainees had been detained for longer than six months, and 2503 for more than three months.[25] These figures were completely unacceptable and needed to change dramatically if the aim of the reforms of the Hungarian criminal justice system was to achieve greater fairness and efficiency of the system as a whole, and to eliminate the *de facto* penalisation of the innocently accused, which is the result of long pre-trial detention. The length of pre-trial detention is one of the main criteria for the assessment of respect of human rights by a criminal justice system, and the periods of such detention indicated above suggest a significant lack of social policy emphasis on the solution to this problem.

Conclusion

Although the reform of the Hungarian criminal justice system has progressed the furthest in the central-eastern European region, this advantage is mainly reflected in the legislative sense: Hungary has progressed the furthest in the reform of its legislation. However, in the area of social policy relating to social control, there is still room for considerable improvement in the existing solutions. These areas will no doubt be the subject of consideration by social policy- and law-makers in the near future, but an awareness of their existence, in light of the aspects of the Hungarian social control system discussed in this chapter, is a basic precondition for the actual implementation of any such improvements.

Notes

1. For example, Los, M. (1988), *Communist ideology, law and crime: A comparative view of the USSR and Poland*, Macmillan, Basingstoke.

2. For example, Szikinger, I. (1994), 'Policing the new democracy in Hungary: Challenges and solutions', paper released by the Hungarian Law Enforcement Research Institute, kindly provided direct to the author. Much of the discussion of crime statistics here is based on material analysed in this paper.

3. See Benke, M. (1994), 'White collar crime and money laundering in Hungary', in *Rendészeti tanulmányok*, no. 4, p. 71.

4. The traditionally military character of the Hungarian police organisation and strategy is still reflected in the fact that police officers have exactly the same ranks as military officers, their uniforms are identical in cut to Army uniforms, the difference being only in colour, and the police chain of command and operational structures are the same as those of the military. The introduction of community policing therefore meant that substantial changes needed to be introduced into the police structures to make them more diverse, accessible from the outside,

localised, and able to be more receptive to the community. All these features are opposed to a rigid military-style of police organisation.

5. See Szikinger, op. cit., p. 9; also Szikinger, I. (1994), 'The police in Hungary today', *Rendénszeti tanulmányok*, vol. 4, pp. 23–35.

6. See Szikinger, I., 'Policing the new democracy in Hungary: Challenges and solutions', p. 14, and Szikinger, I., 'The police in Hungary today', p. 29.

7. *Szonda Ipsos Public Opinion Research Company Statistics, Official police and prosecution statistics.*

8. Szikinger, op. cit., p. 28.

9. Géza, K. (1994), 'Survey on crime-prevention', *Rendészeti Tanulmányok*, vol. 4, pp. 37-40.

10. ibid., p. 42.

11. The Hungarian Constitution, article 51.2.

12. Section 10.1. of the 1978 criminal law. Hungarian criminal legislation is systematised by sections, not by articles.

13. Földvári, J. (1980), 'Observations in relation to the new Hungarian Criminal Code', *Hungarian Law Review*, no. 1–2, pp. 7–8.

14. See section 22 of the 1978 law, and Földvári, op. cit., p. 9.

15. ibid., p. 10.

16. The relevant articles from the Yugoslav and Czech criminal legislation are discussed in greater detail in the preceding chapters. It should be pointed out here that the comparisons between Hungarian and Yugoslav criminal laws are diachronic, and not synchronic, because the subject of analysis here is the Hungarian 1978 criminal law, which has been significantly changed since its original enactment, and which is important because it is the most comprehensive Hungarian criminal law since the introduction of criminal legislation in this country. This law is compared with Yugoslav criminal legislation which is in the process of synchronisation and change but has not yet been fully synchronised and changed. This means that a past legislative situation in Hungary is basically compared with a present legislative situation in Yugoslavia, which presents a diachronic perspective. The reason for this perspective is that the changes to Hungarian 1978 criminal law which have been introduced after 1989 are the subject of a separate discussion, which would ideally correspond to a discussion of the changes to Yugoslav

criminal legislation that are expected through the enactment of the new federal criminal law. It is possible that many of the differences between Hungarian and Yugoslav laws will disappear in this context, or that they will at least undergo a substantial qualitative change once the new federal criminal law is enacted in Yugoslavia. At the moment this law is still the subject of debate.

17. The 1978 Hungarian criminal law, section 38, paragraphs 1–2.

18. Sections 40–46 of the 1978 Hungarian criminal law. The law distinguishes between: (i) 'crimes' in the 'full' sense, defined as those acts that are 'committed intentionally and for which the law prescribes prison sentences of two years and above' (section 11, paragraph 2), and (ii) 'misdemeanours', which include any other offences not qualifiable as crimes in the 'full' sense.

19. A distinction needs to be drawn between the penalty of seizure of particular items, and the one of confiscation of property. The former involves the seizure of certain specific items which were either the subject of the crime, were or are relevant for the crime and the danger to society that the crime or the perpetrator represent. The latter (confiscation of property) involves the confiscation of all property of an individual regardless of the existence or non-existence of any relevant role and instrumental value of that property in the commission of the crime or in the constitution of the danger to society arising from the perpetrator's actions. The latter penalty, for example, includes the confiscation of a house, car, and material means necessary for life. This penalty is characteristic of ideologically exclusive and in certain ways authoritarian régimes. It is extremely problematic from the point of view of human rights, and it is therefore a surprising phenomenon in the 'reform' criminal laws of the mentioned central European countries.

20. It was not entirely clear here what the difference between 'treason' and 'treachery' was.

21. In the same year (1992) changes were made to the 'Rules of expropriation', defined by section 14 of the 1976 Legal Decree number 24. These changes did not relate directly to the 1978 criminal law, but they clearly had a relevant political significance. The changes practically eliminated expropriation, as it was considered to be a remnant of the previous political régime (Act 13, 1992). Act 14 of the same year introduced changes to the criminal law relating to offences against the 'discipline of accounting', 'crime of bankruptcy', and 'illegal preference granted to a creditor'. These changes were not entirely unrelated to the political shift in the country's system of political governance and the composition of the new political system, but they are of somewhat lesser importance for the present discussion, because of the nature of the crimes to which they related.

22. Among the most important such legal technicalities are the two 1991 amendments to the 1973 Act on criminal procedure, the 1992 'Act on the introduction of the procedure of review of the 1973 Act no. 1 on the criminal procedure', and the major 1993 Act no. 32, 'on the amendment of the 1979 Legal decree no. 11 on the execution of penalties and measures'. The last act enforced a far stricter accountability in the implementation of penalties, especially for imprisonment, and imposed restrictions on those penalties which the parliamentarians considered either predominantly ideologically determined, or excessively severe.

23. For more information about the organisation of the prison system, see Boros, J. (1994), 'The organisation: The structure of the Hungarian prison system', *Prison Review*, pp. 3–5.

24. ibid., p. 4.

25. ibid.

5 Social policy and criminality in post-communist societies

When discussing the nature and role of the law in any society, and thus also in post-communist communities, a distinction between various types of law should be kept in mind. Various types of law reflect various functions of the law as the most important system of social control. Examples of various types of law are: 'criminal law', which is of course of primary relevance for this study (its role being social control *par excellence*, perhaps in the most direct and obvious sense); 'regulative law', whose basic function is general social regulation in non-criminal areas; 'welfare law', whose main function is the regulation of the distribution of resources in society; and 'civil law', whose main function is the resolution of private disputes between citizens. This systematisation, of course, does not necessarily correspond with the formal systematisation of areas of the law in any particular legal system. It merely represents a fragment taken from a conceptual division of functions of the law which is often mentioned in the context of jurisprudence and legal policy.[1]

Various streams in jurisprudence have sought to interpret the law in differing ways, from the idealistic and 'reificatory' notion of the law as a self-sufficient paradigm of justice, to more community-orientated conceptions, reflective of the anchoring of the understanding of law in social policy questions. As far as post-communist societies are concerned, the latter understanding of the law, and first of all of the criminal law, is probably the most useful for the comprehension of a fuller picture of how politics, economics, and the demands of justice form various parts of one and the same social and normative body in any society, whether this is understood in the positive or in the negative connotation.

Social policy questions of principle and post-communist transition

Post-communist polities are only semi-polities. These are societies whose internal structure and organisation have been largely destroyed, and from which a new structure is emerging. This new structure is still at an embryonic stage, and is therefore insufficiently distinct and developed to provide full social regulation of societal relationships. Given such an embryonic stage of development of state and societal relationships, and of the social policy of the new political order, there is a large amount of spontaneity in the social dynamics of post-communist societies. Part of that spontaneity is socially destructive. Where more 'western' societies are overregulated, post-communist polities tend to be underregulated, primarily in the fundamental areas of regulation such as business law, protection of contracts and mutual obligation, trade practices regulation. On the other hand, in areas where western societies are underregulated, in matters involving individual liberty and the freedom to compete for limited social resources, post-communist societies often have a strong tradition of overregulation, namely a policy that could be considered as overly intrusive social control.

The legal transformation of the Czech Republic, Hungary, Slovakia, Poland, and other countries of the central-eastern European region has destroyed the semantic and legal syntagmas of communism, such as the principles of 'static' equality and the unconditional right of citizens to basic social services and support, loyalty to state ideology and obligation to the Party. At the same time, however, this transformation has failed to establish new paradigms and syntagmas, which would be able to effectively govern societies used to over-regulation. The term 'overregulation' should not be understood as having an exclusively negative connotation here, because communist overregulation provided a large amount of security and opportunities for creative leisure and education which were once so celebrated by Marx, and which are largely unknown in many capitalist societies.

As a result of the collapse of strong regulatory mechanisms and social policy schemes, which once catered for the most disadvantaged and unequal members of society, the invasion of the ideology of free markets and unrestrained competition has led to a shock wave of poverty, high levels of social stress and stress-related diseases, apocalyptic death rates in the region, and an ever faster spinning circle of social stratification in the former communist societies. Part of the problem was that social reforms, enacted through the new laws, were badly designed, usually in that they tended to follow the western models uncritically, even with a measure of adoration (first of all in the countries of central Europe), while at the same time failing to take into account the different habits and nature of central-eastern European societies from those on the geo-political West. These models also did not adequately take into account that post-communist societies were insufficiently affluent and were lacking the social mechanisms necessary to provide compensation and assistance to those who were most directly affected by the negative effects of social reforms, and these were the poorest parts of the population.

Another and related reason for the relative failure of post-communist societies to provide an adequate 'service' of justice and social regulation was their lack of well-integrated and independent institutions, first of all the *judiciary*. The independence of the judiciary is, of course, always only relative, even in the most democratic and transparent of societies, simply because the judges are always appointed by politicians, either by government or by Parliament, and the courts, obviously, must follow legislation, which in itself is a result of political compromise, rather than following any fully 'independent' postulates of justice. At the same time, the operation of the judiciary can be independent so far as the judges and magistrates are aware of their interpretative and creative function within the legal system, and their relatively secluded position within the political battlefield of interests, to which the formation of legislation itself is fully exposed. Thus, the judges have the opportunity to create a *legal tradition*, consisting of a consistent application and interpretation of the law, which gives citizens the impression that their interests are upheld by a morally integrated, independent social institution, and that the way the judiciary functions stems from the *community's generalised perception of justice*, within the limits of the written laws, and in addition to the mere following of legal regulations. It is at least to some extent true to say that however bad the legislation, if the judiciary is a stable institution marked by integrity, the impression of the implementation of the law and support for the principles of justice in society will tend to be reasonably good. On the other hand, however good the laws might be, if the judiciary is corrupt, incompetent, uncaring, and indifferent, then the very nature of the system of justice in society is bound to decay rapidly.

One way of looking at the judiciary in communist societies is that it was little more than a rubber-stamping institution for decisions made by the government — its job was not very strenuous, and standards imposed on it were lenient. The regulation and control of the judiciary was in the hands of the executive, of the government agencies and ministries, and the main task of the judiciary was to confer a maximum possible amount of procedural legitimacy on these agencies. When the overregulated communist system gave way to liberal and capitalist societal arrangements, the judicial institutions found themselves in the position of not being able to cope with the new duties, especially with their *independence* acquired overnight. Instead of supporting the professional and human standards of justice and insisting on legal scholarship and the inherent legal interpretation of cases, the courts tended to engage in daily politicking, especially in the first years after the beginning of post-communist transition, and especially in central European countries. In such circumstances, community pressures and the general atmosphere often became crucial factors in deciding the fate of those who were caught in the claws of post-communist justice. Affairs such as the earlier-mentioned Kahánek case in the Czech Republic are only indicators of this phenomenon of uncritical submission of parts of the criminal justice system to the political *atmosphere* in the community, primarily relating to social policy. The judges did not see themselves as agents of social justice, in addition to being agents of the law, and did not make use of their presupposed, relatively secluded position within the political system, where they were able to exercise their legal sense of correctness and fairness, and to provide an educatory example of conscientiousness and consistency for the rest of society. Instead, they tended, and still do, to perceive themselves more or less as government employees, fully dependent on the government. In certain situations this is a fatal conception for the judiciary.

The distorted notion of democracy as the right to mimic and implement the values of a narrow, concrete, *de facto* community in official policy only aggravates this problem, because in such situations the retrograde values of relatively small parts of the community could be allowed to exert a very strong influence on important judicial decisions. The control of the judiciary and the integrity of the judicial practice in Hungary appear somewhat better than in the rest of the region, but courts in Hungary are still clogged with unresolved cases, and questions such as those relating to excessive periods of pre-trial detainment cast a shadow on the legitimacy of judicial policy.

These problems of principle and practice have naturally created an impression that post-communist societies are going through a major, and global, crisis of morality, and that this crisis has been brought about by 'brutal' and 'primitive' capitalist competition and 'cut-throat' fighting for limited social resources. In fact, the problem is predominantly cultural, and educational: the new tasks and political priorities are dramatically different from the old ones, and those who are supposed to achieve them are not sure how to respond to the newly created social needs. A legal tradition that would create the impression of the criminal justice system's independence and respect for the inherent principles of law is missing, because in the previous system the law had been made into an instrument of social control which had a clearly identifiable owner, that is the communist elite.[2]

The relevance of the law for social policy has thus become a double-edged sword, which has cut both ways ever since the communist system started to wane. During communist rule, social policy questions were no less important or obvious than they are now. After the political changes, the amount of initiative coming from the government has decreased, and new sources of initiative have emerged throughout society. This phenomenon has been mainly identifiable, or connected, with the processes of decentralisation and privatisation of property and services, processes that have progressed the furthest in central Europe. The community has gradually started to assert a greater degree of control over social issues. A certain deregulation has occurred, which has meant that agencies that had once merely followed government initiatives have had to become sources of initiative themselves. *Social policy* has thus become much more a *community issue*, a community problem, with which the community has had to cope much more directly than under the previous régime. This was a result of democratisation, but that democratisation has had both positive aspects and negative, unpleasant aspects. The 'guardian' role of the Party élite has vanished, but the problems that the Party élite had solved have not disappeared. The societies that were once used to social policy problems being solved on its behalf by the Party élite are now having to face these problems directly, by themselves. This is the starkest contrast between today's central-eastern European societies and these same societies before 1989.

This difference is also partly a result of democratic procedure: the post-communist governments must please the voters, and in solving social policy puzzles they are naturally keen to hear what the public has to say, and what the professionals and professional organisations have to advise. This is not just because the new governments are inherently more benevolent to the community than the communist governments used to be. The reason is rather more simple and less romantic: hearing what the community wants to say about social policy enables governments to make politically informed and strategically considered decisions, whose success is probably somewhat more likely than the success of any decisions that would be made in isolation from the public. Second, and from the government's point of view more importantly, these decisions tend to be much more *politically defensible* if they do *not* succeed than the decisions made behind the scenes.

However, for a number of reasons the benefits of the democratic procedural change are not yet bearing all their fruit in the region. Most of the problems in this context stem from two sources: the agencies, the professionals, and the general public are insufficiently prepared to provide constructive leads across the range of main social policy issues, because they have not yet fully adjusted to their new roles in society. Second, the very identity of the community, in particular the community bonds that have remained after the end of the old system are in such a bad condition, and the amount of mutual confidence in the community is so eroded, that individuals often continue to prefer to act as *discrete agents*, rather than as members of an *organic social unity*.

The lack of a feeling of organic society of individuals means that cooperative relationships are difficult to build, and once they are built, they tend to remain low in intensity. This further means, and this is a crucial consequence for any social system, that social policy questions tend to have very *different meanings* for different individuals and social groups in post-communist societies. In fact, the more these individuals and groups are isolated and discrete, the more they tend to think exclusively in terms of their own interests, the more likely it is that *collective initiatives* and community concerns and priorities will be — *incomprehensible* — to them.

Systems that used to be based on planned economic performance are not the best material for the building of strong, cooperative economic and other relationships in the relatively suddenly changed circumstances, which need to permeate post-communist societies in order to bring them to the levels of efficiency and cohesiveness which would enable them to pick up socially, economically, and politically with the rest of the world. It is precisely at this stage of the process of social and political transition that a certain social paralysis is noticeable today. It is reflected in the widely shared impression that major social policy dilemmas are insoluble. Once this sceptical attitude becomes sufficiently prevalent, various strong-handed governments tend to assume authority. This has happened in all central-eastern European countries, in fairly short periods of time within the past seven or eight years. Some of these countries have recovered and reestablished the foundations for the building of genuine political institutions, while others have continued their plunge into the abyss of internal dissipation of initiatives into a fatal discreteness of mutually indiscernible social and political identities, choices, and priorities. The result — destruction, rising social and other stress levels, devastating military conflicts raging through the region, and political disintegration sweeping across the former communist world.

In situations where heavy-handed authority appears necessary, the law tends to become a weapon in the political struggle of prospective rulers with potential opponents. Those who succeed in assuming control of the law and legislative mechanisms have the greatest chance of becoming effective rulers. Once they have succeeded, the law remains hopelessly isolated from its own mission, namely to ensure just social arrangements and serve earnest social concerns and solutions, including the dilemmas and problems of social policy. In one way or another, unavoidably, instead of being a tool for reintegration, social inclusion, and achievement of greater social cohesion, the law becomes more or less solely a measure of oppressive control. The oppressors and the oppressed may change from time to time, they may even swap places and roles, but the basic principle of oppressive control remains.

In most cases, oppression can be identified with the main currents of social stratification; in other words, those particular social groups which tend to be at the receiving end of social stratification also tend to be at the receiving end of the repressive, and oppressive, function of the law. Societies affected by the post-communist confusion (or anomie) thus fall prey to injustice and degradation, which leads to a further increase in the amount of detachment and discreteness among individuals and groups, thus creating a vicious self-perpetuating system of inequality in all aspects. In such a situation, the function of the law, though not of criminal law, is largely to create compensatory mechanisms, relieving intra-societal influences, to restructure the resources where necessary, and to attach additional burdens where required, all in an effort to prevent rapid social disintegration.

In many ways, social policy dilemmas, ranging from problems associated with the shortage of housing and the explosion of uncontrolled and perhaps uncontrollable rent-seeking behaviour and free riding, to problems associated with drug addiction and high crime rates, are new questions for the post-communist societies in the region. There are many grounds for arguing that these societies are not yet fully constituted civil societies. On the other hand, there is certainly at least some plausibility in saying that the newly discovered civil relationships, to the extent to which they have appeared over the past several years, are still largely incapable of dealing with concrete, and very serious indeed, social policy problems in central-eastern Europe. Societies that were essentially *irresponsible* and *governed*, are suddenly expected to *govern* themselves *responsibly*. The newly established free-market economies are often perceived as suggesting, even heralding, an open season on any security and earned status from the past times. This open season as a specific type of social situation gives greatest opportunities to those in possession of the greatest resources, that is, mainly those who, in legitimate or illegitimate ways, have done extremely well under the previous régime. The enormous differences in starting positions which thus arise lead to very disturbing forms of negative social stratification, leaving scores of formerly welfare-dependent citizens virtually in the streets, plunging through the vast holes in the remnants of the former compensatory and security nets of social policy. These holes are torn through the security mechanisms by the new governments, especially in central Europe, who are keen to rid themselves of any symbols of the former ideology, by the newly rich entrepreneurs, who appeared almost overnight and who are keen to maximise their takings while the social situation is still fluid and intransparent. Finally, these holes in social policy partly arise from the temporary lack of understanding of most citizens of what is really happening in society, a lack of understanding caused by the fast changes that the society is undergoing.

Negative aspects of social stratification, social crisis, and security crisis

The groups most victimised by this negative stratification are those who are disadvantaged in most societies, such as pensioners and elderly citizens in general, the ill and disabled, and the youth who, caught in the tidal wave of depression and denial which is sweeping across central-eastern Europe, opt for accepting the 'loser' label, rather than confronting the new reality, which seems too complex and hostile to cope with. In this way, the crisis of social policy leads to a crisis of morality and spirit, and this, ultimately, further leads to a crisis of security.

All of the factors mentioned earlier, including the inefficiency and inadequacy of the judiciary and other relevant structures in the criminal justice systems in European post-communist countries, have been causes of increased crime rates. However, in many ways it seems appropriate to point out that perhaps the most important cause of criminality is the constantly worsening social crisis in the region, generated by the very social changes that were expected to bring prosperity and peace to the region. As time goes by and the social transition breeds more and more social stratification and more natural redistribution of resources *towards* those who were in the strongest positions to start with, an increasing number of citizens, especially young men, tend to turn to crime and related forms of deviance. This is only partly a form of securing those goods that are necessary for survival in the new system, and which might be unavailable in any other way, at least to some individuals. To a considerably larger extent, the rising crime rates are a result of what is commonly referred to as *relative deprivation*, namely the *perceived inequalities* in opportunities and a *perception of injustice* of the existing, and seemingly irreversible, economic mechanisms for the natural transfer of resources to those members of society who already have the most.

Before proceeding further, it is perhaps necessary to clarify the concept of 'natural transfer of resources'. If one imagines a situation where all parties, or all members of society, have the necessary means for survival, and some of them, because of their privileged positions in the social system, have more than they need, then it becomes clear that once the structural features of the system of distribution change (which is what has happened in post-communist societies), those with a surplus of resources will be able to generate even more resources, while those with the bare minimum necessary for survival will not be able to manipulate their resources to generate capital. In other words, the rich will become even richer, and the poor will be left with what they had from the outset, or less than that. This, after all, is the well-known Marxist dialectic of profits and capital, which, in one form or another, has been recognised by political economy almost since its earliest days. In other words, this seems to be one of the least controversial claims put forward by Marxism.

In communist societies, members of the communist élite and their supporters (many of whom are now in positions of power in contemporary transitional societies) were the mentioned privileged members of the community. They were able to exploit the system, to secure benefits for themselves which were inconceivable for an ordinary citizen.[3] They profited from the inequality between the élite and the mainstream population, which is inherent in every communist political ideology, and which is primarily reflected in the conceptual distinction, characteristic of communist ideology, between the mainstream proletariat and its 'avant garde', that is, the ruling oligarchy.

However, once the system changed, the new liberal ideology emerged. The main assumptions of liberalism are directly opposed to those of communism as an extreme form of communitarianism. Liberalism requires initial equality and respect for the privacy of individuals. Liberal political economy does not call for any redistribution of resources on the basis of their origin and the circumstances of their acquisition (as long as this was legal), but rather for the respect of *existing* differences, equalisation of the *terms* of competition, and a gradual redistribution, according to the principles of *economic efficiency*. This means that those who had the resources from the beginning — and they were very few compared to the mainstream population, which was impoverished and politically victimised under communism — are free to use their resources in accordance with the newly discovered and established rules of the market. These rules imply that those whose basic needs are fulfilled will opt for taking economic risks with the surplus resources, and that in such a situation only those who are able to invest and maintain high stakes at relatively high risk levels can benefit substantially. Most of the population are unable either to invest and maintain high stakes, or to take high levels of risk, because they are forced to think about questions of survival in the most elementary sense. This creates a very unfortunate picture indeed in the process of transition towards liberal-capitalist social arrangements, where former communist supporters and party apparatchiks acquire control of large companies and business organisations, while those who were at the receiving end of social stratification during communism remain at the receiving end of capitalist market forces in the transitional countries of central-eastern Europe today. It is therefore not surprising that there is a considerable longing for the old times among considerable parts of the populations of central-eastern Europe today, and that all countries, perhaps apart from the Czech Republic, have seen a considerable shift back towards political forces that have been at least loosely associated with at least some aspects of the communist times, that is, towards left socialist and social democratic political parties.

For all of the above reasons, it is not surprising that many analysts of contemporary events in central-eastern Europe attribute the social crisis and the alarming state of affairs of civil relationships to a crisis of social policy, and in particular to the critically underdeveloped management of human resources. This includes not only management in the workplace and guidance towards a prompter and fuller adaptation of the workforce to the changed industrial relations and general living circumstances, but also management of labour markets, health care, education, administration of general affairs, etc.[4]

Some of the most obvious problems in social policy concern health care. The earlier régime of state subsidies for health care has largely disappeared in most of the region, leaving behind rather dubious arrangements with various private health funds, many of which were short-lived. The starkest example was that of the Czech Republic, where the main health fund, created after the political changes in 1989, went bankrupt after only six months of operation. The privatisation of health care has led to changes in legislation regulating health care, and this has led to a continually decreasing level of state investment in this area of social policy. As a consequence, large numbers of mainly socially disadvantaged people were left virtually without access to adequate health care. When this phenomenon is viewed in the context of unhealthy living habits in almost all countries of the region, polluted environment, low living standards, and high stress levels arising from changed social conditions, it becomes clear why the region is experiencing death rates unprecedented in its entire peacetime history.[5] This especially applies to working-age men, who are traditionally entrusted with providing for the family, and many of whom were victims of the unemployment wave which first swept across the region after 1989. Today the risk of death for Hungarian men aged between fifteen and fifty-nine is higher than in developing African countries such as Zimbabwe; in the Czech Republic the situation in this respect is worse than in Vietnam. During the past three decades, death rates for men in their late forties have grown astonishingly — for example, in Hungary by 131%, with most increases occurring within the past few years of rapid social transformation.[6]

Economically, these phenomena leave society without its most valuable resource — the human resource. This causes huge economic losses in investment, in training, and in education in the region. Central and eastern European countries have traditionally pursued education and training with great enthusiasm, and have managed to create a tremendous human infrastructure in that sense, which was underused under communism, but which is a major resource for most countries of the region today. The region's population is highly educated, on average far more so than the populations of most western countries. The ideological burden of the past few decades, however, meant that the structure of the demand for education did not correspond to social needs. This has created a situation where there are perhaps disproportionately too many academics and artists in the region today, and too few managers, engineers, lawyers, and accountants, as the latter were considered to be low-ranking professions, and were not in demand during communist times. The high profile of these countries in official educational statistics paints a misleading picture of real employment prospects for educated youth in the region. The high numbers of Nobel Laureates does not mean that new philosophers and sociologists will be able to find jobs, or that the region's countries' educational structures correspond to their social realities.[7]

The new governments in most central-eastern European countries have cut funds for education, along with the general fall in the GDP, both in absolute terms, which is understandable, and in relative terms, which is less understandable. In many countries of the region the *proportions* of the GDP earmarked for education (not just absolute amounts of money allocated to education) are ever smaller, and wealth and resources tend to be transferred more into the business sector and into restructuring the physical, economic, and industrial infrastructure.[8] This means that the new governments are effectively leading their countries towards very high unemployment rates in the longer term, as the uneducated youths, who are missing out today because of the short-sighted redirecting of funds away from education, are the structurally unemployed of tomorrow. Today these problems are not obvious because of the still high proportion of highly educated people who are still relatively young and early in their careers. However, with time, with the ageing of the population, and with the shrinking of funding allocated to education, the educational structure of the populations in the region may change dramatically, and the problems of structural, long-term unemployment, which are so painfully present in all western societies today, could dawn on central-eastern Europe tomorrow. At the same time, the increased presence of structural unemployment would probably exert undesirable influences on the general criminality situation, given that experiences in most countries show a fairly consistent positive correlation between increases in unemployment and increases in criminality. This also aggravates the strategic problems of 'later' crime-control efforts, as the conditions for an increase in criminality have already been created.

It should also be pointed out that criminal policy, as a specific area of social policy, does not come into the focus of public attention in all its important aspects, or frequently enough, unlike many other areas of social policy.

In discussions of criminal policy the real effects on society of particular forms of crime control are often left out of consideration. This includes the effects relating to the prevention of recidivism, and the financial effects, including the considerations and questions of the costs associated with various penal and preventative measures, as well as the costs arising from the lack of success of preventative efforts. This particularly concerns the structure of social stratification in the former communist countries. The materially most damaging crimes, namely those classified as white-collar crime, are the least detectable, and they are the least frequently prosecuted, because of the typically relatively high social positions of typical perpetrators of such crimes, their influence, and ability to conceal their crimes. Public attention is not focused on these crimes, which present the greatest problem in the sense of management of social resources. Instead, public attention is usually focused on the crimes that are attractive for the media, mostly violent and sexually motivated crimes, or on crimes that are the most immediate threat to individual citizens, mainly including street crime. These latter crimes, often described as characteristic of members of the socially most disadvantaged groups, represent only a very small proportion of all reported or detected crimes (in most countries not exceeding 10%), and their financial effect, however unacceptable they may be in their very nature and appearance, is minor when compared with that of white-collar crime.

The effect of excessive concentration of public attention on the need for preventing street crime is the danger that crime control might get out of hand, while any substantial real results in policy management of the concomitant financial crisis and crisis of confidence in society are not achieved. In most societies, and certainly in the contemporary central-eastern European ones, not more than 10% of all detected crimes lead to conviction. This means that, if disproportionate public attention and policy resources are concentrated on violent crimes, and rates of conviction, sometimes even reporting and detection, are low, then however severe the system of penalties as it is defined by criminal legislation might be, the deterrent and regulatory functions of penal policy simply will not be fulfilled satisfactorily. This fact is compounded if it is remembered that most violent crimes are not committed on an entirely rational basis, or by rational individuals. For severe penal policies to have any serious effect in the prevention of reoffending, offenders would have to be rational, which means that they would have to consider the consequences *before* committing the crime. If violent and sexually motivated crimes are largely irrational, that would mean that they generally cannot be deterred and their number reduced by penal policy alone. In many countries where a severe penal policy was introduced, a certain self-perpetuation of violence has occurred, and the result has been a complete crisis of internal security, and sometimes a real explosion of violent and sexually motivated crimes.[9]

The only way to try and close the yawning gap between the desire to secure successful social control on the one hand, and the grim reality of that problem on the other hand, is to attempt to increase the efficiency of policing and investigation. This has been tried many times, in many different social settings, and in many different ways, and has rarely been completely successful. On the other hand, concentrating on violent crimes, whose potential for prevention is so small, means leaving aside many other types of criminality, which are much more rational and premeditated in a more direct sense. These other crimes (including white-collar crime) are the ones that could be regulated more successfully by adequate penal policy. For that to be achieved, the value systems of policy-makers would have to shift towards more realistic control paradigms, which would be less based on daily politics and more on focusing attention primarily on the control effort directed at those crimes that are more capable of successful regulation by repressive social control. These new paradigms would have to provide as many social policy alternatives to repression as possible, in relation to other types of criminality which do not seem to be completely controllable by repression alone.

The social crisis that has been inflicted on the populations of central-eastern European countries has many facets. In essence, the crises in health, educational policy, and criminal justice are much the same in structural characteristics. The weak links in the chain of social policy are corruption, inertia, political opportunism, and ideological obscurantism. Some of these weak links could be subsumed under the category of white-collar crime. The mechanisms that have been put in place to deal with the crimes of the rich and the powerful in the newly liberalised, transitional societies, have not proven too effective so far. What remains to be seen is whether a reordering of priorities will occur in the social policy frameworks of these countries, and whether the governments will re-target their control effort towards those social groups who are inflicting the most damage on society, both in financial terms and in social terms.

Conclusion

Estimates of surging poverty, increasing death rates because of social stress and unemployment, and other indicators of a social crisis in central-eastern Europe abound, but it would probably be too simplistic to attribute the region's security crisis to these factors alone. There is reason to believe that the main cause of increased rates of criminality is not so much the absolute amounts of deprivation and social stress as the relative deprivation, that is, the perceptions of unequal distribution of the burdens of transition. According to the left-realist theory, it is exactly this perception of inequality and injustice that leads to an increase in criminal deviance. The fact that the onset of the security crisis in the region coincided with the social crisis, and the security crisis is the most pronounced where the social differences and restratification are the worst, and where, therefore, the social crisis is the most pronounced, cannot be disregarded. It can thus be concluded that criminality is justifiably seen as a social problem *par excellence* for central-eastern European societies in the period of post-communism, a problem with crucial social policy implications. The creation of an underclass because of the ideological and political restructuring of the region, through increased unemployment, general consequences of social restratification, and loss of access to important systems of social services, such as health care and housing, has led to the spread of perceptions of injustice of social and economic systems. Sometimes these perceptions invite reactions of resorting to criminality, often by young underprivileged men. Urban populations of teenagers are thus often found to be driven to crime by the group and subcultural ethos of rebellion against victimising social conditions and structures. The tormented souls, in other words, sometimes turn to confronting the social evil with which they could not otherwise cope, by resorting to avenues of action that are seen as illegitimate by those on the other side of the divide separating the underclass from mainstream society. This is a familiar phenomenon in the modern history of industrialisation, and much the same phenomenon is occurring in central-eastern Europe at the end of the 20th century.

The crisis sweeping across the central-eastern European region is not only a security crisis. Above all, it is a general social and political crisis, with important elements of an economic and population crisis. Critical parameters of demographic, health, and crude mortality rates are present in all countries of the region. This crisis has a causal influence on rates of criminality, especially on youth crime rates. Almost all countries of the region have experienced a sharp and steady increase in the rates of crimes against property. As it has turned out, the category of offenders who have been to the greatest extent associated with these crimes have been the young offenders. For example, in Slovakia, the proportion of crimes committed by young offenders jumped from 14% in 1989 to 28% in the first half of 1993. In Hungary, this rate was already very high in 1989 (37.7%), and it subsequently rose to 41.7% in 1992.[10]

The welfare outlook for the region is extremely bleak, and this in part probably accounts for the relatively high crime rates. Perhaps, in this situation, the most significant actual causes of criminality are not and may not be able to be captured, or targeted, by legal measures alone. It seems indeed that, as well as legislative and enforcement changes, social policy changes must also be implemented for an improvement in the situation if internal security is to be achieved. If these measures are not instituted with greater promptness and efficiency, the crisis of the region, including its internal security crisis, will inevitably considerably worsen in coming years.

Criminal justice systems are therefore partly inadequate for the task of addressing these issues, for the simple reason that the questions underlying the problems associated with most types of crime today may well not be exclusively legal, or ones that can be solved directly by legal, or exclusively legal, measures. The main questions may in fact be social in nature. Legal and social policy theory might be able to point out the ways in which social policy and criminal legislation could be reformed to avoid victimisation and marginalisation as aspects of the social and political changes that are taking place in central-eastern Europe. In their essence, these questions are philosophical, and they should be answered by a new conceptualisation of the political climate in the region, which would be connected with the actual social policy changes aimed at alleviating the crisis itself.

The legislative changes that have been explored in this book are an example of attempts by the governments to step beyond the conceptual and ideological barriers imposed by the previous régime, and to provide new regulatory frameworks for their societies. These new frameworks would have to be maximally liberal and tolerant in the sense of facilitating the realisation of a liberal, individualist conception of liberty and social reality, with all its dangers and advantages, and yet less stigmatising than they would have to be were they to be based exclusively on the crude laws of market competition and the new capitalist ideology. This is a task many western European societies never even set themselves, let alone achieve. The limited and partial, often very small success in the realisation of this goal by the new central-eastern European governments is thus understandable, given the daunting complexity of the task. The task is not only daunting in size, but the territory through which the social policies of central-eastern European societies have to pass in order to reach it is practically absent from the chart of the journey that has been taken in the past by the more developed capitalist countries on the Continent.

Understandably, the new governments have limited capabilities to overcome the ideological legacy of the former régime, and to reach the ideological compromises for which they search. The establishment of a social-democratic pre-eminence (not to say dominance) in the region, often disguised in parties with socialist names, in countries such as Poland, Hungary, Bulgaria, to some extent, and more recently, even the Czech Republic (in the Parliament), is a sign of searching for this compromise of a market-driven direction on the one hand, and social care on the other. However, some central-eastern European societies are increasingly resigned to the rising rates of criminality, the resulting intra-societal antagonisation, and crisis of internal security, as *inevitable* consequences of the market reforms. At the same time, the new culture, new normative systems created around patterns of deviant responses to social frustration that have been created in the crisis processes since the late 1980s, in the 'post-communist' changes, may become lasting remainders of a poorly managed transition process. All these elements of transition create social structures, new classes of citizens, whose main occupation is crime. They create an atmosphere of desperation, tolerance and permissiveness of crime — a Cosa-Nostra type of mentality, which has already been firmly established in countries that have undergone social and political destruction, such as the former SFR Yugoslavia and large parts of the former Soviet Union. These structures are practically impossible to eradicate at later stages of social development, because they become part of that development itself.

Organised crime thus becomes the final result of an internal security crisis which arises from a social crisis. It becomes an integral part of politics, and an integral part of the reality of everyday life in central-eastern European societies. This is the dialectic of creation of the Mafia that is known from the western European, first of all Italian conditions, and which is still going on in central-eastern Europe. It is important to note that this type of creation of the Mafia is not merely a matter of omissions in the individual forms of control policy during the transition, but rather a structural resultant of the disturbances of relationships between various elements of the entire process of transition. These disturbances primarily arise from the overemphasised role of the 'high ground' of transition, that is, ideology and its strictly legislative encapsulation in social norms, in relation to the 'low ground' of the transition, that is, the concrete social policy. In the gulf between the high and the low grounds of the transition, that is, between the often extremely unclear and inconsistent ideological changes, abuses, and positions, and the social tragedy of the largest part of the population, a new class is constituted — the Mafia of the new post-communist world of the former geopolitically eastern Europe. There should be no mistake in qualifying the evaluative dimension of this statement — equivalent, often structurally very similar forms of creation and regeneration of Mafia-type structures exist in all ideologically western societies, and this phenomenon is therefore by no means specific to eastern Europe. Given the fragile nature of the transitional eastern European societies, however, this phenomenon is proportionally more damaging for these societies than for some others.

Notes

1. For an innovative and informative study of legal policies in Yugoslavia, for example, see Jelić, Z. (1995), *Aktualna pitanja pravne politike u Saveznoj Republici Jugoslaviji*, Ekonomika, Beograd. This book discusses many relevant conceptual issues in the systematisation of areas of the law and its functions.

2. About this phenomenon see, for example, Đilas, M. (1990), *Nova klasa*, Narodna knjiga, Beograd.

3. It was exactly because of these structural characteristics of the positions the communist élite used to occupy, and still occupies in the so-called transitional societies, that Milovan Đilas called the communist oligarchy the most shameless 'new class', although that oligarchy used to call verbally for the abolition of class society — ibid.

4. A number of thorough studies reflecting the importance of these elements of social policy can be found in Barr, N. (ed.) (1995), *Labour markets and social policy in central-eastern Europe: The transition and beyond*, Oxford, Oxford University Press.

5. See UNESCO (1994), *Central and eastern Europe in transition: Monitoring public policy and social conditions*, Economies in Transition Studies, no. 2, *Crisis in mortality, health and nutrition*, Innocenti.

6. ibid.

7. Barr, op. cit.

8. Barr, op. cit.

9. According to the American Federal Bureau of Investigation (FBI), in 1970 there were approximately 16 000 murders in the USA. That number rose to 20 510 in 1975, then up to 23 040 in 1980. In 1985, in a period of a relatively moderate penal policy with a simultaneous emphasis on social policy, the number of murders fell to 18 980, but with the escalation of social crisis, recession, and unemployment, and finally with the reintroduction of the death penalty in some federal states, in 1990 the murder rate jumped to the highest level of 23 440 and according to the same estimates, has been rising constantly, if slowly, ever since (in 1993 it was approximately 24 500).

10. UNICEF, op. cit., p. 12.

References

Atanacković, D. (1995), 'Objektivni uslov inkriminacije i njegovo razgraničenje od posledice krivičnog dela' ('The objective condition of incrimination and its distinction from the consequence of a criminal offence'), *Problemi reintegracije i reforme jugoslovenskog krivičnog zakonodavstva* (*Problems of reintegration and reform of the Yugoslav criminal legislation*), Institute of Criminological and Sociological Research, Beograd.

Atkinson, A. & Micklewright, J. (1992), *Economic transformation in eastern Europe and the distribution of income*, Cambridge University Press, Cambridge.

Auerbach, N.M. (1968), 'Edmund Burke', in Sills, D.L. (ed.), *International encyclopedia of the social sciences*, Macmillan and The Free Press, New York.

Axelrod, R. (1984), *The evolution of cooperation*, Basic Books, New York.

Barr, N. (ed.) (1995), *Labour markets and social policy in central-eastern Europe: The transition and beyond*, Oxford University Press, Oxford.

Benke, M. (1994), 'White collar crime and money laundering in Hungary', *Rendénszeti tanulmányok*, no. 4, pp. 71–80.

Berki, R.N. (1986), *Security and society: reflections on law, order and politics*, J.M. Dent & Sons, London & Melbourne.

Biberaj, E. (1989), 'Yugoslavia: A continuing crisis', *Conflict Studies*, vol. 225, October.

Boros, J. (1994), 'The organisation: The structure of the Hungarian prison system', *Prison Review*, pp. 3–5.

Burkhardt, J. (1955), *Force and freedom: An interpretation of history*, ed. by J.H. Nichols, Meridian Books, New York.

Christopher, W. (1995), 'America's leadership, America's opportunity', *Foreign Policy*, vol. 98, pp. 6–29.

Cohen, S. (1990), *Visions of social control*, Polity Press, Cambridge.

Constitution of the Republic of Hungary.

Cornia, G.A. & Sipos, S. (1991), *Children and the transition to the market economy: Safety nets and social policies in central-eastern Europe*, Avebury, Gower Publishing Group, Aldershot.
Coser, L.(1956), *The function of social conflict*, The Free Press, New York.
Criminal law of the Federal Republic of Yugoslavia.
Criminal law of the Republic of Montenegro.
Criminal law of the Republic of Serbia.
Democracy, economic reform and western assistance in Czechoslovakia, Hungary and Poland: A comparative public opinion survey, Freedom House, New York, 1991.
Deutsche Bank Research, *Official Statistics.*
Đilas, M. (1959), *Anatomy of a moral: the political essays of Milovan Đilas*, ed. by A. Rothberg with an introduction by P. Willen, Thames and Hudson, London.
Đilas, M. (1990), *Nova klasa*, Narodna knjiga, Beograd.
Đorđević, M. (1995), "Osnovna pitanja u vezi sa donošenjem krivičnog zakonika SR Jugoslavije" ('Key issues relating to the introduction of a new federal criminal law of FR Yugoslavia'), in *Problemi reintegracije i reforme jugoslovenskog krivičnog zakonodavstva (Problems of reintegration and reform of the Yugoslav criminal legislation)*, Institute of Criminological and Sociological Research, Beograd.
Eberstadt, N. (1990), 'Health and mortality in eastern Europe', 1965–85', *Communist Economies*, vol. 2, no. 3.
Economic Commission for Europe (1994), *Economic Survey of Europe in 1993–1994*, United Nations, New York & Geneva.
Ellman, M. (1994), 'The increase in death and disease under Katastroika', *Cambridge Journal of Economics*, vol. 18, no. 4.
Földvári, J. (1980), 'Observations in relation to the new Hungarian Criminal Code', *Hungarian Law Review*, 1980, no. 1–2, pp. 5–22.
Forest Keen, M. & Mucha, J. (1994), *Eastern Europe in transformation*, Greenwood, Westport.
Géza, K. (1994), 'Survey on crime-prevention', *Rendészeti Tanulmányok*, vol. 4, pp. 37–40.
Godišnjak Saveznog zavoda za statistiku SRJ (Federal Republic of Yugoslavia's Federal Bureau of Statistics Yearbook) (1994), Beograd.
Hoffmann, S. (1995), 'The crisis of liberal internationalism', *Foreign Policy*, vol. 98, Spring, pp. 159–79.
Hungarian Prison Review (1993), English edition.
International Monetary Fund (1989, 1990, 1991, 1992, 1993, 1994), *Government Financial Statistics Yearbook.*
Jelić, Z. (1995), *Aktualna pitanja pravne politike u Saveznoj Republici Jugoslaviji*, Ekonomika, Beograd.
Jelínek, J. & Sovák, Z. (1994), *Trestní zákon a trestní řad*, edited text as of September 1, 1994, Linde Praha a. s. - Právnické a ekonomické nakladatelství a knihkupectví Bohumily Hořínkové a Jana Tuláčka, Prague.
Jozan, P. (1980–81), 'Some features of mortality in Hungary', Budapest (mimeo).

Katona, G. (1994), 'Survey on crime-prevention', *Rendészeti Tanulmányok*, vol. 4, pp. 37–43.

King, Neil, (1995), 'Slovakia's miracle plan', *The Wall Street Journal's Central European Economic Review*, March, p. 14.

Knežević, A. & Tufegdžić, V. (1995), *Kriminal koji je izmenio Srbiju*, Radio B-92, Beograd.

Krivični zakon Republike Crne Gore (*Criminal law of the Republic of Montenegro*) (1993), *Službeni list Republike Crne Gore*, Podgorica, no. 42, October 11.

Krivični zakon Republike Srbije (*Criminal law of the Republic of Serbia*) (1977), enacted on June 28, 1977 with subsequent changes and amendments.

Krivični zakon Savezne Republike Jugoslavije sa objasnjenjima i uputstvima, (*The federal criminal law of the Federal Republic of Yugoslavia with explanations and instructions*) (1993), ed. by M. Kokolj, *Službeni glasnik SRJ*, Beograd.

Kvaśniewski, J. (1984), *Society and deviance in communist Poland: Attitudes towards social control*, Berg Publishers Ltd, Leamington Spa, Warwickshire.

Law on the acquisition and loss of Czech citizenship.

Lea, J. & Young, J. (1984), *What is to be done about law and order: Crisis in the eighties*, Penguin Books.

Lea, J. & Young, J. (1993), *What is to be done about law and order: Crisis in the nineties*, Pluto Press, London & Boulder, Colorado.

Livi-Bacci, M. (1993), 'On the human costs of collectivisation in the Soviet Union', *Population and Development Review*, vol. 19, no. 4.

Los, M. (1988), *Communist ideology, law and crime: A comparative view of the USSR and Poland*, Macmillan, Basingstoke.

Maier, C.S. (1994), 'Democracy and its discontents', *Foreign Affairs*, July/August, pp. 48–64.

Mason, David (1992), *Revolution in East-Central Europe: the rise and fall of communism and the Cold War*, Westview Press, Boulder.

Milanović, B. (1993), *Social cost of transition to capitalism: Poland 1990–91*, World Bank, Washington, DC.

MONEE Database.

Murray, C. (1990), *The emerging British underclass*, Institute of Economic Affairs, London.

Murray, C. (1984), *Losing ground: American social policy 1950–1980*, Basic Books, New York.

Nell, J. & Stewart, K. (1995), 'Proximate and underlying causes of the health crisis in Russia, 1989–94', *Innocenti Occasional Papers*, UNICEF International Child Development Centre, Florence (forthcoming).

1978 Hungarian criminal law.

Official Hungarian police and prosecution statistics.

Official Statistics for Hungarian criminal justice (1994), *Prison Review*.

Pehe, J. (1994), 'Czech Republic's crime rate slows down', in *Radio Free Europe/Radio Liberty Research Report*, vol. 3, no. 8, 25 February, pp. 43–48.

Rubin, F. (1980), 'The policing systems in Hungary', *The Police Journal*, vol. 53, pp. 20–29.
Rupnik, J. (1988), *The other Europe*, Weidenfeld & Nicholson, London.
Security for Europe project: Initial report (1992), Center for Foreign Policy Development, Brown University, USA, December.
Sekelj, Laslo (1992), *Yugoslavia: The process of disintegration*, Atlantic Research and Publications.
Shoup, Paul S. (ed.) (1990), *Problems of Balkan security: Southeastern Europe in the 1990s*, The Woodrow Wilson International Center for Scholars, Washington.
Sipos, S. (1992), 'Poverty measurement in central and eastern Europe before the transition to market economy', Innocenti Occasional Papers, Economic Policies Series, no. 29, UNICEF International Child Development Centre, Florence.
Škoda Automobilova Statistics.
Statistics of the Hungarian National Bank.
Stevanović, Z. (1995), "Pravno regulisanje mera bezbednosti medicinskog karaktera i problemi njihovog izvršenja", in *Problemi reintegracije i reforme jugoslovenskog krivičnog zakonodavstva*, (*Problems of reintegration and reform of the Yugoslav criminal legislation*), Institute of Criminological and Sociological Research, Beograd.
Stojiljković, S. (1986), *Psihijatrija sa medicinskom psihologijom*, Medicinska knjiga, Beograd & Zagreb.
Szikinger, I. (1994), 'The police in Hungary today', *Rendészeti tanulmányok*, vol. 4, pp. 23–35.
Szikinger, I. (1994), 'Policing the new democracy in Hungary: Challenges and solutions', paper released by the Hungarian Law Enforcement Research Institute.
Szonda Ipsos Public Opinion Research Company Statistics.
Tarschys, D. (1980), 'The success of a failure: Gorbachev's alcohol policy, 1985–88', *Europe-Asia Studies*, vol. 45, no. 1.
Truell, P. & Feduschak, N.A. (1995), 'Big Russian trader is a mystery man', *The Wall Street Journal's Central European Business Review*, March, p. 22.
UNICEF (1993), *Central and eastern Europe in transition: Monitoring public policy and social conditions*, Economies in Transition Studies, no. 1, *Public policy and social conditions.*
UNICEF (1994), *Central and eastern Europe in transition: Monitoring public policy and social conditions*, Economies in Transition Studies, no. 2, *Crisis in mortality, health and nutrition.*
United Nations (1989), *World population prospects*, United Nations, New York.
United Nations Criminal Justice Information Network, *Crime and justice letter*, vol. 1, no. 1/2, section entitled 'Citizens' experience and satisfaction with police', electronic version.
University of North Caroline at Chapel Hill, Goskomstat of Russia, Russian National Scientific Research Centre of Preventative Medicine, The World Bank (1992), 'The Russian longitudinal monitoring survey report on

economic conditions in the Russian Federation, Round 1, July–October 1992' (mimeo).
Vujanović, F. (1995), "Razlicite inkriminacije u KZ Srbije i KZ Crne Gore i pitanje jedinstvenog krivičnog zakona", in the collection *Problemi reintegracije i reforme jugoslovenskog krivičnog zakonodavstva* (*Problems of reintegration and reform of the Yugoslav criminal legislation*), Institute of Criminological and Sociological Research, Beograd.
World Bank (1993), *Ukraine: The social sector during transition*, World Bank, Washington, DC.
World Bank (1993), *World development report 1993*, World Bank, Washington, DC.
Yarmolinsky, A. (1994–95), 'Cold war stories', *Foreign Policy*, no. 97, pp. 158–70.
Yugoslav Bureau of Statistics (1994), *Statistical yearbook*, Yugoslav Bureau of Statistics, Beograd.

For Product Safety Concerns and Information please contact our EU representative GPSR@taylorandfrancis.com Taylor & Francis Verlag GmbH, Kaufingerstraße 24, 80331 München, Germany

Printed and bound by CPI Group (UK) Ltd, Croydon, CR0 4YY
14/09/2026
02216243-0017